I0828071

Additional Praise for
Just Give Me a Chance to Fail

"Sam Mills did not have the size or pedigree to play pro football, yet he played for 15 seasons. Today he has a bust in the Pro Football Hall of Fame and a statue outside Bank of America Stadium in Charlotte. His story, skillfully told by author Paul Domowitch, is truly an inspiration."

—RAY DIDINGER, Pro Football Hall of Fame sportswriter and author of *Finished Business*

"Before Sam Mills told an assembled Panthers team the words 'Keep Pounding'– words that are literally stitched into the fabric of the organization– he lived them. *Just Give Me a Chance to Fail* paints the picture of Mills' indomitable spirit, and the impact he had on so many people in football and in life, a legacy that continues to this day."

—DARIN GANTT, Panthers.com

Navigator Books Pledge of Human Creativity

At Navigator Books we believe that insight, innovation, and creativity are the apex of human achievement. Because of this, we pledge that the fundamental creative efforts that go into the development of this book and all of our books—the ideas, the writing, the editing, and the design elements—are produced for humans, by humans.

No Large Language Models or other Artificial Intelligence systems beyond rudimentary spelling or correction checks, word processing, or image adjustment systems were used in the creative material in this book.

Sincerely,

Brendan J. Cahill
CEO & Publisher
Navigator Books

JUST GIVE ME A CHANCE TO FAIL

Also by the Author

with Leo Carlin
A Bird's-Eye View

JUST GIVE ME A CHANCE TO FAIL

The Life of NFL Hall of Fame Linebacker Sam Mills

PAUL DOMOWITCH

FOREWORD BY
VIC FANGIO

Navigator Books
Philadelphia

Published by Navigator Books LLC
P.O. Box 31, Merion Station, PA

navigatorbooks.com

ISBN 9798994998007

Library of Congress Control Number: 2026908023

Publisher and Editor: Brendan J. Cahill
Copyeditor: David Aretha
Proofreader: Duncan McHenry
Assistant: Catherine Sorrentino

Printed in the United States of America
1st Printing

Set in Minion Pro
Designed by Jon Hahn Design

To Shelley,
the love of my life.

For every hill I've had to climb,
For every stone that bruised my feet,
For all the blood and sweat and grime,
For blinding storms and burning heat
My heart sings but a grateful song—
These were the things that made me strong!

For all the heartaches and the tears,
For all the anguish and the pain,
For gloomy days and fruitless years,
And for the hopes that lived in vain,
I do give thanks, for now I know
These were the things that helped me grow!

—**Ernest Lawrence Thayer**

I always want to be the first person to know how bad I am, and the last person to know how good I am. As long as I can live by that, I will continue to strive to be better.

—Sam Mills

FOREWORD

SAM MILLS AND I were together for 15 years. We both got our professional starts with the Philadelphia Stars in the United States Football League, Sam as a small-school linebacker who had been rejected by the NFL and the CFL because of his height, and me as a 25-year-old entry-level coach. We won two championships together with the Stars.

He did all the heavy lifting. I was just along for the ride.

When the league folded, Stars coach Jim Mora, who had hired me in Philly, got the head-coaching job in New Orleans with the Saints and took me with him to be his linebackers coach. One day early in our first training camp there, he called me into his office and told me he was thinking of signing Sam and wanted to know what I thought.

You know the saying about jumping up on the table? I literally did that. I told him we absolutely should sign him, although he didn't really need me to convince him.

Sam and I were together in New Orleans for nine years. He was part of the best linebacking corps in NFL history. They called them the "Dome Patrol." Sam and Vaughan Johnson, whom we also signed out of the USFL, manned the two inside spots. Pat Swilling, whom we drafted in 1986, the same year that Sam and Vaughan signed, and Rickey Jackson played on the outside.

We were pretty damn good with those four guys. When the Saints had their first-ever winning season in '87 and made the playoffs for the first time, it was Sam and the linebackers who led the way.

We had the same four starters at linebacker in New Orleans for seven years. *Seven years!* That doesn't happen anymore in the NFL. The four of them earned a combined total of 20 Pro Bowl invitations, five by Sam. In 1992, all four of them made the Pro Bowl together. It's the only time in history that four linebackers from the same team have made the Pro Bowl in the same year.

They just meshed together and had a lot of pride in the way they played. Swilling and Jackson had a quiet competition with each other as far as who was better. Vaughan and Sam were tied at the hip. They all fed off one another. But the other three guys all relied immensely on Sam prior to the snap of the ball every play.

Everywhere I've gone in the NFL since then, I'll come across somebody who was coaching or playing back then and they'll rave about that group of linebackers.

After the '94 season, I left New Orleans to become Dom Capers' defensive coordinator with the expansion team in Charlotte, the Carolina Panthers. It was the first year of free agency. Probably because of Sam's age—he was 36 by then, just a year younger than me—the Saints weren't offering him the kind of money he felt he deserved.

I told Dom and Bill Polian, who was the Panthers' general manager, that we needed to sign Sam. Dom had been with Sam in Philly and New Orleans, and like Jim in '86, he didn't really need any convincing. Getting a guy of his stature, his ability, and what he would bring to a new franchise was a no-brainer.

It turned out to be a tremendous acquisition. Hell, they put up a statue of Sam in front of the Panthers' stadium after he retired, which tells you what he meant to that franchise. He was the ringleader of that team. We won seven games in our first season and went to the NFC Championship Game in our second year. That never would have happened without Sam. Never.

Sam was one of the finest men I've ever known. He left an indelible mark on the teams, the franchises, and the communities that he played in. He was somebody whom everybody could relate to. Anybody who met him knew how genuine he was.

The mark he left on New Orleans and Carolina will be there forever. Nobody had a bad thing to say about Sam. Not the janitor. Not the guy serving the food in the cafeteria. Not the equipment guy. No one. They all loved him. But when he got on the field, he loved to knock the crap out of people.

Sam's football story is truly inspirational. It didn't come easy for him. For many of the other great players who have played the game, it usually comes easy. But not for Sam.

Everywhere he went they dismissed him; told him he was too short. Division I schools ignored him when he came out of high school. So, he went to a small school, Montclair State, and became a star.

Still, nobody was willing to look past his height. He went undrafted and then was cut by both the Cleveland Browns and the Toronto Argonauts of the CFL. If not for the Stars and the USFL, that might've been the end of his football career.

Everybody looked at Sam as an overachiever because he was short. But he wasn't an overachiever. He had a lot of talent. He was a very talented player but had an overachiever's mentality and work ethic. Combine that with his talent, and that's why he is a Hall of Famer.

Everybody thought they could take advantage of his height. Maybe an offensive lineman would fire out and try to engulf him because he was bigger. But it never worked.

Teams would try to beat him down the middle with a tight end, thinking they could throw over him. But I can remember just one touchdown that he ever gave up in the red zone in the 14 years we were together. It was to Minnesota Vikings tight end Steve Jordan. Jordan caught a pass on the end line in the back of the end zone against Sam. Every year, there might've been one or two plays where you saw Sam's height as a detriment. But never more than that.

He was small, but he had an incredibly strong lower body. He was a great high school wrestler and never was on the ground. He had the best six-inch pop I've ever seen. He could knock anybody back with it.

It's almost like, when he was going through the assembly line, he was supposed to be 6'3". But they changed their minds at the last minute and made him 5'9". But he already had the hands and feet of somebody 6'3". He had long arms for a short guy. He had big hands for a short guy. He had big feet. He just happened to be 5'9".

Our first year in Carolina, we started 0–5. In our sixth game, against the New York Jets, we were trailing late in the first half when Sam intercepted a pass and ran it back for a touchdown and we won the game. It changed everything. We went on to win seven of our last 11 games. Sam finished fourth in the NFL Defensive Player of the Year voting that year. Our second year there, when we went to the NFC title game, Sam was the main player. He made everybody better. He might've been older, but he still was playing at a high level. Hell, he made first-team All-Pro that year. *At the age of 37!*

He helped everybody in meetings and practices and before the ball was snapped on Sundays. And then he backed it all up with stellar play.

Sam had an incredible knack for making big plays when you needed them. More than 40 years later, I still remember a playoff game against the New Jersey Generals in the '84 USFL playoffs. They had the ball near the goal line. They gave it to Herschel Walker three straight times. And three straight times Sam stoned him and prevented him from scoring. We won that game because of him. We won a lot of games because of him.

When Sam was with the Panthers, we were playing the Atlanta Falcons. Ironhead Heyward was with them at the time. Ironhead weighed something like 280 pounds. He was one of the biggest running backs who ever played in the league. On an important short-yardage play, Sam met Ironhead right in the hole. He clobbered him and stopped him cold. When we beat the Dallas Cowboys in the '96 playoffs to advance to the NFC Championship Game, Sam had the game-clinching fourth-quarter interception against Troy Aikman to preserve the win.

Sam was a master at studying film and exploiting tendencies. His instincts were unreal. He never took a wrong step. The only other guy I've seen in the modern game who had Sam's instincts was Ray Lewis. His instincts and play diagnoses and reactions were second to none at that time. He was a complete player. Equally good against the run and the pass. A good blitzer.

Vince Tobin was the Stars' defensive coordinator when Sam played in Philly. He was the one who convinced Jim Mora to look beyond Sam's size. After the USFL folded, Vince became the defensive coordinator of the Chicago Bears, who had won the Super Bowl the year before he arrived. Vince tried to sign Sam, even though he already had a future Hall of Fame middle linebacker, Mike Singletary. The Bears had played a 4–3 under Buddy Ryan. If Sam had signed with them, Vince planned to switch to a 3–4 and have Mike and Sam playing alongside each other inside. Fortunately for us, Sam decided to go to New Orleans instead.

Singletary went into the Hall of Fame in 1998 in his first year of eligibility. Sam didn't get in until 2022, in his 20th and final year. Mike was in his prime when he played for Vince. He had been the NFL Defensive Player of the Year the year before Vince got there. A couple of years later, I was talking to Vince and he told me that Singletary was a great player, but that Sam definitely was better. He also told me that if I ever told anybody he said that, he'd deny it. Sadly, Vince passed away a couple of years ago. I'm hoping he's not up in heaven right now cursing me for telling that story.

Sam was the leader of the defense everywhere he played, especially in Carolina because of his experience and all of the young players we had. He called everything. He made others better, which I think is an important quality. And he knocked the shit out of people. Everybody in the locker room looked up to him, even though he was 5'9".

I was with him for 15 straight years—two with the Stars, nine with the Saints, and four with the Panthers, including the year after he retired and was on the coaching staff with me. He coached pretty much the way he led on the field. It was a quiet, analytical approach. Never yelling, never screaming. He had the players' respect because of who he was as a player. But that runs out quickly if you can't prove you're a good coach who can help make them better. He made them better. There's absolutely no doubt in my mind that if he had lived, he would've been a successful head coach in the NFL.

He was a fighter right to the end. When he was diagnosed with cancer in August 2003 at the age of 44, they gave him three months to live. They didn't think he'd make it to Christmas. Well, he not only saw that Christmas, but the next one as well. He lived a year and nine months before the cancer took him.

Even toward the end, he would still run sprints and train between chemo treatments. I would talk to him every week when he was going through it. I went to Charlotte twice to see him when he was getting the chemo. He was beat up from the treatment. But his attitude was tremendous. After we got over the emotions of the situation and what he was going through, the next day or two I would spend with him were like normal.

It shouldn't have taken Sam 20 years to make the Hall of Fame. Anybody who coached with or against him, anybody who played with or against him, knew what kind of player he was. If we had had any kind of success in the playoffs when we were in New Orleans, I think there would've been a different dialogue about Sam and he would've gotten into the Hall of Fame a lot sooner. But since we never won a playoff game, he wasn't on the national stage much.

The truth is, he was the best, or one of the two best, linebackers of his time in the league.

I've got Sam's picture on the wall of my office in Philadelphia. I've had it on my office wall everywhere I've been since before he died.

He's always with me.

Back in 2019, in my first year as the head coach of the Denver Broncos, we started 0–4. We were getting ready to play our fifth game against the Chargers. At the Saturday night meeting, which is the last time I really get to talk to the team before the game, I put together a video of Sam, both of him playing and the things he had said and done and the way he battled his cancer. It was about a 10-minute video. Boy, it really had an effect on our players. I told them Sam's story, from getting cut by the Browns and the CFL to his unforgettable "Keep Pounding" speech with the Panthers during the 2003 playoffs after he was diagnosed with cancer.

We went out the next day and beat the Chargers and won seven of our last 12 games.

That became our motto that year. *Keep pounding.*

Even after his death, Sam could still inspire people. Over the years, I've had a lot of agents call and try to sell me on their 5'9" linebacker client. But Sam was one of a kind. I miss him.

Vic Fangio
Philadelphia
June 2025

INTRODUCTION

> *It used to be the goal of an offense to run the ball 40 times and finish up with the passing game. Now, it's throw the ball 40 times and finish up with a running game. It requires a different animal at linebacker today.*
>
> —Hall of Fame coach Dick Vermeil

FOOTBALL HAS CHANGED much more than almost any other sport over the last 60 years.

A sport like baseball has a constancy to it that football does not. While baseball has tinkered with a rule here and there—the DH, a pitch clock, bigger bases—the game itself has remained largely unchanged for more than a hundred years. It's still, in essence, pitching and hitting. For its fans, that timeless consistency has been an important part of what they love about the sport.

You can't really say that about pro football. While a lot about the game has remained unchanged—it's still 11-on-11, still played on a 100-by-53.3-yard field with 10-yard end zones, still four downs to make 10 yards—it was a very different game in the '60s, '70s, '80s, and early '90s than it is today.

Back then, it was largely a land war with minimal deception or trickery. It was power versus power, with all the glorified bone-jarring violence that goes along with it. CTE was just three letters of the alphabet back then. In the '70s and '80s, NFL Films' hottest-selling VHS/DVD series was called *The Best of Thunder and Destruction: NFL's Hardest Hits*, which was a compilation of the league's most vicious collisions. Today, the league would get crucified if it ever tried to sell something like that.

The forward pass had been legal since the 1920s, but it still played second fiddle to the run back then. Woody Hayes, the legendary Ohio State coach, famously said, "Three things can happen when you pass the ball, and two of them are bad."

NFL coaches weren't quite as anti-pass as Hayes, but even in the late '80s, the vast majority of them preferred to throw the ball only on third-and-long, or as an occasional change of pace from the plethora of sweeps and counters and traps. In the Miami Dolphins' back-to-back Super Bowl wins over the Minnesota Vikings and the Washington Redskins in 1972 and 1973, the Dolphins ran the ball a total of 89 times in those two games and threw it just 18. Today, it's not uncommon for a quarterback to throw 18 passes before halftime.

The great Green Bay Packers quarterback Bart Starr, a first-ballot Hall of Famer, started 157 games in his career from 1956 to 1971. He averaged just 16 passes a game and threw 30 or more passes just 15 times in his entire career. In 1975, NFL teams ran the ball nine more times a game than they threw it. Every single one of the league's 26 teams averaged more than 30 rushing attempts per game. As recently as 1988, more than half of the league's teams were still averaging 30-plus carries a game.

"Back then, you had a basic offense that you ran almost every week," Vermeil says. "I might change the formation that we ran something from. We might use a different motion or a different shift. But it was basically the same play. We called it the Dirty Dozen. I was oriented in NFL offense by [Hall of Fame coaches] Chuck Knox and George Allen. [Their approach was] run the ball and play great defense and special teams and only throw if you have to."

Defenses of that era were literally built around the middle linebacker. The primary job of a middle/inside linebacker was to stop the run. The archetypal middle linebackers of that era were ill-tempered, 240-plus-pound human wrecking balls like Dick Butkus, Ray Nitschke, Jack Lambert, Sam Huff, Bill Bergey, and Matt Millen. Big men who took great delight in inflicting pain on whoever happened to have the ball.

They weren't Olympic sprinters, but they didn't need to be. It wasn't really a speed game back then. It was about power. Most of the action took place between the hashmarks. When a running back tried to go outside, it was the job of the defensive end and outside linebacker to turn the play back inside. Butkus ran a five-second 40-yard dash. Today, linebackers who run five-flat 40s spend Sunday afternoons in the fall watching the game at home on television.

By the same token, many of today's faster-but-smaller NFL linebackers would've had a difficult time surviving the down-after-down physicality of the game when Butkus played.

"The day of the big-guy linebacker, the MIKE linebacker, 250-pound guys à la Levon Kirkland and Matt Millen and those guys, they wouldn't be playing now," Philadelphia Eagles defensive coordinator Vic Fangio says. "Your typical linebacker now is between 225 and 235 pounds. The game is played more in space than it used to be. You need linebackers who can run."

In the '60s and '70s, offenses typically lined up with just two wide receivers, a slow-footed tight end, who basically was an extension of the offensive line, a blocking fullback, and a carry-the-load running back. Teams used two-back formations with the quarterback under center.

There were exceptions, of course. Sid Gillman, a Hall of Famer who coached the San Diego Chargers in the '60s when they were part of the American Football League, is credited with being one of the innovators of the vertical passing game. Former San Francisco 49ers coach Red Hickey introduced the shotgun formation in 1960. But it wasn't regularly used for another decade and a half until Dallas Cowboys coach Tom Landry installed it in his offense with Roger Staubach in 1975. Today, more than 70 percent of the snaps in an NFL game typically are from shotgun.

Don Coryell had one of the NFL's most lethal passing offenses with the Chargers in the late '70s and early '80s with Hall of Famer Dan Fouts as his quarterback. In the mid-'70s, Bill Walsh developed what came to be known as the West Coast offense when he was the Cincinnati Bengals' offensive coordinator. It featured a timing-based horizontal passing game. He would later perfect it in the '80s as the head coach of the 49ers, with whom he won three Super Bowl titles in an eight-year period with multiple Hall of Fame players including Joe Montana and Jerry Rice. But Walsh's 49ers still ran the ball a lot by today's standards. In 1984, when they won the second of their three Super Bowls under Walsh, their 534 rush attempts were the fifth most in the NFL.

Mouse Davis, a college coach at Portland (Oregon) State in the late '70s, developed a pass-heavy offense called the Run-and-Shoot, which featured empty backfields, five receivers, motion, and option routes. He took it to the major college game in 1981 as Cal's offensive coordinator, then to the Canadian Football League with the Toronto Argonauts and to the United States Football League with Jim Kelly and the Houston Gamblers in '84. The Gamblers averaged nearly 40 pass attempts per game with Davis as their offensive coordinator.

This was the football world Sam Mills grew up in. But the game was evolving, and Sam would find himself right in the middle of its evolution.

Despite being just 5'9", Mills thrived, excelled, and adapted to the changes in the game. He played most of his career at around 228 pounds, which was light for middle/inside linebackers of his era. But he could hit blockers and ball carriers with every bit of the power and ferocity of Butkus and Lambert. He was built like a tank. A small tank, but a tank nonetheless. He had huge arms, a massive chest, an 18-inch neck, and legs as thick as tree trunks. He could bench-press 400 pounds. All of that just happened to come in a diminutive 69-inch package. He was also whip-smart and instinctive, and unlike many of those 240- to 250-pound linebackers, he had the speed to play sideline to sideline and cover any tight end or running back, regardless of their size or elusiveness.

While traditional coaches and scouts were slow to realize it, Mills didn't have to bend his knees to get under a blocker's pads and gain leverage on him. As his head coach with the Philadelphia Stars and New Orleans Saints, Jim Mora, would famously say, "Low man wins."

That low man, almost always, was Sam Mills.

Sam would regularly take on an offensive lineman who was six inches taller and 100 pounds heavier, slip off that block, and make the tackle. He also possessed a lethal six-inch punch to the solar plexus that had a stun-gun effect on anyone trying to block him. Bart Oates, a five-time Pro Bowl center who played both with and against Mills during his career, said offensive linemen would often look at Sam and expect to physically dominate him because of his size.

"I learned a long time ago you weren't going to do that," Oates says. "You were at a disadvantage if you went straight at him. Your best hope was to get an angle on him. That was always my game plan when we played against each other in the NFL. But that was easier said than done."

The NFL hadn't yet embraced analytics when Sam came out of tiny Montclair State College in 1981. It didn't keep track of things like missed tackles. Even quarterback sacks didn't become an official league statistic until 1982. But Mills seldom let a ball carrier get away from him. He was as close to a technically perfect tackler back then as there was.

In addition to being short, Mills also didn't have very long arms, which almost certainly would get him dinged by scouts if he were coming out of college today. But back in the early '80s, arm length wasn't yet a key scouting measurable. Terry Bradway, who was a young personnel assistant with the Philadelphia Stars when Sam played for them in 1983–85, and has been an NFL scout and personnel executive for five decades, can't recall how long Mills' arms were. He just remembers that he never missed tackles.

"He'd always body up people," he says. "He never lunged. He would get there and make the play."

The game started to change in the late '80s and '90s as offensive coaches like Walsh became more schematically innovative and less fearful of throwing the football. Vermeil experienced the transformation firsthand. In 1980, even with Sid Gillman as his quarterbacks coach, Vermeil's Philadelphia Eagles went to the Super Bowl with an offense that averaged 33 rush attempts per game and just 29 passes.

Nearly two decades later, after coming out of retirement to coach the St. Louis Rams, Vermeil won a Super Bowl with the Rams and their prolific "Greatest Show on Turf" offense that included Hall of Famers Kurt Warner, Isaac Bruce, and Marshall Faulk and seven-time Hall of Fame finalist Torry Holt. Bruce, Faulk, and Holt had a combined 2,711 career receptions. The '99 Rams averaged just 26 rushing attempts and 33 passes per game on their way to the Lombardi Trophy.

In the late '90s, more and more teams began emulating the offensive innovations of the college game, phasing out the fullback and using spread formations and empty backfields with four and sometimes even five wide receivers. By 2015, the NFL clearly had transformed into a pass-first league. The league's 32 teams averaged nearly 10 more passes per game than runs in '15. Over the next 10 years, no more than six teams averaged 30-plus rush attempts in the same season.

"They're still running the ball, but it's different," says Fangio. "It's without the fullback."

For every action, there is a reaction. As NFL offenses started spreading people out and throwing the ball more, defenses had to adjust. And those adjustments had a major impact on the linebacker position. With the explosion of three- and four-wide receiver sets, defenses countered with more nickel (five defensive backs) and dime (six DBs) packages featuring fewer linebackers. And the linebackers who stayed on the field had to be able to run and cover as well as stop the run. When Fangio was the San Francisco 49ers' defensive coordinator in 2011, he used nickel only about 50 percent of the time.

"We were one of the first teams to play nickel on early downs when I was in New Orleans," said Fangio, who was the Saints' linebackers coach on Jim Mora's staff from 1986 through 1994. "It's been a slow evolution. But in the last five to eight years, everybody's playing predominantly nickel."

The Saints played a 3–4 defense when Fangio and Mora were there. Their four linebackers—Mills, Rickey Jackson, Vaughan Johnson, and Pat Swilling—were so versatile and good that they all stayed on the field on passing downs. The Saints would sub in an extra defensive back for one of the linemen.

Today, most NFL defenses, including Fangio's with the Eagles, play nickel or dime anywhere from 75 to 90 percent of the time. Many defenses, including the Eagles, regularly employ a 4–2 front that features two off-the-ball linebackers and a third 'backer who essentially is a defensive end that will occasionally drop into coverage. Those two off-the-ball linebackers have to be sturdy enough to play the run, but they also need to be fast enough to play in space in the passing game.

As the NFL's offensive emphasis switched from the ground to the air in the 21st century, a league that once chuckled at the idea of a

5'9" linebacker like Mills suddenly became more open-minded about the relevance of size at the position. When Mills played for the Saints and Carolina Panthers from 1986 through 1997, linebackers under six feet were scarce. In 2025, there were 14 starting off-the-ball linebackers in the league under six feet.

Mills had a lot to do with that, as a precedent for a defensive revolution that remade the linebacker position.

His success with the Saints and Panthers opened the door for other undersized players. A year after Sam retired following the 1997 season, Vermeil's Rams signed a 5'9 ½" linebacker out of Division III John Carroll University in Cleveland named London Fletcher. Fletcher was a key member of the Rams' Super Bowl-winning defense in '99 and played 16 years in the league and went to four Pro Bowls.

"I think it's a little easier being an undersized [linebacker] today," says Fletcher. "Especially if you can play in space and know how to tackle. There are a ton of 220- to 225-pound linebackers today. It's not as physical in the run game as it used to be."

When Fletcher was in college, he was inspired by a *Sports Illustrated* story on Mills, in which he talked about his size and the technique he used to get off blocks.

"I still remember the confidence I got from reading that article," says Fletcher. "I was thinking, *Man, maybe I can do this.*"

Fletcher played in a 4–3 defensive alignment most of his career. Mills, on the other hand, played his entire professional career—three years with the USFL's Philadelphia Stars, nine with the Saints, and three with the Panthers—in a 3–4 scheme. Originally devised by University of Oklahoma coach Bud Wilkinson in the 1940s as a 5–2—the two outside linebackers played up on the line—the 3–4 became widely used in the NFL in the '70s and '80s.

Jim Mora ran it in New England in '82 when he was the Patriots' defensive coordinator under Ron Meyer, and he brought it with him to Philadelphia the next year when he took the head-coaching job with the USFL Stars. He later used it in New Orleans with Fangio. Mills became its centerpiece.

The central concept of the 3–4 was for the three defensive linemen to occupy blockers and allow the four linebackers to make plays. It worked to perfection in New Orleans with their four stud linebackers. The 3–4 alignment declined in popularity in the '90s as teams began to throw the ball more, before experiencing a resurgence in the 2010s as defensive coaches like Fangio tweaked it to fit the modern game.

Evaluating football flesh, regardless of size, has always been an inexact science. Today, NFL teams have a seemingly infinite amount of information and data on players prior to the draft, as well as the technical wherewithal to review every single snap the guy has taken since he came out of the womb.

And yet, the draft still remains a crapshoot. There are as many mistakes made now as there were 40 years ago. Maybe even more, according to many NFL personnel executives. For every Peyton Manning there is a Ryan Leaf. For every Justin Jefferson there is a Jalen Reagor. For every J. J. Watt there is a Vernon Gholston.

Even with all the information teams have at their disposal, when they gather inside the draft room to make their decisions, they're still relying on the human element of the evaluators. It's easy to convince yourself of something that ultimately turns out not to be true.

"How many draft rooms have you seen where picks are made and everybody is high-fiving and saying they can't believe the kid was still on the board, and then, a year or two later, he's out the door?" Terry Bradway says. "So, there still are lots of mistakes made. You try to minimize them as much as possible. You try to have a good, solid process. But not everybody's process is consistent."

The problem very often is the same one today as it was back when Mills was playing: There is an overreliance on metrics such as size-and-speed numbers rather than experienced scouts just trusting what they see with their eyes. Too many players are judged by how big they are or how fast they can run a 40-yard dash rather than by on-field performance and production.

For decades, NFL teams shied away from shorter quarterbacks because they didn't feel they'd be able to see the field and throw the ball effectively over taller offensive and defensive linemen. Doug Flutie, a 5'10" Heisman Trophy-winning college legend in the early '80s at Boston College, essentially had to go to Canada and play at an elite level there for eight years before the NFL would finally take him seriously.

Then other undersized quarterbacks like Drew Brees came along. Brees was just a shade over 6'0" and was passed over by every team in the NFL in the first round of the 2001 draft and almost had his career cut short by a shoulder injury. He would recover and throw for 80,358 yards and 571 touchdown passes in a spectacular 20-year Hall of Fame career that included 13 Pro Bowl invitations, eight All-Pro selections, two NFL Offensive Player of the Year awards, and a Super Bowl title.

Thanks largely to Brees and others, the size of a quarterback is no longer considered a deal-breaker. The Seattle Seahawks won the Super Bowl in 2013 with 5'11" Russell Wilson as their quarterback. Wilson threw 292 touchdown passes and just 87 interceptions in 10 seasons with the Seahawks. Kyler Murray, who at 5'10" is the same size as former 11th-round pick Doug Flutie, was the first overall pick in the 2019 draft. In 2025, a quarter of the NFL's season-opening starting quarterbacks were no bigger than Brees.

It's been a similar situation for quarterbacks who can run. For many years, mobility was a negative on a quarterback's resume. Scouts felt running quarterbacks didn't have the pocket discipline to go through their reads and would take off at the first hint of pressure.

(The fact that many mobile quarterbacks happened to be Black also led to accusations of racial bias in the scouting process.)

They preferred 6'5" statues who could be counted on to stay in the pocket and go through their progressions, even if it was only because their lack of speed left them with no other recourse. In 2004, just two quarterbacks—Michael Vick and Daunte Culpepper—rushed for more than 300 yards. Twenty years later in 2024, there were 13.

Today, pure pocket passers are practically extinct. If you don't have a quarterback with enough mobility to elude a rush and pick up an occasional first down with his feet, you're at a grave disadvantage. In 2024, 10 quarterbacks had 25 or more rushing first downs, led by Jalen Hurts of the Philadelphia Eagles, who had 62 in the regular season and 14 more in the playoffs en route to being named Super Bowl MVP. Speedy and agile linebackers are critical to defending both designed and ad-libbed runs by the new generation of mobile quarterbacks.

The same reasoning regarding short quarterbacks also long applied to undersized linebackers like Mills. Scouts wondered how they would be able to see over the massive defensive linemen in front of them. How would they locate and get to a running back? It didn't seem to occur to scouts at the time that maybe the running back might have an even bigger problem locating the undersized linebacker.

Bradway will never forget a scouting report he saw on Mills in the early '80s.

"Good player," the scout wrote in his report. "But can he tackle Earl Campbell?"

Campbell would retire the year before Sam arrived in the NFL, so he never got the opportunity to tackle the man who was dubbed a "One-Man Demolition Team." But during the 12 years he played in the league, Mills cut down more than his share of big, powerful backs.

Low man wins.

Despite the prolific success of undersized players like Mills and Fletcher, most defensive coaches even today still prefer their 'backers taller rather than shorter, if only to more easily deal with the influx of athletic 6'5" and 6'6" pass-catching tight ends. There were 43 starting linebackers in the league in 2025 who were 6'2" or taller. But if a bigger linebacker can't run and play in space, they're not going to be around very long.

Almost every NFL personnel department has preferred size and weight parameters for each position. Those parameters are more etched in stone with some teams than others.

Hall of Fame coach Bill Parcells always had to have tall linebackers. No exceptions.

During the eight years he coached the New York Giants from 1983 to 1990, he told the Giants' scouts and personnel people not to bother drafting or signing a linebacker who was shorter than 6'2". The Giants won two Super Bowls under Parcells, in 1986 and 1990. Every one of the starting linebackers on those two championship teams was 6'2" or taller. Gary Reasons and Carl Banks were both 6'4". Lawrence Taylor and Pepper Johnson were 6'3". Harry Carson and Steve DeOssie were 6'2".

"I wanted bigger, faster players," Parcells says unapologetically. "It didn't make any difference what position they played. I was looking for bigger, faster guys. That's the way the pro game was evolving when I was in it."

Brett Senior, Sam Mills' longtime agent, also did some advisory work for Parcells. He remembers a conversation he had once with Parcells about Mills. Parcells told him that Mills was one of those guys you turn on the film and watch, and "as an old football guy, you just smile. You say, 'That is a football player.'

"But I would've been too stupid to bring him into camp because of his size."

During the 1989 draft, Parcells and George Young, the Giants' general manager who, like Parcells, is in the Pro Football Hall of Fame, had a memorable shouting match in the team's draft "war room" after Young overruled his coach and used a fifth-round pick on a 5'7" running back out of Towson State named Dave Meggett. Parcells thought Young had lost his mind.

"Just tell me one thing," Parcells loudly asked Young just before storming out of the room. "Where the fuck is he going to play?"

As it turned out, Parcells found a lot of things to do with Meggett. He played 10 years in the NFL, the first six with the Giants, and became one of the league's top third-down backs and one of its most dangerous punt and kickoff returners. His seven career punt returns for touchdowns are still the seventh most in league history. When he became a free agent in 1995, it was none other than Parcells, then the head coach in New England, who signed him.

Parcells was hardly alone in believing that football was a big man's game at the time. And no one would come to know that better than Mills, who was a constant victim of that narrow-minded thinking.

He spent much of his career being dismissed because of his size. Even though he was one of the most dominant prep players in the state of New Jersey in the mid-'70s at Long Branch High School, Division I schools shunned Mills. Syracuse coach Frank Maloney spoke for most of his fellow big-school coaches back then when he told a reporter, "Mills is just too small to play linebacker at our level of competition."

Hall of Fame general manager Bill Polian thought the same thing in 1981 after watching Mills at a pre-draft tryout camp. "You could tell he was a good athlete and really smart," says Polian, who was a scout for the Kansas City Chiefs at the time. "But we just thought he was too short. Shame on us."

Maloney and Polian were hardly the only ones who refused to believe their eyes when it came to Mills. Shunned by the big schools coming out of high school and undrafted after a spectacular college career at Montclair State, he was cut by both the Cleveland Browns and the CFL's Toronto Argonauts, not because he wasn't good enough, but because he wasn't tall enough.

Even after he finally made it, and became one of the best linebackers of his generation, even after five Pro Bowl invitations and four All-Pro selections, even after having a statue built in his honor by one of the teams (Carolina) he played for, respect still came painfully slow to Mills. He didn't make the Pro Football Hall of Fame until 17 years after his death, in his 20th and final year of modern-era eligibility.

Every game, every down mattered to Sam, because he always took the attitude that he was just one bad practice away from being cut, even when he knew deep down that he wasn't. He outworked and outstudied everyone. His leadership and passion for the game would leave a legacy among those who played with and against him, the coaches and football staffs who worked with him, and the fans and franchises who loved him. His greatness would emerge alongside the transformation of the position he played, and his success would pave the way for the many other undersized players who followed him.

All he needed was a chance to fail.

1

Mom worked hard. She was the working lady, the hardest-working person I've ever known. I truly believe that's where Sam got his work ethic. She would do anything that came up to help our family make it through the day.

—LEON MILLS, SAM'S YOUNGER BROTHER

SAMUEL DAVIS MILLS JR. was born and raised in Long Branch, New Jersey, in a place called Seaview Manor. The name suggests a large beachfront estate with extensive grounds, extravagant architecture, and a gorgeous vista where you can sit on the veranda sipping Pappy Van Winkle as you watch the boats go by.

In truth, Seaview Manor neither had a view of the sea nor bore the slightest resemblance to a manor. Distance-wise, it sat only a mile from the Atlantic Ocean. But it might as well have been a million miles from it. Seaview Manor was a cramped government housing project that was built next to a toxic-waste-spewing coal gasification plant. The residents there called it SMU—Seaview Manor University—because, as Sam's younger brother Leon remembers it, "it was a pretty tough place."

Long Branch is a popular North Jersey beach town that was visited by several US presidents. In the late 19th century, Ulysses Grant, Rutherford B. Hayes, Benjamin Harrison, and William McKinley all summered in Long Branch during the Gilded Age. James Garfield was brought there in July 1881 after he was shot in the back by Charles

Guiteau, in the hope that the fresh air and quiet might help him in his recovery. It didn't. He died three months later.

The Long Branch that Mills grew up in the '60s and '70s was a mostly blue-collar town. Elberon, which is located in the south part of Long Branch, was mostly white and upscale. But the majority of the town was a mix of blacks and whites. Seaview Manor and two other nearby government housing projects, Garfield Court and Grant Court, which were bordered by Central Avenue and Liberty and Rockwell Streets, were predominantly black.

The Jersey shore was no different than the rest of the country back in the '60s and early '70s. There was racial tension. Maybe a little less of it in Long Branch than in other parts of the shore like Asbury Park and Neptune. But it was always there, one incident away from boiling to the surface.

While he is more closely associated with Asbury Park, where he launched his career at the legendary Stone Pony nightclub in 1974, Bruce Springsteen was born in Long Branch and wrote "Born to Run" in a key cottage in the town's west end section. He has said the town's working-class atmosphere and Jersey shore setting inspired his songwriting.

Sam was the ninth of 12 children born to Juanita Bennett Mills. The births spanned nearly a quarter-century, so not all 12 lived in the tiny apartment in Seaview Manor simultaneously. Juanita had her oldest, Wallace, when she was just 14, and had Sam when she was 34. But when Sam was growing up, there were usually seven or eight kids living together at SMU, including nieces and nephews.

Juanita was the daughter of South Carolina sharecroppers. She had moved to Long Branch when she was 11. Sam's father, Sam Sr., who was seven years younger than Juanita, was also from South Carolina. He served in both the Army and Air Force and fought in the Korean War.

He was stationed at Fort Monmouth Army Base, five miles west of Long Branch. After he was honorably discharged, he moved to Long Branch, where he met Juanita. Sam Sr. held several different jobs over the years that included working for a local plumbing and heating company, driving a school bus, and doing other jobs for the Long Branch school district.

Sam Sr. was in and out of his children's lives. He and Juanita didn't live together much of the time. She was the one who primarily raised them.

"My pop wasn't really influential in what me and Sam did," says Leon, who was three and a half years younger than Sam. "He wasn't a father that was going to go to our games and root us on and support us. He wasn't abusive or anything. He was just kind of there."

Juanita's oldest son, Wally, who was 20 years older than Sam, served as a surrogate father to Sam and Leon. He would take them to their games and practices and could always be heard cheering them on.

"He was everywhere," Leon says of Wally. "My brother's college teammates still talk about Wally. Nobody cheered louder than him."

Juanita worked as a private-duty nurse for Stouffer Registry, a local company that provided nurses and aides to local hospitals, nursing homes, and individuals. She primarily took care of the elderly, often as a live-in caretaker, which is difficult work. Juanita regularly worked 70 to 80 hours a week to support her large family. "We lived in poverty early on," Leon says. "It was tough."

Juanita loved all her children, but she had a special place in her heart for Sam, and vice versa. They were two peas in a pod. Sam's future wife, Melanie, likened them to twins. Their mannerisms were identical. They had the same walk. They had the same quiet personality. Melanie once described her mother-in-law as "Sam in a wig."

"She wasn't a big talker," says Melanie. "She said very few words, but they were key words."

Sam was born without any hair. His family nickname as a child was "Clean," as in Mr. Clean, the cartoon mascot for the popular household cleaner. His siblings would clip an earring on one of his ears for fun.

A lack of hair was the least of little Sam's problems growing up. He also struggled with vision problems and asthma. He had to wear glasses from a very young age, and he also had to use a special device to help him cope with his breathing problems. None of that, however, deterred him from playing sports.

Sam and Leon, who was the spitting image of his older brother, were inseparable growing up, despite their age difference. Sam included Leon in everything. He mentored him. He taught him how to drive and cut his own hair. He taught him how to shave and how to work out the right way when they both started playing competitive sports.

"He was almost like, not just a big brother, but like a father to me," says Leon.

Seaview Manor didn't have any grass fields. A few patches of grass here and there, but it was mostly concrete. That didn't stop Sam and the other kids at Seaview Manor from playing tackle football. Juanita was forever running to the drugstore to get Band-Aids and antiseptic.

Mills attended Gregory Primary School (K–6), which was located on 7th Avenue, a few blocks from Seaview Manor. The school was racially mixed, with students from Seaview Manor and the nearby neighborhoods.

Sam eventually would move on to organized football. He began playing Pop Warner when he was still attending Gregory School.

The town's Pop Warner teams were sponsored by the Italian American Memorial Association of Long Branch; the letters IAMA were prominently displayed on the front of their jerseys. The club was formed shortly after the end of World War II in honor of the Italian American servicemen and servicewomen of Long Branch who had fought in both world wars. The IAMA youth football program was one of the best in the state in the '70s.

Mills was a bit heavy as a child—thick, not fat. But he often had trouble staying under the maximum weight for his age group and would have to play up a year.

"It wasn't a big problem for him," says his friend Ed Balina. "Sam held his own. It benefited him in the long run to be playing against older kids."

It had long been Juanita's dream to save up enough money to one day get her family out of Seaview Manor and into a bigger, better place. It took years, but she finally saved enough to buy a duplex at 143 N. 5th Avenue in the early '70s. The duplex was only a few blocks from Seaview Manor, but it had a lot more room and was in a better neighborhood.

Sam was 14 or 15 then. Juanita lived upstairs with Sam and Leon and some of the other younger children. Sam's sister Carol, who was 17 years older than him, lived downstairs.

"My sister did a whole lot of cooking, so we spent a lot of time downstairs in her place eating her fried chicken," says Leon.

Like her mother, Carol was a private-duty nurse. She would later join the ministry and spend 20 years as the pastor of Pentecostal Faith Church in Long Branch. Carol was a big influence on Sam with respect to his faith.

Sam met his future wife, Melanie, at a local roller rink shortly after his family moved into the duplex on N. 5th Avenue. Mel was a year younger than Sam and lived in nearby Ocean Township. One of Melanie's cousins, who knew Sam from sports, introduced them.

They had just started dating when Mel's mother died. She was just 16 at the time. She had relatives in California and briefly moved out there and lived with them. But she said she felt "like a fish out of water" on the West Coast and returned to New Jersey the following summer.

She didn't really have any relatives she could stay with, so Sam approached his mother about the possibility of Mel moving in with them. His mom gave her approval, and she moved in while finishing school at Long Branch High.

Sam's mother was a humble, private woman who didn't often share her feelings with other people. Melanie said it wasn't until several years into her marriage to Sam that she finally received Juanita's official approval.

"One day, out of the blue, she turned to me and said, 'I'm glad you married my son,'" says Melanie. "I told that story at the rehearsal dinner for my [younger] son Marcus because I wish I had heard that from her sooner. I told Marcus' wife that's why I was saying it [to her] now."

2

Sam became a hero to all of the kids in Long Branch. He became somebody for all of them to be like. He showed every one of them that they can get a chance to better themselves too. He changed the whole character of the town.

—Frank Glazier, Sam Mills' high school coach

SAM MILLS WAS an exceptional all-around athlete. Beyond his football prowess, he could've played any sport and excelled at it. Even though he was only 5'9", he could dunk a basketball. If he hadn't played football, Ed Balina believes he could have been an exceptional soccer player. In track, he became proficient enough to take fifth place in the javelin at the Shore Conference tournament his senior year with a throw of 176 feet after just a couple days of practice.

Mills was also an outstanding wrestler at Long Branch High School. He won two district titles and made it to the state finals as a senior in the 188-pound weight class, where he lost to Sparta High School's Craig Blackman, 4–1.

Sam had wrestled Blackman in a tournament the previous summer, with Blackman beating him by a couple of points. Blackman went on to wrestle at Franklin & Marshall, where he was an EIWA champ and finished fifth in the NCAA Division I tournament. He would also compete on the USA Junior World team.

"It was a great match," remembers Balina, who was the district champ at 148 pounds that year as a junior. "Blackman was a strong kid. They went at it. It was the first time I had seen someone match strength with Sam."

Blackman was 6'3", which gave him a six-inch height advantage on Mills. Dealing with height disadvantages would become the story of Mills' athletic life. The six inches he was giving away to Blackman made it difficult for him to shoot in and grab his opponent's back leg for a takedown. Mills was in on him the entire match. He kept getting the single leg but couldn't penetrate and get the double leg to finish the takedown because of Blackman's size.

Blackman remembers well his state championship battle with Mills. He said the most impressive thing about Sam was how explosive he was. Though a little lacking on technique, he was an incredible athlete.

"In terms of physical tenacity, he was a scary dude," says Blackman. "I think if he would've had the right coaching, he could've been a terrific collegiate wrestler. But football clearly was his passion."

Mills' wrestling background would be a huge asset for him on the football field. His balance, leverage, and ability to stay on his feet were all honed on the wrestling mats at Long Branch High.

"Wrestling is a thinking man's sport," Mills said. "You have to understand how to do it. You have to learn how to use your body leverage, which also is the key to playing linebacker.

"In wrestling, you have to look at your opponent's eyes to know where he wants to go, just like you have to look at the quarterback's eyes as a linebacker to know where he's going with the football. And wrestling puts an unbelievable desire in you. I was always having to make weight. That was good training for preseason camp."

Many times before wrestling matches at Long Branch High, Mills and Balina would drive over to the Fort Athletic Club in nearby Oceanport and sit in the sauna and try and sweat off a pound or two to make weight.

Blackman was right. Football was clearly Sam Mills' first passion. He was a fullback on the freshman team at Long Branch Junior High, then switched to linebacker as a sophomore. From the first day he strapped on pads, the Long Branch High coaches knew they had a special player. Since Balina was a year younger than Sam, they didn't play together when Mills was a sophomore and he was a freshman. But he remembers his two older brothers coming home from varsity football practice and talking about how Mills was "just killing people."

Ken Schroeck was the Long Branch High head football coach when Mills arrived as a sophomore. Schroeck didn't like to play sophomores, even though it was evident from the first preseason practice that Sam was far from your typical underclassman. Schroeck moved him from linebacker to the defensive line because he already had two pretty talented seniors starting at linebacker.

But in the second game that year against Lakewood High School, one of the Green Wave's starting linebackers got hurt. Schroeck reluctantly inserted Mills. Sam was already built like a block of granite at that point, naturally strong and quick with great timing.

Bob Biasi was an assistant coach on that team and was up in the coach's box that night communicating with Schroeck via his headset. Just two plays after Mills went into the game, he remembers an impatient Schroeck not being happy with something Sam had done and screaming, "He's killing us!" Biasi convinced Schroeck to take a deep breath and calm down.

"He knows what he's doing," Biasi assured him.

He did. Mills ended up with a team-leading 13 tackles against Lakewood and went on to start several games at linebacker for the Green Wave that year.

In a move that would ultimately change Mills' life, Schroeck was forced out after the '74 season and replaced by Frank Glazier.

Schroeck coached at Long Branch for nine seasons and had a respectable 41–39–1 record. But the football program wasn't the powerhouse it had been in the late '50s and early '60s, largely because of regionalization. When Shore Regional High School opened in 1962, students from neighboring towns like Monmouth Beach, Oceanport, Sea Bright, and West Long Branch that had been going to Long Branch High were sent to Shore Regional, which was located in West Long Branch.

The opening of the new school benefited Long Branch High as far as alleviating the overcrowding that had forced the school district to go to double sessions. It also dramatically improved the teacher-to-student ratio. But it had a negative impact on many of the school's sports teams, particularly football. With fewer students, the talent pool shrank.

Glazier was a coaching nomad when the then 41-year-old was hired to replace Schroeck shortly before the 1975 season. He had been a very successful high school coach in Maine, Florida, Delaware, Massachusetts, and New Jersey, losing just 19 of 82 games. He also had coached at the college level, serving as a defensive coordinator at Pennsylvania Military College (now Widener University) and Springfield (Massachusetts) College.

The president of the Long Branch Board of Education trumpeted Glazier's hiring, calling him "one of the most astute and knowledgeable coaches along the entire eastern seaboard." He said the board envisioned "a complete about-face in the Green Wave's ability to produce champions" with him as head coach.

Glazier would end up staying at Long Branch just three years before moving on again, but he left an indelible imprint on both the program and Mills. Mills would play for some excellent coaches during his prolific career, including Jim Mora, Vic Fangio, Dom Capers, and Steve Sidwell. But none of them would have as huge an impact on him as Glazier.

He was a brilliant coach who was ahead of his time with respect to many of the things he did and taught. He was bullish on weightlifting before it really became a standard part of football training. He emphasized the importance of film study. He would hand out thick scouting reports to his players before games. He was a fanatic about conditioning.

Glazier taught Mills and the rest of the Long Branch High players how to work out the right way. He showed them new training techniques and drills that they had never seen before.

Long Branch High School didn't have a weight room when Glazier got there in 1975. Well, not much of one, at least. It kept a few barbells and a Universal weight machine in a small classroom for its sports teams to use, but that was it.

"If you had five people in there, it was packed," says Balina, a running back on the football team and, like Mills, a wrestler.

What the school did have was three gyms.

Shortly after he was hired, Glazier convinced the Board of Education to take the third gym, divide it in half, and build a weight room on one side and a wrestling room on the other. When it was completed, Long Branch's weight room would become the envy of every high school sports program in the state of New Jersey.

"I remember it being featured in magazines as one of the best on the East Coast, including colleges," Balina says.

Glazier would have his players do circuit training in the weight room. Top, then middle, then legs. This was long before circuit training really became the norm in football strength training.

After that, he'd take them to the wrestling room and have them do bench jumps, which was one of Glazier's favorite workout drills. He would extend a string about 18–20 inches off the ground and have his players jump back and forth over it laterally. The purpose of the drill was to improve foot speed.

"We'd be dying after those workouts," Balina says. "But we were in shape. I don't know how many games we won in the second half because we were in better shape than the other team."

Leon Mills said Sam used to come home from practice every day and do bench jumps with him. Leon said everything that Glazier taught Sam he would bring home and do there.

Glazier worked his players hard. Preseason practices began with a two-week "boot camp." Three practices a day. A 6 a.m. mile run that every player had to complete in less than six minutes. Skull sessions. The first year, they slept on cots provided by a local merchant. The next year, he brought in beds. The parents would rotate making and serving meals.

"It was brutal," says Balina. "The coaches would blow the whistle and wake us up every morning at 5:30. We'd be on the track at 6 and running the mile. If you didn't run it in six minutes, you had to run it again after the third practice at night. I felt sorry for the linemen because they had to run it in six minutes too."

Years later, when Mills was in the NFL, Balina happened to be talking to him and asked him about Glazier's boot camps.

"Sam, you've played at every level for a lot of teams," Balina said. "Do you guys do what we did in those camps?"

"Nothing even comes close to what we did," Mills responded. "I still do most of the drills we learned from Glazier, including bench jumps."

Glazier tended to play fast and loose with rules and regulations, which probably had something to do with why he never stayed in one place very long. He held spring practices, which were forbidden by the New Jersey State Interscholastic Athletic Association, the state's governing body for high school sports.

Merrick Tomaine, who was the athletic director at Long Branch High in the mid-'70s, didn't get along with Glazier. Even though it was his own coach, he reported Glazier to the NJSIAA for practicing in the spring. But it didn't stop Glazier. One of the players on the team lived in upscale Elberon and had a huge backyard. The team moved its spring practices over there.

"We would call it Field X," remembers Balina.

Glazier even brought his own quarterback with him to Long Branch. Timmy Wilson was a high school player from Springfield, Massachusetts, where Glazier had previously coached. He knew Wilson's mom and dad, and they agreed to let Glazier become Timmy's guardian so that he could move with him to Long Branch and play football there. Wilson was a very good player. He became the Green Wave's starting quarterback in 1975 and later played at Syracuse.

"Timmy was a great quarterback," Balina says. "He was fantastic."

Glazier's demanding approach to football wasn't for everyone. The boot camps, the three practices a day, the spring practices, the early-morning mile run, triggered a mass exodus of players who wanted no part of The Glazier Way. They ended up with only about 25 players on the team that first year. But the ones who stayed, like Mills and Balina, were all in.

"A lot of seniors quit," says Balina. "They were used to the old regime, the old ways. It was disappointing because we had talent. But a lot of them just didn't like Glazier and didn't like the hard practices."

Glazier knew right away that he had a once-in-a-lifetime player in Sam Mills. One of the first things he did after he was hired was ask Jim Simonelli, a Long Branch native who had played linebacker for him at Pennsylvania Military College and had been on Schroeck's staff a few years earlier, to work with Mills on technique, reading offenses, and recognizing tendencies. Glazier asked Simonelli to teach Mills how to read "the triangle"—the two offensive guards and the running back—at the same time. For an inside linebacker like Mills back then, if you could master that, it was like getting your hands on the colonel's secret recipe.

"That's why Sam became so good at the upper levels [college and the pros]," Simonelli said before he died in 2025. "He could diagnose things. He was so intelligent. He was a quick study.

"When he learned to read that triangle, he became a beast. You couldn't stop him. He was a step ahead of everybody. It was hard enough to block him when he was standing in front of you. But when he was moving away from you or diagnosing the plays and moving to the football, he was just incredible."

If you're a defensive player, your eyes are your most important tool. They take your body where it needs to go. Mills always excelled at that. He never took a wrong step. He never got fooled.

Glazier believed that football was as much about the brain as it was about the body. Film study wasn't nearly as big in the '70s as it is today, especially at the high school level. For starters, the technology was much more primitive. You had to sit in a dark room with a whirring projector and watch games the same way you watched your family's grainy vacation film.

But Glazier understood the importance of getting inside the mind of your opponent and knowing his tendencies. It was like being able to predict the future. He knew how valuable that information could be to a cerebral linebacker like Mills.

Glazier taught Sam how to watch film. He would give his players those thick scouting reports before a game. It was Greek to most of them, but not to Sam. He and offensive lineman Randy Mickens, a future Columbia grad, were the only ones on the team who could read the whole thing and understand it.

"Sam was such a tremendous diagnostician," said Simonelli. "He would do his film work. And he *really* knew how to watch film. Some people watch film and they watch themselves running around and don't really see anything. Sam would watch film and he would study the movement of the guards. He would study the backs and look for them to tip what they were going to do."

Mills' instincts and his ability to absorb everything were rare, particularly for someone at his young age. Sam made all of the calls on the field for the Green Wave defense. Every defensive signal. The coaches would just point to Sam, and he would make the call based on the other team's formation and tendencies and personnel package.

"He could just diagnose it and analyze it—*boom!*—right there on the field," Simonelli said. "He could make the call and have them in the right defense every time."

Mills was more than just a smart player. In addition to being a strong tactician, he had excellent technique and was impossible to block. No one is exactly sure who taught Mills how to tackle. He got excellent coaching at the Pop Warner level, so it might've been there. Regardless, by the time he arrived at Long Branch High School, his tackling technique was absolutely flawless.

"You teach kids to wrap, keep your feet moving, nose on the ball," says Bob Biasi. "The real good ones learn to roll their hips. Sam was doing all of that in our very first tackling drill. He had that quick twitch. He was just a very technically sound player."

Even at a young age, when Mills hit people, they *felt* it. Their next of kin felt it. Long before he was knocking college and professional running backs into the middle of next week, he was doing the same to high school players, including fellow teammates.

Balina recalls a halfback drill where the running back had to take on a linebacker head-on. Balina and three or four other running backs would be lined up over on the side. Mills would be the one and only linebacker.

Glazier would be standing there watching. The first back ran at Sam and ended up on the ground. The same with the second and third backs.

Balina was next up. He knew that if he went at Sam at anything less than 100 percent, the same thing that happened to his teammates would happen to him. His only chance was to go at Sam with everything he had.

"I hit him and it was literally like running into a brick wall," he recalls with a smile. "He didn't budge an inch."

Glazier motivated and inspired Mills. He showed him that he could do great things, regardless of his size or other people's opinion of him. Before Glazier came along, Sam hadn't been sure about that. If enough people tell you you're too small, if enough people tell you that you can't do something, you start to believe it. But Glazier kept telling Sam: *You can do it; you can do it.*

Mills was the heart and soul of Long Branch High's football team in 1975 and 1976. In addition to playing linebacker, he was also a standout guard on offense and dealt out the same kind of punishment on that side of the ball that he did on defense. Even playing with just 25 players, the Green Wave finished 4–4–1 in the tough Shore Conference in '75, Sam's junior year.

The Green Wave ran the "veer" offense, which was created by University of Houston coach Bill Yeoman in the '60s. It was a triple-option system that used split backs and was based on reading the defensive end and linebacker. It was the original version of the RPO [run-pass option] and zone-read principles now heavily used by NFL offenses.

Opposing defenses dreaded it when the Long Branch offense would run a counter play with Sam leading the way as the pulling guard. "I think he was 215 pounds back then," Simonelli said. "He was like a freight train coming down the tracks. God help you if you got in his way."

The Green Wave became a dominant team in Glazier's second year at the helm, winning nine of 11 games and making it to the playoffs. Mills recorded 88 solo tackles and assisted on 99 more as a senior. He was a first-team All-Shore Conference selection that year, though interestingly, not as a linebacker. He was a first-team pick as an offensive lineman.

One of Long Branch's nine wins in '76 was over Matawan High School, which took a 24-game win streak into the game and was the top-rated team in the state at the time. Long Branch was ranked eighth. The game drew one of the biggest crowds in school history to Long Branch's Bresett Stadium. It was the Shore Conference Game of the Week and broadcast on Asbury Park-based WJLK, which was a very big deal back then.

Balina said he was out on the field with the specialists about an hour before the game, and the place was already packed. When the Green Wave came back out for the start of the game, fans were standing four-deep around the fence that ringed the field.

"People couldn't even get near the stadium that night," remembers Balina. "I had a friend who ran cross-country. They had a meet that morning and were coming back on the bus. The bus turns onto High Street, which was two blocks over from the stadium. The bus couldn't get down the street because it was jammed. Everybody got out of the bus and ran to the stadium to make it for the opening kickoff."

Matawan ran the single-wing offense. They had one of the best quarterbacks in the state—Ken Mandeville. A year earlier, he had led Matawan to an 11–0 record and the Central Jersey Group IV title. Mandeville was a versatile quarterback who could beat you with his arm or legs.

But Mills and the rest of the Long Branch defense shut Mandeville down that day. Late in the game, with Long Branch up by 12 and Matawan driving, Mandeville's line created a hole for him with the potential for a big play. But Sam came up and made the tackle to clinch the 18–6 victory.

Long Branch made it all the way to the Central Jersey Group III championship game that season, where they faced undefeated Carteret High School. The game was played at Carteret. The school had a pair of huge 330-plus-pound offensive tackles and the best quarterback in the state—Tim Fedroff. They had a half dozen Division I prospects, including Fedroff, who went on to play at the University of Maine. They averaged nearly 30 points a game on offense, and their defense forced 45 turnovers that year, including 33 interceptions.

In an interview years later, when asked to name the toughest guy he ever had to tackle, Mills didn't name any of the countless NFL running backs or quarterbacks or receivers he played against, many of whom are in the Pro Football Hall of Fame. He mentioned Fedroff.

Fedroff was a 1976 version of Lamar Jackson. He was 6'4" and had jackrabbit speed and moves. Glazier moved Sam from linebacker and put him on the line against Carteret because Long Branch couldn't match them physically up front.

Biasi said Mills was "a beast" on the line that day. But when he was moved to the line, the Long Branch defense lost his pursuit ability at linebacker. Whenever Fedroff would break containment and get to the edge, they didn't have Sam there to stop him.

Long Branch trailed by two touchdowns late in the fourth quarter. Bert Grandinetti caught a one-yard touchdown pass from Timmy Wilson with one second left to make it a seven-point game. But Carteret recovered the onside kick and hung on for a 29–22 win.

"We were down and we were out, but we never surrendered," Glazier said after the game. "When they had us down 29–8, it would have been easy to just quit. But we never gave up. We fought to the bitter end."

Until his senior year at Long Branch, Mills really hadn't given a lot of thought to going to college. He was a pretty good student. But the one thing he loved to do besides play football was work on cars. He was considering going to a trade school and learning to become an auto mechanic, and maybe eventually open his own garage.

Glazier talked him out of that.

Glazier said that he once gave Sam a car to work on when he was in high school and "he destroyed it." After that experience, Glazier yanked him out of all of his vocational classes, put Sam in the school's college-prep program, and told him in no uncertain terms that he would be going to college and playing football.

Given all that he accomplished at Long Branch High, Mills should have had his pick of Division I football offers. And if he had been three inches taller, that almost certainly would've been the case. But he was 5'9", and that scared the crap out of coaches and recruiters, just like it would later scare pro coaches and scouts.

Mills had been doubted his whole life because of his size, so it didn't come as a shock to him that college recruiters weren't beating a path to his door. The truth is, Sam himself wasn't convinced that he was good enough to play Division I football. Says his brother Leon, "His whole thing was that as long as he got an opportunity somewhere [he would be happy]."

Glazier and his staff did their best to find a Division I suitor for Mills, but they came up empty.

"If you're a coach and you watched his high school film—if you took any game he played and watched it—you were gonna go: *holy mackerel*," Simonelli said. "He hit people. Heads snapping back. Very rarely, if ever, did I ever see Sam go backwards. But everybody was so fixated on his height. We couldn't convince anybody."

Glazier had a ton of college contacts. He could pick up the phone and get Pitt's Johnny Majors or Penn State's Joe Paterno or Notre Dame's Dan Devine on the line. That's how respected and plugged in he was.

But when it came to Sam, no one would buy what Glazier was selling.

3

A lot of people figured I wouldn't get into a big school. And it turned out I didn't because of my height. But I enjoyed playing at Montclair and never, ever regretted going there.

—Sam Mills

MANY OF THE stories written about Sam Mills suggest that he was a walk-on at Montclair State. While technically true, it's not accurate. Division III schools like Montclair don't award athletic scholarships, then or now. So every athlete at a Division III school is technically a walk-on. But while they can't give out scholarships, Division III programs can recruit players. And Montclair most definitely recruited Mills.

Fred Hill, who was starting his second season as Montclair's head football coach in 1977, was well aware of the undersized tackling machine from Long Branch. Hill had been a high school coach in North Jersey for 10 years before taking the Montclair job, including six at Pequannock Township High School, which was just an hour and change up the Garden State Parkway from Mills' Long Branch stomping grounds.

Hill had watched Mills play his senior year at Long Branch and came away very impressed. "They got a real good football player over there," he told one of his assistants, Rick Giancola.

While the big schools weren't willing to take a chance on a 5'9" linebacker, Hill didn't have the same reservations. Division III ball, then as now, is filled with runts of the litter and kids who aren't considered fast enough, strong enough, or good enough to play at Notre Dame, Georgia, Alabama, or Ohio State.

Hill's first Montclair team the year before Mills arrived went 4–5–1. After watching Mills play at Long Branch, he felt the small playmaking linebacker was someone he could build a solid defense around.

Giancola, who would succeed Hill as Montclair's head coach in 1983, was assigned to hand out helmets and shoulder pads to the incoming freshmen on the first day of preseason practice in '77. He didn't immediately recognize Mills when he showed up for his equipment. Giancola, who was Montclair's line coach at the time, mistook him for an offensive lineman.

"Hey, congratulations. Glad to have you," Giancola said. "How would you like to play guard?"

"Coach, I'm a linebacker," Mills responded.

Fred Hill wasn't the only coach at Montclair excited by Sam's arrival on campus. So was the school's wrestling coach. Montclair had one of the top small-college wrestling programs in the country at the time. They had won the Division III national championship two years earlier.

The wrestling coach, Rich Sofman, started drooling when he found out Sam was coming to Montclair. He was well aware of his prowess on the mat. He'd been there at Princeton's Jadwin Gymnasium when Sam lost to Craig Blackman in the state finals.

Sofman was hoping he could convince Mills to wrestle *and* play football at Montclair. While Sam liked wrestling, he really wasn't interested in competing in two sports in college. He wanted to focus on football.

He would participate in the school's annual intramural wrestling tournament. When word would get out that he planned to compete, the other wrestlers signing up for the tournament would ask what weight class Sam was entering so they could be sure to wrestle in another weight class.

Like Frank Glazier, Fred Hill knew right away that he had something special in Mills. Sam became an immediate starter at Montclair as a freshman, beating out a senior who had been a starter for Hill the year before. The senior whom Sam beat out was also from Long Branch. He wasn't happy, but it didn't take him very long to realize Mills was a much better player than he was.

Mills was a natural leader. His teammates gravitated to him. He inspired them. That would be the case throughout his career.

He would be the first player on the practice field every single day, and he always—always—practiced hard. The other players saw his intensity. They saw his ability to make plays. He didn't say much, but he didn't have to. His play and his actions spoke volumes.

Montclair won five of its first six games in Sam's freshman year. They gave up a total of just *16 points* in those six games. Sam seemed to be in on every play.

In just his third game at Montclair, Sam turned in one of the greatest individual performances in the school's history against Southern Connecticut State. He recorded 22 tackles and had a long interception return for a touchdown for the only points of the game in a 7–0 victory.

Vinny DeMarinis, who was also a linebacker on that '77 Montclair team, said the performance reminded him of the time he saw New York Giants Hall of Famer Lawrence Taylor beat the Detroit Lions with a 97-yard interception return.

DeMarinis and Mills played together at Montclair for four years and became good friends. They would later spend another three years as teammates with the Philadelphia Stars.

They were very different types of players. DeMarinis was 6'4" and was a self-described "balls-to-the-wall" player, who relied on his aggressiveness to make plays. "If the guy is going this way, I'm going after him," he says. That style of play occasionally can lead to mistakes, but because of his aggressiveness, DeMarinis also made a ton of plays.

The 5'9" Mills played more under control. He always took the proper angle. He never got cut back on. Ever.

Montclair went 6–4 in Mills' freshman year. He led Montclair in tackles as a freshman and was a first-team All-New Jersey Athletic Conference selection.

He also became a father for the first time. Melanie became pregnant with their first child that fall. Sam III would be born the next spring.

"Every weekend, Sam would disappear after the game," says Terrence Porter, who was a wide receiver on the Montclair football team and one of Sam's close friends. "The rest of us would be out doing our thing, enjoying ourselves and living the college life as successful football players. But Sam would just vanish.

"I finally asked him, 'Hey, man. Where do you go every weekend?' That's when he told me that Mel was pregnant and he was going home to be with her."

Sam's outstanding play at Montclair as a freshman didn't cause any of the Division I schools who ignored him a year earlier due to his size to reconsider and offer him a scholarship. But one school did come knocking.

One of Montclair's New Jersey Athletic Conference rivals, William Paterson College, had hired a new football coach in August of '78. It was Frank Glazier, Mills' old high school coach at Long Branch.

Ed Balina had initially planned to join Mills at Montclair and play football with him. He had enrolled at the school earlier that summer, but he didn't receive an invitation from Fred Hill to Montclair's preseason camp. After Glazier got the job at William Paterson, he called Balina and asked him to join him there. Balina would star at running back for Glazier as a freshman.

Hill knew how close Glazier and Mills were and was concerned that his best player might transfer. He was concerned enough to ask Mills straight out.

"Are you thinking of leaving to play for Coach Glazier?" Hill asked Sam.

"Coach, I made my commitment to Montclair. I shook your hand," he said. "I'm staying at Montclair."

And that was that.

After getting the William Paterson job, Glazier would make one attempt to persuade Mills to transfer. But he wasn't surprised when Sam told him he was going to stay at Montclair.

"He knew Sam, knew the kind of person he was," said Simonelli. "He wasn't going to do that to Montclair. Glaz' didn't try and pressure him. He respected his decision."

Since they were in the same conference, Glazier's team had to play against Sam and Montclair every year. They were never able to beat them. The best they could do was a 7–7 tie in Mills' junior year.

During Mills' sophomore year, Glazier made Sam the primary focus of his team's pregame preparation the week before their meeting with Montclair.

Every day from Monday on, Balina said Glazier talked about Sam to his players. Hard to block. Nobody faster running sideline to sideline. Can take on a block and get off it.

By Thursday, the William Paterson offensive linemen were tired of hearing about Sam. Guys were coming up to Balina and saying, "Hey, I know you're friends with this guy and played with him in high school. But how good can he be?"

Balina leveled with them. He told them that Glazier wasn't exaggerating. He said Sam was faster than anybody he'd ever seen running sideline to sideline. He told them he knew where the ball was going before the snap.

"If you think you can block him, you might get a piece of him,"

Balina said. "But he'll be off of you like *that*, and he's going to be playing wherever the ball is going."

He received skeptical looks from his teammates. Balina looked at them and shrugged.

"Okay," he said. "You'll see on Saturday."

They did.

Glazier threw every trick in his playbook at Sam that day. He used reverses, flea-flickers, and a bunch of halfback passes by Balina. Anything to try and keep Sam off-balance.

For a while, that strategy worked. For a while. William Paterson even had a slight lead at halftime. But in the second half, Sam was all over the field making plays. Montclair, which would finish 8–2 that year and win its first NJAC title, won 38–24.

After the game, Balina and his William Paterson teammates were back in the dorm licking their wounds and rehashing the game.

"Coach was right," offensive tackle Dennis Hart said. "Sam was great. I'd fire out. I'd be in him, or at least think I was in him. I'd hit him hard. And just when I hit him and close my eyes for a split second, he'd be gone. I had no idea where he went."

"Hey, I'll tell you where he went, Den," Balina said. "He was coming after my ass, man."

4

Even before he signed with Cleveland, one of the things Sam used to say, pretty much every day, was, 'Man, I wish they would just give me a chance to fail.' That was his thing. Just give me a chance to fail. If I can't do it, then I can't do it. But don't just tell me I can't do it.

—Leon Mills

MONTCLAIR LOST A total of five games in Mills' final three years there, winning two NJAC titles. Sam was one of the most dominant college players in the country. He recorded 501 tackles in four years. He was the New Jersey Collegiate Football Writers Defensive Player of the Year three years running. He was a two-time first-team Kodak All-American.

But none of that mattered to NFL scouts, who typically paid little attention to Division III prospects, especially ones with a 5 and a 9 next to their height. Mills sat by the phone at his parents' home in Long Branch during the 1981 draft as 332 players, including a whopping 45 linebackers, were taken. Nobody called the house on N. 5th Avenue.

Even after the draft, none of the league's then 28 teams showed any interest in signing Mills as an undrafted free agent. Much like Frank Glazier and his staff did four years earlier when they tried to stir interest from Division I schools in Sam, his coaches at Montclair worked the phones, reaching out to every NFL contact they had.

Mills' position coach at Montclair was McKinley Boston. Boston had been a first-team All-Big Ten defensive lineman at the University of Minnesota. He was a 15th-round pick of the New York Giants in 1968 (the NFL draft had 17 rounds back then) and played in 27 games for them in 1968–69.

He had left Minnesota 18 credits short of his bachelor's degree. After the Giants cut him, he found his way to Montclair, where he became an assistant on Fred Hill's staff while he finished up work on his bachelor's degree and then got his master's.

One of the people Boston called about Sam was Jim Garrett, who was the running backs coach for the Cleveland Browns. Garrett had been on the Giants' coaching staff when Boston played there.

"Coach, I have a player here at Montclair who I think you should give a shot," Boston told Garrett.

"How big is he?" Garrett asked.

"Well, Coach, he can really play," said Boston.

"That's fine, but how big is he?" said Garrett.

"Well, he's about 225 pounds."

"How tall is he?"

"He can really play, Coach."

Boston desperately tried to keep from telling Garrett how tall Sam was. When he finally did, he fudged a little bit.

"I said he was about 5'11"," he said.

Garrett didn't say yes, but he didn't say no either. He told Boston that he would talk to his boss, Browns head coach Sam Rutigliano, and get back to him.

Like Mills, Garrett was a Jersey boy. He was born in Passaic and went to Rutherford High School, which was just three and a half miles from Giants Stadium and 55 miles from Long Branch.

Garrett and his wife, Jane, had eight children, including four football-playing boys—Jim III, John, Jason, and Judd. A big family needs a big house. Shortly after Garrett was hired as an assistant coach on

Alex Webster's Giants staff, he and his wife bought a large three-story house in Monmouth Beach, New Jersey, which bordered Long Branch.

The Garrett house was known to locals as the "Whale House" because of a large blue wooden whale that hung on one side of the house. The Whale House sat on Ocean Avenue, right across the road from the beach, and included an immense side yard that Garrett turned into a practice field for his sons and others.

"It was a big ol' house," says Jason, who was a quarterback at Princeton and played in the NFL for 14 years. He later was the Dallas Cowboys' head coach from 2011 to 2019. "It was falling down when my dad and mom bought it. But I had seven brothers and sisters, so there was no shortage of labor."

Jason's brother Jim was seven years older than him. He played college ball at Davidson and Oberlin. Jason, John, and Judd were each a year apart in age. They were all in their early teens at the time and had fallen in love with the sport their dad coached. Not long after moving into the Whale House, Jim Garrett started orchestrating backyard workouts for his sons.

The workouts initially were for kids who were around Jason, John, and Judd's ages—seventh-, eighth-, and ninth-graders—plus some contemporaries of their older brother Jim. Then older players from the Monmouth Beach area started coming around. Then players from neighboring towns. Then players from around the state.

"It was a structured practice format where these guys could get better," Jason says. "My dad, being a pro coach, obviously knew how to run something like that. As I reflect back, it was such an incredible opportunity for us, learning from all those players and getting better working with those guys."

The workouts became so popular that people would often stop by and watch on the way to the beach.

"Jim will give any kid a chance," Mills would say years later. "As long as they're about business and effort, he will let them come over there and practice. You saw a whole variety of talent over there over the years. But the one thing was, he let you take a shot."

Garrett's backyard workouts were very productive. He found some talented players for the teams he worked for. Dino Hall, who was from Pleasantville near Atlantic City, was a 5'7", 165-pound standout running back for Glassboro State (now Rowan University). He made the 80-mile drive up to the Whale House and worked out for Garrett and became the Browns' main punt and kick returner from 1979 to '83.

After speaking with Rutigliano, Garrett called McKinley Boston back and agreed to bring Mills over to the Whale House for a workout. The first thing Garrett realized after Sam got there was that Boston had fibbed about the kid's size. Sam wasn't anywhere close to 5'11". He wasn't even really 5'9". Closer to 5'8 ½", he thought.

But Sam impressed the hell out of Garrett that day. Everything Boston had said about him over the phone, with the exception of his size, was spot on.

"My dad really took a liking to Sam," Jason Garrett says. "We all did. I was 14, 15 years old at the time. Sam was 225 pounds. Carved out of a mountain. He was a physical presence. He was something else. For us, it was such a unique opportunity to be around him in those early years. He made such a positive impact on us."

Garrett called Rutigliano and convinced him to sign Mills and bring him to the Browns' training camp at Kent State University that summer. Just as McKinley Boston had fudged about Mills' height to him, Garrett did the same when he talked to Rutigliano. He figured his boss would find out soon enough.

All Sam wanted was an opportunity, and Garrett and the Browns seemingly were giving him one.

5

Don't look at how tall a guy is. Look at how fast he is and look at how he hits. Sam Mills was a guy who could knock your dick off.

—Browns offensive tackle Doug Dieken

KENT STATE UNIVERSITY is located in Kent, Ohio, 21 miles northeast of Akron and 51 miles southeast of Cleveland. The school got the worst kind of national attention in 1970 when four students were killed and nine others wounded by Ohio National Guardsmen during an antiwar rally on campus. It became forever known as the Kent State Massacre. Twenty-eight National Guard soldiers fired 67 rounds at protesters in a span of 13 seconds.

The Browns moved their training camp to Kent State in 1975 after training for more than 20 years at Hiram College. The Browns' camp at Kent State wasn't much different than any other NFL training camp back then.

All but three of the league's 28 teams trained on college campuses, or in the case of the New Orleans Saints in 1981, at the Los Angeles Dodgers' spring training facility in Vero Beach, Florida. Most coaches liked holding training camp away from home. They felt having the players live together for five to eight weeks in college dormitories and eating three meals a day together in the college cafeteria helped build camaraderie.

Times have changed. Today, most teams prefer the convenience of holding camp at their training facility. In 2025, 27 of the league's 32 teams, including the Browns, held training camp at home.

Sam Mills showed up at Kent State in the summer of '81 filled with hope. But the harsh truth was, no matter how well he played that summer, the size issue was always going to be there.

The Browns were coming off their best season in nearly a decade. Nicknamed the *Kardiac Kids* because so many of their games had gone down to the wire the previous season, they had finished 11–5 in 1980 and won their first division title since 1971 before losing by two points to the eventual Super Bowl champions, the Oakland Raiders, in the divisional round of the playoffs.

Quarterback Brian Sipe had the best season of his career in 1980. He had thrown for 4,132 yards and 30 touchdowns and finished with an NFL-best 91.4 passer rating. In that heartbreaking loss to the Raiders, the Browns had the ball at the Oakland 13-yard line late in the game. But a Sipe pass into the end zone for Hall of Fame tight end Ozzie Newsome was picked off.

The '80 Browns' defense hadn't been quite as good as the offense. It finished 12th in points allowed and 22nd in takeaways, but it had been very good against the run. Their four returning inside linebackers, the position where Mills would be competing for a roster spot, were four-year starter Dick Ambrose, '77 first-round pick Robert L. Jackson, 1980 third-round pick Cliff Odom, and Bill Cowher, the future Super Bowl-champion coach.

Cowher had signed with the Philadelphia Eagles in 1979 as an undrafted free agent out of North Carolina State. He was the last linebacker cut by them that summer. In '80, he signed with the Browns, made the team in training camp, and was a special teams standout on their division title team. At 6'3" and 225 pounds, Cowher was more of a prototypical linebacker than Mills, but he wasn't as fast as Sam.

Cowher, who would play four seasons in the NFL, primarily on special teams with the Browns, got to know Mills well that summer. They became friends. Or as close to friends as two players competing for the same roster spot can become.

They sat together in the same meeting room every day, right behind Ambrose and Jackson. "Sam was just a good guy," Cowher remembers. "A guy you wanted to root for."

When Mills walked into the Browns' training camp locker room for the first time that summer, he drew amused looks from the other players. *Hey, who's the little guy? Since when did we start signing circus midgets?* But Sam was used to the skepticism and the jokes. He didn't let it bother him. He didn't let it make him feel like he didn't belong there. Because he knew he did. Even if the coaches would have difficulty realizing it.

The amused looks from the Browns players quickly disappeared when Mills got on the practice field and started running around and hitting people. He punished ball carriers and stunned blockers with his six-inch punch. Because of his size, they often didn't see him coming until it was too late.

Jason Garrett and his brothers accompanied their father to Kent State that summer and followed Mills closely. They rooted for him. After meeting him at the Whale House, he quickly became their favorite player. The fact that they were as tall as he was helped them identify with him.

Cowher got hurt in the Browns' third preseason game that summer and would miss the entire '81 season. His misfortune appeared to be a huge break for Mills. Cowher told Sam as much. He told Sam that with him on injured reserve, he was a lock to make the Browns roster. He wasn't just blowing smoke up Mills' ass. Cowher truly believed it.

Mills called his brother Leon every day that summer and kept him abreast of how training camp was going. "I think he started, like, 10th on the depth chart, but kept moving up every day," Leon says. "Every day he was doing something special and would call me and tell me about it. He'd say, 'I had a nice interception,' or, 'I made some big tackles; I think they like me.' He was flying high."

The Browns' first preseason game that summer was against the Atlanta Falcons in the Hall of Fame Game in Canton, which wasn't far from their Kent State training camp. Mills was all over the field in that game, recording a dozen tackles. It wasn't a one-time thing. Every time Sam stepped foot on the field that summer, he flashed.

Matt Miller, Cowher's future brother-in-law, was an offensive guard on that '81 Browns team. When they were doing a light practice the day before a game, Miller came around the corner on a play and Sam jacked him up and put him on the ground.

"That goddamn Mills," Miller muttered later on the sideline.

"Matt, he's already underneath your pads because he's only 5'9"," Cowher told him. "He's just touching you."

"I know, but it's just so damn frustrating," Miller said. "I can't get him off his feet. I can't get underneath him because he's so damn short."

Cowher told Miller, "You can't tell Sam to slow down."

"I knew what he was doing," Cowher says. "He was trying to make the team. He was trying to make an impression. He was going to try and stand out however he could stand out."

One of Mills' nicknames at Montclair was "Cement." The other Browns linebackers found out the hard way why he was given that nickname. Their linebackers coach, Dave Adolph, would have his players do a headbutt drill. This was long before anyone understood the dangers of long-term brain damage from concussive hits to the head. Three linebackers would line up in front of a fourth linebacker and take turns running at him and headbutting him. Any time Sam was the guy the other linebackers had to run into, they would desperately try to avoid the line.

"It seemed like his head was made of solid rock," Ambrose remembers. "Any time you hit him it was an instant headache. Looking back on it now, it probably was the stupidest thing you could do."

Ambrose didn't have prototypical linebacker size, either. He was just 6'0". His nickname was "Bam-Bam," like the tiny but Hulk

Hogan-strong *Flintstones* character. But 6'0" was still three-plus inches taller than Mills.

Mills took advantage of every opportunity he got with the Browns that summer. He continued to flash in practices and games. After playing well in the Browns' fourth preseason game against Buffalo, and with Cowher now out for the season, Mills began to believe he was going to make the team.

Then, two days after the Bills game, Cleveland made a trade with the Dallas Cowboys for another linebacker, Bruce Huther. The 6'1", 221-pound Huther had spent four unremarkable seasons with the Cowboys. Like Cowher, he was primarily a special teams guy, with zero career starts. His biggest claim to fame was that he was one of the few players in NFL history with a degree in zoology (from the University of New Hampshire).

The day after acquiring Huther, Rutigliano called Mills into his office and informed him that they were going to be releasing him, but not until after the team's final preseason game that week against the Green Bay Packers.

The news absolutely devastated Mills. Because the Browns weren't going to cut him until after the Packers game, Mills had to suffer the ignominy of flying to Green Bay with the team and suiting up for a game he wasn't going to be allowed to play in. He was only being kept around in case something happened to one of the other linebackers.

After getting the news, Sam called his brother Leon and told him.

"He was in tears," Leon says. "He had dealt with a lot in his life, but I never heard him so down. It was like, *What more can I do? I had a great camp. I did everything they wanted and more. And they still cut me.* He was crushed."

Mills also called Ed Balina and told him. He broke down and cried on the phone with Balina as well.

The Browns' decision to cut Mills was 90 percent about his height and 10 percent about his lack of experience. They felt they needed more experience at the backup spot behind their two starting inside linebackers, Ambrose and Jackson. That's why they'd made the trade for Huther.

Huther started two games for the Browns in '81. He was used primarily on special teams. The '81 season didn't go nearly as well for the Browns as '80. They finished 5–11. The defense wasn't very good. They finished 23rd in points allowed, slipped from sixth to 18th against the run, and gave up the fourth most touchdown passes in the league. But all of that was little consolation to Mills.

After the '81 season, the Browns traded for the rights to linebacker Tom Cousineau, who had been the first pick in the 1979 NFL draft by the Buffalo Bills. Cousineau signed with the CFL's Montreal Alouettes after the Bills tried to lowball him, and spent three seasons in Canada. When the Browns signed Cousineau, Huther asked for a trade. The Browns obliged, sending him to the Chicago Bears.

Dave Adolph had pounded the table for Mills. He told the team's defensive coordinator, Marty Schottenheimer, to ignore Sam's height and judge him on his training camp performance, which had been off the charts. While Schottenheimer acknowledged that Mills had had an impressive camp, he just couldn't get past 5'9".

Schottenheimer would go on to win 200 games as a head coach with the Browns, Kansas City Chiefs, Washington Redskins, and San Diego Chargers. But he screwed up badly when he decided to let Sam Mills go.

Ironically, the guy who hired Marty to be the Chiefs' head coach in 1989, Carl Peterson, was also the guy who would give Mills his big break with the USFL's Philadelphia Stars a year and a half later.

"I never let Marty forget it," Peterson says. "I used to kid him and say, 'You sure have a great eye for talent, man.'"

For what it was worth, Mills did manage to make a significant impression on Rutigliano. "Before I left camp, he told me not to give up," Mills said. "He told me I had talent and that I could play football.

I was really disappointed about getting cut. But those words meant a lot to me."

After getting released, Mills packed up his old Thunderbird for the long, seven-and-a-half-hour drive back home to Long Branch. He didn't know what was next for him. He had Melanie and three-year-old Sam III to support. He couldn't keep chasing a dream at their expense. He had played his ass off with the Browns, certainly well enough to make the team. And they cut him simply because they didn't think he was big enough.

As Mills was pulling out of the parking lot to head home, Jim Garrett flagged him down and asked him to come into his office for a second. When he got in there, Garrett put his arm around him and complimented him on how well he had played.

He gave him a similar pep talk to the one Rutigliano had given him earlier. He told Mills he had played well enough to make the team. He told him the Browns had made a mistake in cutting him. He told him he knew how disappointed he was but urged him not to give up football. He assured him that he would get another chance somewhere.

Mills wasn't so sure about that. But he promised Garrett that he wouldn't give up on his dream.

6

Sam made us all look bad. He made people in two countries look bad. He was internationally messing with everybody.

—Dale Lindsey, Toronto Argonauts defensive coordinator, 1980–82

THE LONG, SEVEN-AND-A-HALF-HOUR DRIVE from Kent, Ohio, back to Long Branch, most of it on I-80 through rural Pennsylvania and New Jersey, gave Mills a lot of time to think. He was used to dealing with doubters. But getting cut unexpectedly by the Browns, well, that was a gut punch.

He had promised Garrett he wouldn't give up on his football dream. But much of it was out of his control. He needed another team to give him a chance. And he needed that team to judge him on what he did on the field rather than on his size. After what had happened with the Browns, he wasn't sure that would ever be possible. He knew he had played well there. As well as he could. His coaches knew that too. In the end, it still hadn't mattered.

But first, he needed to take care of his family. Sam, Melanie, and Sam III were living upstairs in his mother's duplex on N. 5th Avenue. He took a job as a substitute teacher and worked odd jobs to pay the bills, including one as a uniformed security guard on the Long Branch pier.

Sports heroes like Mills weren't supposed to wind up as rent-a-cops. Bill Hill was a good friend of Sam's. They had played against each other in high school when Hill was a star running back at Howell

High School, and they became lifetime friends. They worked out regularly together. Sam had introduced Hill to Jim Garrett, who also had signed him with the Browns.

"I was living in a high-rise at the time," Hill says. "I was down on the boardwalk one night and saw Sam in that security guard outfit. When you see a guy like him in a security uniform, it's kind of crushing. I knew it wasn't what he wanted to be doing."

No, it wasn't. But Mills wasn't about to feel sorry for himself.

He taught school during the day and patroled the Long Branch pier on nights and weekends. In between, he made sure to create enough time each day to work out. Mills enjoyed working out. He loved the weight room. He hardly was a workout fanatic, but he understood the importance of being strong and in shape. Frank Glazier had ingrained that into him.

His entire career, from his days at Long Branch High with Glazier to his final NFL stop with the Carolina Panthers, Mills outworked everyone. Part of it was the work ethic he got from his mother, Juanita. But a bigger part of it was that he always felt he had to. Because he knew that no one was ever going to give a 5'9" linebacker the benefit of the doubt.

"I'm just one bad practice from getting cut," he would say regularly.

Despite the encouraging words from Garrett and Rutigliano after he was cut by the Browns, Mills knew Cleveland was not going to invite him back to their training camp in 1982. They had made up their mind about him: *Good player, but just too short to play in the NFL.* And a growth spurt at the age of 23 wasn't in the cards. Sam hoped that maybe another NFL team that had seen him on film in the Browns' preseason games that summer might have been impressed enough to give him a shot. But that didn't happen.

In early February 1982, he got a call from his agent, Grassella Oliphant, who told him the Toronto Argonauts of the Canadian Football League were interested in bringing him to their training camp. The

CFL season started earlier than the NFL season—in early June. As a result, their training camps opened in late April, as opposed to NFL camps, which opened in mid- to late July.

It wasn't the NFL, but it also wasn't something Mills felt he could afford to thumb his nose at if he ever hoped to eventually play in the NFL. He knew the NFL signed players out of Canada. Maybe he'd catch someone's eye up there.

Unlike the Browns, who were coming off an 11–5 season and a playoff appearance the year before Mills went to camp with them, the Argos were a mess. They had finished 2–14 the previous year. Toronto had been one of the CFL's elite franchises in the '40s and early '50s, winning five Grey Cups in eight years from 1945 to 1952. But that was a generation ago. They hadn't had a winning season in eight years and hadn't won a division title since 1971.

The previous year, they had hired former Detroit Lions coach Tommy Hudspeth to be their head coach. But he was shown the door after just one season and was replaced by Bob O'Billovich, a 42-year-old former CFL defensive back who had been an assistant with the Ottawa Rough Riders.

The CFL game had some significant differences from the NFL. The most notable: It was played on a larger field. A CFL field is 110 by 65 yards with 25-yard end zones. An NFL field is 100 by 53.3 yards with 10-yard end zones.

The Canadian game also has just three downs rather than four. So, the CFL game has always been more about the pass and less about the run, even back in the early '80s when most NFL offenses were still leaning heavily on the three-yards-and-a-cloud-of-dust approach. The CFL also had a limit on how many American players a team could have on its roster. It generally fluctuated between 40 and 45 percent.

With a little less enthusiasm than a year earlier with the Browns, Mills packed up the old Thunderbird, kissed Melanie and Sam III goodbye, and drove north to Toronto from Long Branch, feeling reasonably confident that he'd be able to make the team.

That said, when O'Billovich and his defensive coordinator, Dale Lindsey, got their first up-close look at Mills, they had the same reservations as the Browns: *too short.*

Lindsey remembers Sam as a very astute player, but he had zero experience in the Canadian game.

"It's a totally different game up there," says Lindsey. "The field is much larger, and we felt we needed somebody taller and with more range."

Which begs the question: Why did they even bother inviting him to camp in the first place? Didn't they bother to check his measurables? Then again, this was an incompetent organization that had had one winning season (7–5–2 in 1973) in the previous 10 years. There were a lot of things they apparently missed.

Like the Browns the year before, Toronto ended up trading for another linebacker and eventually releasing Mills. Lindsey would later work as an assistant with five NFL teams. Cutting Sam definitely wasn't the proudest moment of his career.

"We cut Sam Mills," he says, "which tells you how dumb we were."

Lindsey's and Mills' paths would cross many times when both of them were in the USFL, Mills as a linebacker for the Philadelphia Stars and Lindsey as a coach for the Boston Breakers (1983) and New Jersey Generals (1984–85).

"Every time we played them, I'd be thinking, 'What a dumbass you are, Dale,'" he says. "'The guy is running around making plays and you didn't know enough to keep him when you had the chance.'"

Mills was disappointed when Toronto released him, but not nearly as disappointed as he was when Cleveland had cut him. He wasn't all that fired up about the prospect of playing in Canada. But once again, he had played well enough to make the team, and was being sent home because the coaches couldn't get past 5'9".

Returning to Long Branch, Mills figured his dream of ever playing professional football almost certainly was over. He resigned himself to getting on with the rest of his life. He'd find a teaching job, become a high school coach, and focus on his family.

7

Sports aren't easy, man. There's a lot of bad, a lot of obstacles along the way. A lot of guys don't get past what Sam got past to get there.

—Terry Bradway, longtime NFL personnel executive and scout

After getting cut by the Toronto Argonauts in the early spring of 1982, Mills thought his playing career was over. "I kept telling myself that the end has to come for everybody," he said.

He started to get on with the rest of his life, finding a job at East Orange (NJ) High School teaching black-and-white photography and helping coach the football team. He still held out a sliver of hope that someone might give him one more shot. But there weren't a lot of playing options left for him, aside from maybe a $50-a-game semipro league. The NFL had decided he was too short. So had the CFL.

Then along came the United States Football League.

In May of '82, shortly after the Argos had cut Mills, a New Orleans antiques dealer named David Dixon, surrounded by a dozen investors from around the country, held a press conference at the 21 Club in New York City to announce the formation of a new league called the United States Football League. It would play in the spring rather than head-to-head against the NFL in the fall and have 12 teams in New York/New Jersey, Boston, Chicago, Detroit, Washington, DC, Los Angeles, Phoenix, Birmingham, Oakland, Denver, Tampa, and

Philadelphia. All but Birmingham, an SEC college football hotbed, were proven pro football markets.

Dixon announced that the new spring league would start play in March of '83 and already had television deals in place with ABC and ESPN, the fledgling all-sports channel that had launched in 1981.

The day after the announcement, Mills got a call from Grassella Oliphant telling him about the new league. Oliphant represented several small-college players, including Mills and his former Montclair teammate Terrence Porter.

Oliphant wasn't your typical agent. He was a former jazz drummer who had played in the '50s and '60s with Sarah Vaughan, Gloria Lynne, Shirley Scott, and others. He released a couple of soul jazz albums in the '60s and was part-owner of a small jazz club in East Orange.

"Grass was a good man," says Porter. "He repped a lot of the unknown players from the New York/New Jersey area who were just looking to get a shot with somebody or at least get into a camp. He cared about us. He got us in the door, got us a look. That's all you can ask for at that level."

When Oliphant told Mills about the USFL, Sam was skeptical.

"Right away, I said, 'The USFL? What's that, some kind of semipro league?'" Mills said. "'What is this thing?'"

The Philadelphia franchise, which was named the Stars, was owned by Myles Tanenbaum, a tax lawyer turned shopping mall developer. He hired Carl Peterson, who had been the Philadelphia Eagles' player personnel director the previous six years and had helped Dick Vermeil build the Eagles' 1980 Super Bowl team, to be the team's president and general manager.

Peterson was the perfect architect to build a football team from scratch. After serving as an assistant coach on Vermeil's staff at UCLA, he went with him to Philadelphia when he took the Eagles' job in 1976. Vermeil moved Peterson from the sideline to the front office as the team's personnel chief, and Peterson's keen eye for talent was invaluable. He helped Vermeil turn around a hapless organization that had had nine straight non-winning seasons and had traded away most of their top draft picks before they arrived. Four years later, they made it to the Super Bowl.

Peterson knew where the bodies were buried. As a former NFL personnel man, he had a lot of friends in the league, which was a big help when he began building the Stars. Lynn Stiles replaced Peterson as the Eagles' player personnel chief after he went to the Stars. Stiles and Peterson were close friends. They had worked together for Vermeil at both UCLA and the Eagles. Stiles would give Peterson a sneak peek at the NFL waiver wire so that he could sign players before they were claimed by other NFL teams.

Oliphant contacted several teams, including the Stars, about Mills. A couple of months passed with no response. Finally, Peterson and the Stars called back and invited Sam to one of the tryout camps they were holding at Penn Charter High School in Philadelphia.

Browns coach Sam Rutigliano hadn't forgotten about the undersized linebacker he had cut the previous year. He called Peterson that summer and recommended Sam. He told Peterson that the only reason they cut him was because his defensive coordinator (Schottenheimer) didn't think he was big enough to play. Rutigliano asked one favor of Peterson.

"If you do sign him," said Rutigliano, "don't cut him until you've seen him hit."

Peterson brought in a number of NFL castoffs, including fullback David "Duck" Riley, offensive guard Chuck Commiskey, safety Mike Lush, tight ends Steve Folsom and Ken Dunek, and wide receiver Tom Donovan.

He drafted and signed top young college players, such as running back Kelvin Bryant, offensive linemen Irv Eatman and Bart Oates, linebackers Mike Johnson and George Jamison, defensive back Antonio

Gibson, defensive end William Fuller, and punter Sean Landeta. He persuaded veteran NFL players like quarterback Chuck Fusina, linebacker John Bunting, nose tackle Pete Kugler, and wide receiver Scott Fitzkee to jump to the new league.

Fusina had an impressive 29–3 record as a three-year starter at Penn State. He had been the 1978 Heisman Trophy runner-up to Oklahoma's Billy Sims in one of the closest Heisman votes in history.

Sims was the first overall pick in the 1980 NFL draft. He rushed for 1,000 yards in three of his first four seasons. Fusina was taken in the fifth round of the '79 draft by the Tampa Bay Bucs. He spent three seasons with the Bucs as Doug Williams' backup, playing in just seven games and attempting a total of five regular-season passes. When Peterson called him and offered him the opportunity to be the starting quarterback for the Stars, Fusina, who was tired of riding the bench in Tampa, jumped at it.

Before he signed Fusina, Carl Peterson picked Joe Paterno's brain about his former quarterback. JoePa told him that Fusina "doesn't look good throwing the ball and he doesn't look good running with it. All he'll do is win games for you."

That was good enough for Peterson.

The tryout camps at Penn Charter that the Stars held during the summer and fall of '82 were mainly to find a few diamonds in the rough—a few obscure players who might be able to compete for a bottom-of-the-roster spot in a new spring league.

Mills still wasn't sure what to make of the USFL. Was it legitimate? And even if it was, did he really want to risk getting his heart broken a third time?

But Oliphant and others convinced him that he had nothing to lose by driving down to Philly and participating in the camp.

Tanenbaum initially tried to get Paterno to be the Stars' head coach. Paterno was at the height of his popularity in the early '80s. The Nittany Lions had finished in the top five in the national rankings three of the previous five years, including a No. 3 finish in 1981. Tanenbaum offered JoePa a boatload of money. He even threw in a beach house at the Jersey shore. Paterno was tempted but ultimately decided to stay in Happy Valley.

Peterson eventually persuaded Tanenbaum to go with a coach with NFL experience. That ended up being Pittsburgh Steelers assistant head coach/defensive coordinator George Perles.

Perles had hired just one assistant when the Stars held their tryout camps. That was his offensive coordinator, Joe Pendry, who previously had been the OC at Michigan State. Pendry ran the drills at the tryouts. He also provided the temporary "office" that Peterson used at the tryouts to sign players.

Pendry had a conversion van with captain's chairs, which were popular back then. The van also had a table right behind the captain's chairs. After the tryout, if there were any players they were interested in signing, Pendry would send them over to the van, where Peterson would be sitting in one of the captain's chairs with a player contract and pen.

"My son was in the sixth or seventh grade at the time," says Pendry. "We didn't have a lot of help. So, I had him writing the 40 times down and telling the guys to go see Carl. My son is 54 now, but he still talks about that. He's the one who went to Sam and told him to go see Carl."

Mills aced the tryout. After it was over, he was sent over to the van by Pendry's son to talk to Peterson, who offered the future Hall of Famer a two-year deal that would pay him the princely sums of $18,500 the first year and $22,000 the second year, plus a $500 signing bonus.

By comparison, the NFL rookie minimum in 1983 was $30,000, not including the player's signing bonus. Walker Lee Ashley, who was a linebacker out of Penn State taken in the third round of the '83 NFL draft by the Minnesota Vikings, received a $50,000 signing bonus. John Elway, the first overall pick in the draft that year, signed a five-year, $5 million deal that included a $1.5 million signing bonus.

If Peterson was expecting Mills to grab the pen and say, *Where do I sign?* he was disappointed. Mills told him he'd have to think about it and would get back to him. He did say it very respectfully.

It wasn't really the small contract Peterson offered him that gave Mills pause. It was the situation. It was the fact that it was a brand-new league. He knew before he drove down to Philly for the tryout that they wouldn't be offering guys like him NFL money. He just wasn't sure he wanted to go through the whole grind again and risk getting told once more that he was too small, this time by a startup league. And there was no guarantee the USFL was even going to survive longer than a millisecond.

He had his young family to consider. Melanie was now pregnant with their second child. After a year of being a substitute, he had the security now of a full-time teaching job, which paid a lot more than the Stars were offering him. And he was coaching, which he really enjoyed. What if the league went belly-up a month into the season? This was a team that was signing players out of a *conversion van.*

Mel had been very supportive of his pro football dream. At the same time, family had always been incredibly important to Sam, and he wondered whether it would be fair to them to walk away from the security of a teaching job for whatever the USFL was.

Mills went back home to North Jersey after the tryout and spent the better part of two months debating whether to sign with the Stars.

He talked to a number of people after he returned from the Stars' tryout camp. One of them was Jim Garrett. Mills had become a regular workout visitor to the Whale House, which was just a few miles from his home in Long Branch. Mills told Garrett he wasn't sure about the whole USFL thing. Garrett encouraged him to give the spring league a shot.

"I still remember that dynamic between him and my dad," Jason Garrett says. "My dad said, 'You've got to do it, Sam. You've got to give it one more shot.'"

Garrett was convincing. He made Mills realize that if he didn't sign with the Stars, he would always regret it.

"I looked at what could happen if I didn't make it, and I looked at what could happen if I did make it," Mills would say. "So much happened in those two months. There was so much I was thinking about. I could've easily made the decision to keep teaching. But I realized I loved playing football too much to give it up yet. It was a gamble. But it was a gamble I had to take."

8

I was 6'2". I could run a 4.5 40. I could get to the ball and make plays. While I developed, they were willing to work with me. But when you're 5'9" and you're learning stuff, they're not willing to work with you. They just say he can't do it. He's too short. Keep it moving.

—Two-time Pro Bowl linebacker Mike Johnson

THE IDEA OF a spring football league in the early '80s was a good one. People can't get enough football, regardless of what time of the year it's being played. Even today, as the NFL plays on almost every day of the week, there doesn't seem to be a saturation point.

While it would only last three years, the USFL was a lot of fun to watch, and it gave a lot of good players an opportunity to extend their careers. The quality of play was very good. The USFL managed to lure dozens of players from the NFL. It outbid the NFL for a significant chunk of the top college talent. And it developed stars who had been shunned or had fallen between the NFL cracks, like Sam Mills.

The Stars would become the best team in the short-lived league. They would make three USFL title-game appearances and win two of them. Twenty-nine of their players would go on to play in the NFL after the league folded. Five of their players would appear in a total of 18 Pro Bowls. Eighteen players would play in at least 30 NFL games and/or make 15 NFL starts.

The Stars' talent wasn't just on the field. They produced four future NFL general managers—Peterson (Chiefs), Bill Kuharich (Saints), Bradway (Jets), and Rod Graves (Cardinals). They also produced four NFL head coaches—Jim Mora (Saints, Colts), Vince Tobin (Cardinals), Dom Capers (Panthers, Texans), and Vic Fangio (Broncos). Several more of Mora's assistants with the Stars would become NFL coordinators. Mills is one of five former USFL players in the Pro Football Hall of Fame, along with Reggie White (Memphis Showboats), Gary Zimmerman (LA Express), Jim Kelly (Houston Gamblers), and Steve Young (LA Express).

Because it initially was viewed as a second-class league, the players in the USFL developed an us-against-the-world mentality. It brought them closer together than they might've been under ordinary circumstances.

"We all had a collective chip on our shoulders," says Mike Johnson, who signed with the Stars out of Virginia Tech. "I remember talking to Reggie White about it once. It was something we all carried with us out of the USFL. Because people were questioning: *Can you play?* And the last thing you want to do with people that can play is question that they can't."

Mills was used to being doubted. It drove him throughout his entire career. Even after he became successful, he continued to take the attitude that he had very little margin for error. *One bad practice.*

The weather in Philadelphia in February wasn't ideal for a football training camp. So, the Stars and several other cold-weather USFL teams copied baseball and headed to Florida and Arizona to prepare for the league's initial spring season in '83. The New Jersey Generals trained in Orlando. The Birmingham Stallions and Michigan Panthers were in Daytona Beach. The Washington Federals were headquartered in Jacksonville.

The Stars hunkered down at Stetson University in Deland, Florida, a small town about 25 miles southwest of Daytona Beach. Deland, which is part of the Deltona-Daytona Beach-Ormond Beach metropolitan area, was the county seat of Volusia County. The population of Deland back then was about 15,000. The highlight of the 30-minute drive from Daytona Beach to Deland is going past Daytona International Speedway, home of NASCAR's Daytona 500.

Stetson is a private university that spans 175 acres. Named for the famous hatmaker, John B. Stetson, it has 2,300 undergraduates and had roughly the same number back in the '80s when the Stars trained there.

Stetson didn't have a football program in 1983. They had discontinued the sport in the '50s and wouldn't bring it back until 2013. The school gave the Stars use of some of its fields to practice on. Because school was in session when they were there, the Stars couldn't use Stetson's dormitories to house their players, coaches, and staff. So, they bunked at a couple of local hotels during training camp. The team's coaches and staff stayed at a Holiday Inn. The players were at a Motel 6 across the street from the school's fieldhouse.

The Stetson tennis coach let Carl Peterson use his office in the fieldhouse while the Stars were in town. The school found the team other rooms in the fieldhouse to hold meetings.

The Stars used two different practice fields, one for their morning practice and another for the afternoon session. The second field was in the middle of town. The team would take school buses back and forth.

Peterson and Tanenbaum had to scramble to find a new coach after Perles abruptly resigned in early December to take the head-coaching job at his alma mater, Michigan State. In mid-January, just two weeks before the team was scheduled to open its first training camp, they hired New England Patriots defensive coordinator Jim Mora. Peterson knew Mora. They had worked together on Dick Vermeil's UCLA staff in the mid-'70s.

Because Mora was hired so late, Peterson had to put together most of his coaching staff for him. The only assistant that Mora personally hired was his running backs coach, Jim Skipper. The first time Mora met the rest of his staff, including his offensive and defensive coordinators, Joe Pendry and Vince Tobin, was when he arrived in Deland the day before the start of training camp in early February.

It was the same with all his players. He didn't meet any of them until he walked onto the practice field at Stetson. Terry Bradway was still making copies of the offensive playbook with Pendry right up until they boarded the plane for Deland from Philadelphia.

"That was kind of nuts," Bradway remembers. "But that was the reality of the situation."

The coaching staff came from all over. Tobin and offensive line coach Jim Erkenbeck were hired out of the CFL. Tobin had spent the previous six years in Canada as the defensive coordinator for the BC Lions. Erkenbeck had been an assistant with the Calgary Stampeders.

Defensive line coach John Pease, quarterbacks and receivers coach Carl Smith, defensive backs coach Dom Capers, and special teams coach Joe Marciano were all college coaches. Pease had been at the University of Washington, Smith at North Carolina State, Capers at Ohio State, and Marciano at Temple.

"Nobody knew each other," says Tobin, who also coached the team's linebackers in addition to being the defensive coordinator. "We were all thrown together."

Prior to coaching in Canada, Tobin had spent six seasons as the defensive coordinator at his alma mater, the University of Missouri. He had been a running back at Mizzou and played in the same offensive backfield with Tigers quarterback Jim Johnson. Interestingly, both Johnson and Tobin would go on to become two of the most respected *defensive* coaches in the NFL during their careers.

Mora was an ex-Marine, and he ran a grueling training camp. He wanted the practices to be harder than the games. He felt that if you survived his practices, the games would be a piece of cake.

Hard practices were just fine with Mills. It provided him with more opportunities to prove that he belonged, which was all he ever wanted.

There were a lot of players in Deland like Mills. With the exception of Oates and a few other draft picks like Eatman, and some NFL veterans like Bunting and Fitzkee who had switched leagues, the camp was full of players who had been cut once, twice, three times, or more by NFL teams.

For Mills, the biggest difference with the Stars compared to his training camp experiences with the Browns and Toronto Argonauts was that he had an immediate supervisor—Tobin—who didn't give a shit about the fact that he was only 5'9".

When Tobin was hired by the Stars, he immediately began trying to put together the best defense he could. He would've played with a 4'6" linebacker if the guy could get off blocks and tackle people.

Tobin might not have had any objections to a 5'9" linebacker, but Mora was a different story. The Stars coach initially felt there was no way the Stars could possibly keep Mills on the roster, let alone start him. He wanted to cut him.

Every night after practice, the Stars coaches and personnel people would gather around a table in a room at the Stetson fieldhouse and evaluate their players at each position. Because Tobin also coached the linebackers, he would be asked to rate that position's players. Every night, from the first practice on, Mills would be his top-rated linebacker.

And every night, Mora would look at Tobin in disbelief and tell him that they couldn't play with a 5'9" middle linebacker.

"We just can't do that," Mora would say. "We've got to get somebody better. People will laugh at us."

Tobin would reiterate that Mills, regardless of his size, was the best linebacker they had on the roster. He looked at his boss, whom he barely knew at that point, and told him, "If you want to get rid of every other linebacker we've got and start over, that's fine. But as long as I'm evaluating them, he's our best player."

This went on for the first couple of weeks of camp. Every night Mora would say they couldn't keep a 5'9" linebacker, and every night Tobin would inform him that Mills was not just his best linebacker, but his best defensive player. Mora kept looking for a reason to cut Mills, but Sam wouldn't give him one. At every single practice in Deland, he was the best defensive player on the field.

"If Vince hadn't been there, I'm not sure anybody would've stood up for Sam," says Bill Kuharich, who was a 29-year-old assistant general manager for the Stars. "But Vince wasn't afraid to stand up to anybody, including Jim. With Vince, it could've been Tom Landry or Bill Walsh he was talking to. He believed what he believed. He stood right up to Jim."

As that first training camp drew to a close, Mora would grudgingly admit that Tobin was right about Mills. That didn't mean he was crazy about the idea of starting a 5'9" linebacker. But his attitude was: *He's obviously the best we've got, so let's go play with him and see what happens.*

While Mora might've been slow to come around to the idea of playing with a 5'9" linebacker, the defensive players in the Stars' training camp weren't. They watched Mills, whom they affectionately nicknamed "Field Mouse," fly around the practice field every single day, drilling ball carriers and beating blockers who were more than a half-foot taller than him. Mills wasn't crazy about his new nickname, but he didn't object too strongly.

"Nobody was going to call him Field Mouse unless Sam was okay with being called that," says Duck Riley.

Mills took his share of kidding over his size, but he was used to it. His jersey number with the Stars was 54. Running back Allen Harvin used to ask him whether that was his number or his height. The irony there was that Harvin was the same size as Mills.

"I used to tell him, 'When you walk into a room, even little babies are trying to measure themselves up against you,'" Riley laughs.

In addition to the Field Mouse nickname, Sam's new teammates also called him "Little Daddy Love." Whenever the Stars would play on the road and the bathroom in their locker room would have a little boy's urinal, Riley would put a sign on it that read: "Reserved for Sam Mills and Allen Harvin."

Mills' off-the-field personality was very different from his on-the-field personality. Stars center Bart Oates said Sam was a "gentle, easygoing, go-with-the-flow guy" off the field. He would wear big horn-rimmed glasses that made him look more like an accountant than a professional football player.

"He didn't have that intensity until he got on the field," Oates says. "When he was on the field, he became someone who was very different than what his normal nature was."

John Bunting signed with the Stars two weeks into the '83 season after spending 11 seasons with the Eagles. He had started 116 games for the Eagles at linebacker. He was 32, almost 33, and at the tail end of his career. Bunting had been one of the Eagles' defensive leaders who helped Dick Vermeil's 1980 team make it to the Super Bowl.

Bunting's first impression of Mills after he signed with the Stars was the same as everybody else meeting him for the first time. "He was so short," says Bunting. "I'm like, *really*?"

Bunting thought Peterson had brought him in to be the Stars' defensive signal caller. That's what he had done with the Eagles. That's what he was very good at, besides beating the shit out of the tight end and playing zone coverage and reading plays and tipping off his teammates. But he quickly realized that on the Stars' defense, that job already was taken.

By Mills.

He also realized after getting in the huddle with Mills that Sam was a guy who demanded attention and was as sharp as a tack. Bunting was immediately impressed with his mental acuity.

"He was always calm," Bunting says. "He never got mad. He never got flustered. He never got excited. That's what a signal caller needs to do. He reminded me of myself a lot. And I appreciated that."

Stars offensive tackle Joe Conwell, who would start 21 games for the Eagles in 1986 and 1987, said Mills was the best teammate he ever had, and he believes most of the other people who ever played with Sam would say the same thing.

"He so quickly and thoroughly proved himself that everybody totally bought into Sam and looked up to him," says Conwell. "Combine that with the fact that he was the most fundamentally sound football player that you can imagine—from reading keys, to pursuit angles, to block-shedding, to tackling, to filling holes, to huddle management, to game preparation—it's like it all came naturally to him."

Mills was like a coach on the field. He had an uncanny knack for reading what the offense was going to do and would quickly relay the information to his teammates. No defense he ever played on was caught off guard by the offense.

Glenn "Moe" Howard, who played alongside Mills at the other inside linebacker spot in Tobin's 3–4 scheme, remembers Mills telling him to watch for particular plays depending on what he saw pre-snap from the offense.

"We'd always be communicating back and forth," Howard says.

Like so many others on that Stars team, Mills and Howard were football rejects. They had been cut by other teams. They had been told they weren't good enough, big enough, or fast enough. They were on their second, third, or even fourth try at living out their childhood dream of playing professional football. The Stars and the USFL gave all of them that.

Mills' training camp roommate was another NFL reject, George Cooper. Cooper, a linebacker out of Michigan State, had been cut by the Steelers the year before. "Sam didn't talk a lot, and neither did I,"

Cooper says. "But we became close. That was the time of our lives, those three years [with the Stars]. Just an unforgettable experience."

Sam would be the best man at Cooper's wedding, and George would be the godfather to Sam and Melanie's son Marcus, who was born during the Stars' first season in '83.

The entire defense bonded very quickly. Many of them would hang out in the locker room after practice and play chess. That was their outlet. It was a terrific team-building exercise.

They ribbed each other and constantly played practical jokes on their teammates. Mills became one of the ring leaders. "You'd be hustling to get out to practice, and Sam would hide your shoe or something like that," Howard says.

Even though they were only in their 20s, both Sam and Duck Riley were already losing their hair. Rex Patterson, who was the Stars' equipment manager, would throw towels to the players after they came out of the shower. When Mills and Riley would come out, he'd throw them washcloths to dry their hair.

"Sam and I would be next to each other by the sinks in the locker room looking in the mirror," Riley says. "Sam always would say, 'Yours is leaving quicker than mine.'"

"Every day there was something going on in that locker room," Riley recalls. "Nothing inappropriate or mean or anything. But we had fun. Coach Mora's practices were grueling. He had to always be thinking, *I don't understand. I'm killing them. Why are they in such a good mood?*"

9

When I walked into the Stars' camp, from day one, I felt I was the last person. It's better to feel that way than to think you're on top and then find yourself on the bottom.

—SAM MILLS

HERSCHEL WALKER WAS the USFL's biggest signing in 1983. About three weeks into training camp, the New Jersey Generals, who were owned by Oklahoma oilman J. Walter Duncan, persuaded the Heisman Trophy-winning running back from the national champion runner-up, the University of Georgia, to leave college early and sign a three-year, $5 million contract that made him the highest-paid player in professional football at the time.

The NFL was very upset about Walker's signing. NFL rules at the time prevented college players from entering the NFL draft until they had completed *all* of their college eligibility, or their class had graduated. So, Walker had been off-limits to them. But the USFL had no such rule. The NFL's PR machine tried to portray the new spring league as football pedophiles.

Walker arrived at the Generals' Orlando training camp in grand fashion, flying in on Duncan's helicopter, which dropped him off on the 50-yard line of one of their practice fields at the University of Central Florida. Duncan would end up selling the Generals to New York real estate developer Donald Trump after the USFL's first season.

Two weeks before Herschel Walker signed with the New Jersey Generals, the Stars also signed one of the nation's top college running backs, albeit at a much lower price.

In addition to holding a regular college draft, each USFL team was assigned a handful of "territorial" schools. Two of the Stars' territorial schools were Penn State and North Carolina. As it happened, Penn State's Curt Warner and UNC's Kelvin Bryant were considered two of the top four college running backs in 1983, along with Walker and SMU's Eric Dickerson.

Just as they did with Paterno, the Stars made a hard run at Warner. At one point, Myles Tanenbaum believed Warner was going to sign with the Stars. Warner and the Nittany Lions had just won the school's first national championship, beating Walker's Georgia Bulldogs in the Sugar Bowl.

At the last minute, Warner got cold feet about signing with the new league and ultimately chose to wait for the NFL draft, where he was selected by the Seattle Seahawks with the third overall pick. Warner was the real deal. He would rush for 1,449 yards and 13 touchdowns for the Seahawks as a rookie and would go on to have four 1,000-yard seasons in his first six years in the NFL.

After getting rejected by Warner, the Stars quickly turned their attention to the 6'2", 195-pound Bryant, a versatile three-time All-ACC tailback coming off three straight 1,000-yard rushing seasons in Chapel Hill. Bryant signed a three-year, $2 million deal with the Stars a week into training camp.

The NFL was still very much a run-first league in the early '80s. So, there was a higher premium placed on running backs back then than there is now. Future Hall of Famer Eric Dickerson was the second pick in the NFL draft that spring, right after Stanford quarterback John Elway and right before Warner. Bryant also likely would've been a top-10 NFL pick if he hadn't signed with the Stars. He was a big, fast running back who seemed to glide across the football field.

"Kelvin just had a different gear," says Duck Riley. "He had that *it* factor."

Before Bryant arrived at the Stars' training camp, there were about 10 tailbacks and two or three fullbacks on the team's roster. The day after Kelvin got there, there were three tailbacks and about 13 fullbacks.

"Kelvin was our best player on offense by far," says Chuck Fusina. "He did things that made me and our offensive line look better. He blocked well. He ran well. He didn't make mistakes. And he could catch the ball as well as a wide receiver. Everybody talked about Herschel Walker. But Kelvin never had to take a back seat to him."

Along with Mills and Fusina, Bryant would become one of the keys to the Stars' success in the USFL's three-year existence. He would amass 5,325 rushing and receiving yards and score 47 touchdowns in 47 games. That's 113 rushing and receiving yards and one touchdown per game.

When Bryant signed with the Stars in '83, Mills wasted little time introducing himself. On Kelvin's second day in camp, Sam gave him a concussion. Bryant hit the hole on a practice run and never saw Mills, who came through the gap and leveled him. Bryant lay motionless on the ground for 15–20 seconds. With help from a couple of his new teammates, he slowly got up and mumbled, "I'm done, man. I don't even know where I'm at."

Back then, Mills probably gave every offensive player on his team at least one concussion at some point, not to mention the opposing running backs he plastered with his picture-perfect tackling technique and power. He wasn't a mean player, but he only knew one way to play—hard.

Duck Riley used to joke that all the Stars' running backs started out 6'4", but after a couple years of practicing with Mills, they shrank two or three inches. Very seldom would Mora practice in shells and shorts. But even when they did, that meant little to Mills.

"That's why we always preferred to come out in full gear," Riley says. "If we were going to be doing blitz drills, you'd better tighten up your chin strap. Because Sam was going to be coming hard."

Vince Tobin had a pair of contact drills for his linebackers during pregame warmups. One was from a basic stance where you'd reach with your hands and separate from the blocker. The other was a forearm drill. One linebacker would have to block another linebacker. The second linebacker would hit the first linebacker with his left forearm. Then he'd have to block him again, and the second linebacker would hit him with his right forearm.

Bunting always seemed to have the misfortune of being matched up against Sam in the drill.

"By the time we'd get done with the forearm drill, my freaking helmet would be turned around," says Bunting. "Vince would be standing there laughing his ass off. He loved watching Sam kick my ass."

Bunting said Mills was the best tackling linebacker he'd ever seen. He led with his face every time. Again, a different era. Today, because of concussion fears, defensive players are taught to get the head out of the way and lead with the shoulder. But Mills always hit ball carriers hard, and he always—always—wrapped up.

"You talk about meeting a runner and accelerating your feet at the same time and putting them down on the ground hard," Bunting says. "That was Sam."

The Stars were a new team in a new league. Peterson thought he had assembled a good team. But no one, including Mora and Peterson, really had a very good feel for how they stacked up with the rest of the league. The USFL didn't play any preseason games. It went straight from training camp to a grueling 18-game regular-season schedule. At the time, the NFL played a 16-game regular season, preceded by four preseason games.

A couple of weeks into training camp, Peterson agreed to a scrimmage in Orlando at the Citrus Bowl against one of the USFL's other teams, the Tampa Bay Bandits, who were coached by former Heisman Trophy-winning quarterback Steve Spurrier, who would later win a national championship at his alma mater, the University of Florida. The Bandits were owned by Canadian businessman John Bassett. Bassett was the father of tennis star Carling Bassett, who was the No. 2 junior women's player in the world in the early '80s and a US Open semifinalist in 1984.

Mora approached the scrimmage as little more than a joint practice. But Spurrier and the Bandits didn't get the memo. They were trying to draw interest in their team and promote what they called "Bandit Ball," and this was an opportunity to give people a glimpse of their exciting new product.

The Bandits treated the scrimmage as if it were a regular-season game. They sold tickets and kept score. Their defense blitzed the hell out of Fusina. On offense, Spurrier trotted out every exotic formation and trick play in his playbook. Mills and the rest of the defense got its head handed to them by the Bandits' offense.

The only thing Tobin had installed to that point was his base defense. He hadn't even installed a nickel defense or a blitz package yet. His defense was out there playing its base 3–4 scheme, and Spurrier was spreading his receivers all over the field. The Stars had to cover wideouts with linebackers.

It wasn't pretty.

"They beat the shit out of us," Tobin said.

The defense got beat up even worse in the Philadelphia newspapers after the scrimmage. When linebacker Glenn Howard arrived at the team's defensive meeting the next day in Deland, he said to Tobin, "Coach, we sure are in the doghouse, aren't we?" Tobin didn't disagree but understood that there were extenuating circumstances.

This was before the internet age, but it didn't take long for word to get back down to Deland about the poor reviews on the team's performance in the Philly papers. That was just fine with Mora and his coaching staff. After all, nothing is a better motivator in sports than criticism. Mora made a point of having the team's public relations director, Bob Moore, and his assistant, Mike Kaine, make photocopies of the most critical newspaper articles and put them up all over the locker room for the players to see.

Somebody on the defense—Howard thinks it might've been linebacker Jon Brooks—came up with a clever name for the unit after the fiasco in Orlando: the "Doghouse Defense." Brooks even had T-shirts printed with "Doghouse Defense" on them and distributed them to all the defensive players.

The scrimmage against the Bandits ended up being an aberration. Tobin's defense turned out to be very, very good. In their first year, it held opponents to a league-best 11.3 points per game and forced an unheard of 67 turnovers in 18 games. That's almost four a game! Nevertheless, the players kept the Doghouse Defense nickname.

"We had a good mix of some really good players and some who were lunchpail types of players who got everything out of their ability, like [safeties] Scott Woerner and Mike Lush," Tobin said. "And it worked. It blended together very well. I was very proud of that defense."

Mills quickly became the leader of the defense. "We looked to him for inspiration and big plays," says Howard.

He provided both.

The Stars and the USFL were the perfect storm for Mills, especially after what he'd experienced in Cleveland and Toronto. He was a guy who had been dismissed as too small his entire career. What better place for an underdog than in an underdog spring league on a unit that called itself the Doghouse Defense? To his eternal credit, Tobin saw the greatness in his little linebacker from day one. He turned his defense over to him. Mills ran with it.

10

Everybody always thought Sam was an overachiever. He wasn't an overachiever. He had a lot of ability and he achieved up to the level of that ability and beyond. He could run. He could cover guys. He could play the run. He was the ideal player to coach. He was just an amazing guy.

—Jim Mora

AS THAT FIRST training camp went on, Sam Mills' job security with the Stars improved dramatically. While Jim Mora didn't love the idea of going to war with a 5'9" middle linebacker, he recognized by the end of camp that he didn't have any better options.

And frankly, the more he watched Mills, the more he liked him. Five-foot-nine or not, the guy hit people like no one Mora had ever seen in his life. And while there were some initial concerns about how he would perform in pass coverage against taller tight ends, his size certainly wasn't any kind of disadvantage against the run. And stopping the run still was a defense's top priority back then.

Mills never took anything for granted. He went to training camp hoping for the best but prepared to be prejudged yet again by coaches who didn't believe a 5'9" linebacker could play professional football. If that happened again, so be it. There would be no tears this time. His wife was pregnant with their second child. He had a teaching job he could go back to. He would be fine. Life would go on and he would have no regrets.

When the Stars shuttered their training camp in Deland and headed back to Philadelphia to get ready for their first season, Mills had not only survived Jim Mora's early skepticism and made the team, he also was one of their starting inside linebackers in Vince Tobin's 3–4 scheme. And the defensive play-caller.

Due largely to that unimpressive performance in the scrimmage against Tampa Bay, there was still uncertainty both inside and outside the Stars organization as to how good Mills and the Stars' defense really were.

With the exception of Bunting, who was now at the tail end of his playing career, they didn't have any defensive players with long-term NFL experience. All of the top college players they brought in that first year—Bryant, Eatman, and Oates—were on the other side of the ball. But right from the beginning, regardless of the quality of their resumes, the defense had a sense of confidence. And it all started with Mills.

Many of the Stars players, including Mills, moved into the Cobblestone Apartments on Lindbergh Boulevard, which was near the Philadelphia airport and only about 10 minutes from Veterans Stadium, where the Stars and Eagles played and practiced.

Melanie, who gave birth to their second child, Marcus, that April, stayed in Long Branch that first season. Mills shared an apartment at the Cobblestone with his training camp roommate, George Cooper.

The Stars linebackers were a close group. All of them ate breakfast together every day during the season. The team catered lunches for the players at the stadium. But they were on their own for breakfast. The linebackers would pick up breakfast sandwiches on the way to work and sit in the locker room and talk.

Veterans Stadium, where the Stars played their first two seasons, was also the home of baseball's Phillies and the NFL's Eagles. The Vet, as it was known to fans, was owned by the city of Philadelphia.

The Phillies didn't have any objections to the Stars playing at the Vet, even though their season overlapped with the Stars' February-to-July schedule. The Eagles, however, were another story. Their owner, Leonard Tose, didn't like the idea of another professional football team playing in "his" stadium, even if it was during a different time of year. He did everything he could to prevent the city from letting the Stars use the Vet.

Not long after Myles Tanenbaum was awarded Philadelphia's USFL franchise, he happened to run into Tose at Bookbinder's, the iconic Philly seafood restaurant. Tose had had a little too much to drink and staggered over to the table where Tanenbaum was sitting. He offered to bet the Stars owner a million dollars that his team never would play a game at the Vet. Tanenbaum should've taken the bet, because a few weeks later, the Stars signed a lease agreement with the city to play their games there. The city also built offices and locker rooms for the Stars at the stadium.

Tose, a trucking magnate and a compulsive gambler who would lose his entire fortune at the casinos in nearby Atlantic City, would eventually be forced to sell the Eagles in 1985.

The Stars played their first game on the road against the Denver Gold. The game, which was televised nationally on ABC on March 6, 1983, drew more than 45,000 people to Mile High Stadium despite a heavy snowfall the day before. The skies had cleared and the snow from the previous day's storm was piled up behind the end zones. Sam's former position coach at Montclair, McKinley Boston, flew to Denver to watch him and the Stars' other former Montclair linebacker, Vinny DeMarinis, make their pro debuts.

The Stars beat Denver 13–7, thanks largely to Mills and the Doghouse Defense. Trailing by six late in the fourth quarter, the Gold, who were coached by former Broncos head coach Red Miller, drove from their own 35 to the Philadelphia 1. But the Stars stuffed a pair of run plays, with Mills right in the middle of both stops. A fourth-down pass by Denver quarterback Ken Johnson, a CFL veteran, fell incomplete. Mills and the defense forced six turnovers in the game and held Denver to 215 total yards.

"I can't say enough about them," Mora said of his defense after the game. "They've been taking a lot of—I don't want to say crap—but they had something to prove today."

11

Nobody appreciated it more than Sam did. He knew what it felt like to have it taken away from you. He knew what it felt like to have someone tell him, 'No, you can't do this.'

—Stars linebacker George Cooper

A WEEK AFTER THEIR win over Denver, the Stars faced Herschel Walker and the New Jersey Generals at the Vet. Walker would lead the USFL in rushing that first season with 1,812 yards, nearly 400 more than the Stars' Kelvin Bryant (1,442), who was runner-up.

But aside from Walker, the Generals didn't have many good players. The Stars beat them easily in their Week 2 meeting, 25–0, and would beat them again two months later, 23–9. Mills and the defense held Walker to 60 yards on 13 carries in the first game and 75 yards on 25 carries in the second game. Even with Walker, the Generals would finish 6–12.

Despite becoming the league's most prolific running back and rushing for 5,562 yards in three seasons, Walker would struggle mightily against Mills and the rest of the Stars' defense. Walker averaged 107.4 rushing yards per game against the rest of the league. But in eight games against the Stars, including a pair of playoff losses, he was held to 79.9 rushing yards and had just two 100-yard performances. In the Stars' two playoff wins over the Generals in '84 and '85, Mills & Co. held Herschel to 2.9 yards per carry.

Jim Mora was an old-school coach who didn't have much use

for flashy, spread-'em-out offenses. He believed you won with a tough, opportunistic defense that forced turnovers and a ball-control offense.

Even though he wasn't hired by Mora, his offensive coordinator, Joe Pendry, was from the same conservative school as Mora. The Stars didn't have a flashy offense. Center Bart Oates says the Stars were "a run team that passed when they had to." Most of their games were close that first season. There were few blowouts.

They had a stud running back in Bryant and didn't need to get pass-happy. Quarterback Chuck Fusina would average just 25 attempts per game in his three seasons as the team's starter. Pendry admitted he might've been a little *too* conservative early on and eventually opened things up a little bit after realizing that Fusina was perfectly capable of handling whatever he threw at him.

With Mills and the defense consistently keeping teams out of the end zone, the Stars didn't need to score a lot of points. They gave up more than 10 points in just six of their 18 regular-season games in '83.

Mills would lead the Stars in solo tackles (141 ½) and assists (54) in '83. He also had five fumble recoveries, four forced fumbles, three interceptions, and 4 ½ sacks. He was a unanimous All-USFL selection. He finished second in the league's Defensive Player of the Year balloting to Michigan Panthers linebacker John Corker, who had a league-high 28 ½ sacks.

Corker's career would quickly fizzle out after that. He had only eight sacks the next year and five in '85. When the USFL folded, he signed with the Miami Dolphins but was soon cut. He played in a couple of games for the Green Bay Packers in 1988 but would quickly be cut by them as well.

Sam Mills' career would take a very different turn.

The Stars would win 11 of their first 12 games in '83, and finish with the best regular-season record in the league, 15–3. No other team had fewer than six losses.

In their first playoff game, they played the Chicago Blitz. The Blitz were coached by NFL legend George Allen, who had coached the NFL's Los Angeles Rams and Washington Redskins and would be inducted into the Pro Football Hall of Fame in 2002. They had barely beaten the Blitz in an earlier regular-season meeting, needing three touchdowns in the fourth quarter for a 31–24 comeback win.

It would take an even bigger comeback by the Stars in their playoff rematch. Thanks to an uncharacteristic seven Stars turnovers, Allen's Blitz held a seemingly insurmountable 38–17 lead with 12:04 left in the game. Mills and the defense, which had held the Blitz to just 13 first downs and 218 total yards, rose up and didn't allow Chicago another point.

Meanwhile, Fusina threw three touchdown passes to tie the game and send it to overtime. The Stars marched 73 yards on 14 plays on their first overtime possession and won the game on a one-yard touchdown run by Kelvin Bryant, who finished with 142 rushing yards.

Allen would call the game "one of the greatest comebacks in history."

The win over the Blitz put the Stars in the first USFL Championship Game, where they faced Corker and the Panthers. The game was played in Denver's Mile High Stadium, where the Stars had opened the season. The Panthers' quarterback was Bobby Hebert, who, in a twist of fate, would later be Sam Mills' teammate and Jim Mora's starting quarterback in New Orleans for five seasons. The Panthers beat the Stars 24–22 on the strength of three touchdown passes by Hebert, who was the USFL Championship Game MVP.

A few days before the title game, Mills was asked about his successful first season with the Stars. "Everybody dreams of a way they'd like things to turn out," he said. "But this season has gone way beyond anything I dreamed. I feel I showed a lot this year to a lot of people who had question marks about me. I knew I had to make people believe I could play. I knew I had to make people look past my size."

That first season with the Stars changed Mills' life forever.

The previous summer, his friends had felt sorry for him after he got cut by the Toronto Argonauts and was working as a security guard on the Long Branch pier. A year later, he returned to his hometown after leading the Stars to the USFL Championship Game and received the kind of Jersey shore welcome reserved for Springsteen or Bon Jovi.

He said many of the people there knew his statistics better than he did.

"Everybody follows me," he said. "I went to the pier a couple of weeks ago, and I couldn't even make it up there. People kept stopping me, wanting to talk.

"But that's okay. I like this a lot better than last summer."

12

Like everything else he's ever been involved in, Donald was in it for Donald. He clearly didn't give a shit what the other owners thought.
—Bob Rose, USFL director of communications, 1984–85

THE USFL'S FIRST season went pretty well if you don't count all the money that the 12 teams lost.

The average attendance for games had been just over 25,000, which was excellent for a first-year league, and the TV ratings on ABC and ESPN were very respectable. ABC's 6.0 Nielsen rating for the season exceeded the network's initial goal of 5.0. The USFL Championship Game between Michigan and Philly got an 11.9 rating.

"For a 4 ½-month-old baby, the USFL has done quite well," ABC Sports Senior Vice President Jim Spence proclaimed after the season.

When the league was formed in 1982, the owners agreed to a five-year plan that called for judicious spending on players early on. The idea was to crawl before it walked and walk before it ran. One big signing per team in the first year, two in the second, and three in the third.

But teams quickly blew that plan to smithereens.

It wasn't just the Generals breaking the bank for Herschel Walker. The Michigan Panthers signed three players off the Pittsburgh Steelers' starting offensive line. Other teams quickly followed suit. While the league did an impressive job of acquiring talent in its first year, the revenue generated by ticket sales and television rights fees wasn't able to keep pace with player costs. Every team lost money the first year, and many lost a lot.

Some of the league's owners had deep pockets and could absorb the losses. But many could not. They were desperate to find a way to stop the bleeding. Expansion provided a short-term fix. After just one season, the league added six more teams in Houston, Jacksonville, Memphis, Oklahoma, Pittsburgh, and San Antonio. The 12 original teams split the expansion fee money, which stopped some of the bleeding, but certainly not all of it.

Two months after the Panthers' title game win over the Stars, Donald Trump, a New York City real estate developer, bought the New Jersey Generals from J. Walter Duncan for $9 million. By comparison, Leonard Tose would sell the NFL's Eagles to South Florida car dealer Norman Braman a year and a half later for $65 million.

Trump raised the league's profile in the country's largest media market and regularly put the Generals on the back page of the city's tabloids. He was a master promoter, even if what he was promoting seldom was real.

Not long after buying the team, he had some people believing that he was close to hiring away Don Shula from the Miami Dolphins to coach the Generals. Trump was invited to appear on CBS's *The NFL Today*, which was the top-rated football pregame show at the time. Trump went on the show and said he had "great negotiations" with the future Hall of Fame coach. He said they had agreed on all of the "business points" of a contract. He claimed there was just one sticking point that he couldn't agree to—a supposed demand by Shula for a unit in Trump Tower. He then spent the next five minutes turning *The NFL Today* into an infomercial for Trump Tower.

In truth, Shula never had any interest in working for Trump or owning an apartment in Trump Tower. He eventually ended up hiring Walt Michaels, who had been fired by the New York Jets two years earlier after six seasons as their head coach, to be the Generals' head coach in 1984.

Trump made it clear from the moment he bought into the USFL that he felt the league had no future in the spring. He called the spring a "wasteland" for football.

"If God had wanted football in the spring, he wouldn't have invented baseball," Trump famously said.

If he didn't believe in the concept of spring football, why then, you might ask, did he even buy the Generals? It was because he saw the USFL as a way of getting what he really wanted, which was an NFL team. He felt that if the league moved to the fall, it could eventually force a merger with the NFL.

He had previously tried and failed to buy both an NFL and Major League Baseball team. The USFL was his attempt to force his way into a club that wasn't offering him admittance.

Trump called for a vote to move the USFL to the fall at the very first owners meeting he attended after buying the Generals. "Even if we had cut our losses in the spring, there was no foreseeable chance of making a profit," Trump would claim in his 1987 book, *Trump: The Art of the Deal.*

At about the same time, one of Trump's associates, Jay Seltzer, sent a memo to Stars owner Myles Tanenbaum, a staunch spring advocate, about the potential outcome of a merger with the NFL if the league moved to the fall. Seltzer said a handful of teams would be absorbed by the NFL and the rest would be left out, but presumably would receive some sort of compensation.

Tanenbaum wrote back to Seltzer that Trump's merger strategy "troubles me greatly."

After the first season, the agreement by the owners to adhere to an informal salary cap had basically been thrown out the window. Led by Trump, USFL teams got into a full-scale bidding war with the NFL. Because they held their draft in January, four months before the

NFL's, they were able to sign many of the top college players, including quarterbacks Steve Young and Jim Kelly, Tennessee defensive lineman Reggie White, Oregon offensive tackle Gary Zimmerman, and yet another Heisman Trophy-winning running back, Nebraska's Mike Rozier.

They also raided NFL rosters. Trump signed quarterback Brian Sipe away from the Browns, linebacker Jim LeClair and center Dave Lapham away from the Bengals, and three-time Pro Bowl safety Gary Barbaro away from the Kansas City Chiefs.

The USFL was already in a very difficult financial place even before Trump's arrival. Based on their contract with ABC, they needed their big-city franchises to be successful. But many of those franchises were the ones struggling the most. Steve Ehrhardt, who was initially the executive director of the league and later became the president and general manager of one of its expansion teams, the Memphis Showboats, had to personally take $30,000 in cash to Chicago before the Blitz's opening game in the league's second season just so they could pay for their uniforms.

Tanenbaum and Peterson didn't go nuts with player spending like many of the league's other teams. But they did upgrade their roster ahead of their second season. They made the league's No. 1-rated defense even better by signing former Penn State nose tackle Pete Kugler away from the San Francisco 49ers, and drafting North Carolina defensive end William Fuller and linebackers George Jamison and Mike Johnson. Jamison was from the University of Cincinnati. Johnson was from Virginia Tech.

Johnson and Jamison were college stars who joined a Stars linebacking corps in '84 that easily could have been resentful toward their arrival. They were both just 21 when they signed with the team. But Mills welcomed them with open arms, and the rest of the linebackers followed suit.

"Everything we saw in Sam inspired us and influenced who we became as men," says Jamison.

Kugler had started 16 games for a 49ers team that had made it to the NFC Championship Game the previous season. Fuller, Jamison, and Johnson all went on to become successful NFL players after the USFL folded.

"We had the best defense in the USFL in '83," says Terry Bradway. "Then we added Kugler, Fuller, Jamison, and Johnson. We were loaded for bear in '84."

Despite his outstanding season the year before, despite leading the Stars to the league championship game, many still questioned Sam Mills. NFL scouts continued to insist that while he may have managed to excel in "that spring minor league," he would never be able to survive against the best of the best in the NFL.

Mike Johnson, who played 10 years in the NFL and went to a pair of Pro Bowls, doesn't think those doubts were what really drove Mills.

"I just think he wanted to play," says Johnson. "And when he played, he wanted to play well. I wouldn't want to diminish everything he accomplished by saying he did it because he felt he had something to prove to people. He was just a great player."

Sam and Melanie, who had been together for six years, got married after the '83 season. Along with five-year-old Sam III and newborn Marcus, they moved into an apartment in Clementon in the South Jersey suburbs. Sam got an offseason job working at the Roosevelt Paper plant in northeast Philly.

He'd work at the paper plant from 7:30 AM to 4:30 PM, then drive down to Veterans Stadium to work out. Tose being Tose, he refused to let the Stars use the Eagles' weight room at the Vet, so the city put up some drywall and built them a closet-sized one that barely had enough room for a bench and free weights. Mills would also work out at the Cherry Hill Spa in South Jersey, which was owned by former Eagle Vince Papale, who was the Stars' radio analyst

Mills would go over to Veterans Stadium on Sunday mornings in the offseason and work out with Joe Marciano, who doubled as the Stars' special teams and strength and conditioning coach that first year. Sam would work out, shower, and then walk around the stadium and watch the Eagles game if they were playing at home. Marciano said Mills was the only player interested in coming over on a Sunday in the offseason to work out.

"I invited a few other guys, but they said no," Marciano says. "Sam told me one time, 'You know what, Coach Joe? I do my best work when no one's watching.'"

Mills would do anything for his teammates. Glenn Howard remembers talking to him on the phone one time during the offseason. Mills was back in Long Branch with his family. Howard was in Paulsboro, New Jersey, across the river from Philadelphia, doing some repair work on a rental property he owned. Howard told Mills he had to put down a new floor in the bathroom. Sam hung up the phone, got in his car, and made the 90-minute drive to Paulsboro to help his buddy lay the floor tiles.

"That's the kind of guy he was," Howard said. "That's the kind of friend he was."

13

There's no doubt we are the best team in the USFL. Our attitude since we lost by two points last year in the championship game was to get back here and win. They would not be denied.

—Jim Mora

EVERY PLAYER ON a team that comes up short in a championship game will tell you after the loss that the only thing they care about is getting back to the title game and winning.

But that's easier said than done, particularly in football. It is the ultimate team sport. A handful of injuries can easily short-circuit a team's championship hopes. The physical demands and effects of one season bleed into the next.

But nothing was able to prevent Sam Mills and the Stars from making it back to the USFL title game in '84 and winning. They won 16 of their 18 regular-season games, then outscored their three playoff opponents 71–20, making short work of the Arizona Wranglers in the league title game. Their average margin of victory in their 19 wins was 16.5 points. Eleven of their 19 wins were by 14 points or more. Few teams have ever been so dominant.

Chuck Fusina threw 31 touchdown passes and just nine interceptions that year. His 31 TDs were the second most in the league behind only Jim Kelly's 44. Kelvin Bryant finished second in rushing to Birmingham's Joe Cribbs with 1,406 yards. He also had 48 receptions for another 453 yards.

But the defense led the way.

Led by Mills, the Doghouse Defense finished first in points allowed (12.5 per game) and yards allowed (225 per game) for the second straight year. It had 46 takeaways in 18 games, including 28 interceptions.

For the second straight year, Mills was one of the league's most dominant defensive players, earning another All-USFL selection. He led the league in tackles with 211. To give you an idea of the impressiveness of that number, fellow linebacker George Cooper finished second on the Stars in tackles with 110. Sam had double-digit tackles in 13 of the Stars' 18 regular-season games. He had 19 tackles in a 24–7 regular-season win over Arizona. He had 17 tackles against the Michigan Panthers in a 29–20 win. He had 15 against Reggie White's Memphis Showboats and also against the Washington Federals. In a 41–7 win over the Chicago Blitz, he recorded 12 tackles, two interceptions, and a fumble recovery.

Carl Peterson might've had the best description of what it was like for a blocker or running back to try to move Mills. "It was like running into a fire hydrant," he said.

Mills was an unselfish player who was willing to do whatever was needed to help his team. Despite being his team's best defensive player, he volunteered to moonlight on special teams.

When they played the Houston Gamblers and their run-and-shoot offense, which sent five receivers out on almost every play, the Stars coaching staff actually considered not suiting up Mills that week because they were going to be replacing their linebackers with safeties and cornerbacks much of the time.

But Mora had a hard time wrapping his arms around the idea of not dressing his best player. It was Joe Marciano who came up with a solution. He suggested they use Sam on special teams.

"Whoa, whoa, whoa, Joe," Mora said. "You're not going to put our best player on special teams. I'll get crucified if he gets hurt and we lose him for the season."

Mora eventually relented and agreed to let Marciano use Mills as a blocker on punt and kickoff teams. He was the personal protector—the blocker directly in front of the punter—on punts. He was so good at it that he would continue to do it for the rest of the year.

"At the end of the year, you grade all your players," Marciano says. "Pluses and minuses, percentages, all that crap. [Sam] graded out with 99 percent of his blocks being made [on special teams]."

The Stars' lone two regular-season losses in '84 were to the same team—Trump's Generals. They lost to them up in the Meadowlands in Week 3 by three points, 17–14, then reeled off 14 wins in a row. They would lose to them again in a meaningless game in the final week of the regular season at Veterans Stadium, 16–10.

The Generals were much improved in '84 with Brian Sipe at quarterback. Sipe had started 112 games for the Browns and led the NFL in passing in 1980. But even with those two wins over the Stars, the Generals still finished two games behind Philadelphia in the Atlantic Division with a 14–4 record.

Herschel Walker would finish third in rushing that year behind Birmingham's Joe Cribbs and the Stars' Bryant. The Stars bottled him up in both regular-season meetings against the Generals, holding him to 56 yards on 17 carries in the first meeting and 62 yards on 16 carries in the Week 18 rematch.

The Stars and Generals would face each other a third time in the first round of the playoffs. Because the Stars had finished with the league's best record, the game was going to be in Philly. But the Stars' home field, Veterans Stadium, wasn't available for the game. The Phillies were already scheduled to play a three-game series there against the Houston Astros that weekend. So, the playoff game was moved to Franklin Field on the University of Pennsylvania campus, five miles down the Schuylkill Expressway from the Vet.

Trump was irate. He felt that if the game couldn't be played at

Veterans Stadium, it should be moved up the Jersey Turnpike to Giants Stadium, where the Generals played.

Franklin Field was hardly inadequate. It had 52,000-plus seats, which was more than enough for the game. The Eagles played there from 1958 through 1970 before Veterans Stadium was built. It was the site of the famous 1960 NFL championship game between the Eagles and Vince Lombardi's Packers. In addition, Trump was a Penn grad.

Given his association with the Ivy League school, you would've thought Trump would've liked the idea of playing the game on the campus of his alma mater. But he disparaged the stadium, calling it a "dump" and "a bush-league place to play."

The league had no sympathy for his whining. The game was played at Franklin Field.

Much to Trump's embarrassment, the Stars clobbered the Generals. Jim Mora's team rattled off 21 unanswered points in the second quarter and won going away, 28–7. Walker was once again frustrated by Mills and the Doghouse Defense. He was held to 50 rushing yards on 15 carries.

Mills set the tone early in the game when the Generals drove down to the Stars' 2-yard line and were threatening to take the lead. Sipe handed the ball to the 6'2", 220-pound Walker three straight times. Three straight times he was stoned for no gain by Mills.

"He didn't make an inch on Sam," Carl Peterson would say later. "Not an inch."

After the game, a classy Walker walked over to the Stars' locker room to congratulate Mills. He hugged Sam and said, "Man, I ain't never been hit so hard in my life."

Sam smiled and shook Walker's hand.

The next week, playing the semifinal game once again at Franklin Field because of another scheduling conflict with the Phillies, the Stars beat the Birmingham Stallions 20–10. Mills & Co. were again outstanding, forcing five turnovers and holding Cribbs, the league rushing champ, to 72 yards on 21 carries. Stallions quarterback Cliff Stoudt, who had started 15 games for the Pittsburgh Steelers the previous year, completed just 10 of 26 passes for 109 yards and was sacked six times.

"There isn't a team in this league that can run against our defense well enough to beat us," left tackle Irv Eatman said. "They just can't do it. Sam and the defense are just too good."

He was right.

A week later, the Stars played the Arizona Wranglers in the USFL Championship Game in Tampa. Most of the members of the Wranglers actually had been on the Chicago Blitz team that blew a 21-point fourth-quarter lead to the Stars in the '83 playoffs. That's because the Blitz were involved in one of the weirder transactions in professional sports history.

The Blitz were initially owned by renowned Arizona-based heart surgeon Ted Deitrich. Deitrich had worked with Michael DeBakey in the development of the human heart transplant. When the USFL was formed, Deitrich had expressed interest in owning the Arizona franchise near his Phoenix home. But it had already been awarded to Jim Joseph, a West Coast real estate developer. So, Deitrich agreed to own the USFL franchise in Chicago.

The Wranglers weren't very good in '83, finishing 4–14. Their average attendance was below 10,000. Joseph lost millions and wanted out. The league came up with a solution: Deitrich would become the owner of the Wranglers and be allowed to keep the Blitz's entire coaching staff, including head coach George Allen, as well as most of the team's better players, as part of an asset swap with the Blitz's new owner, James Hoffman, who also happened to be a surgeon.

The '84 USFL title game wasn't competitive at all. The Stars beat the Wranglers 23–3. Mills and the Stars' defense held Arizona to 119 total yards. The Wranglers had two 1,000-yard rushers that season—Tim Spencer and Kevin Long. Spencer was a 6'1", 221-pounder out of Ohio State. Long was a 6'1", 210-pounder who had played five seasons with the New York Jets. The Stars held the pair to a combined 62 yards. Mills would finish with 27 tackles in the Stars' three playoff wins.

Their win over Arizona in the championship game actually wasn't the Stars' final game that season. The publicity-hungry USFL had scheduled an exhibition game between the Stars and the Tampa Bay Bandits at London's Wembley Stadium the week *after* the title game.

In the Stars' locker room after the win over Arizona, none of the players were thinking about the game in London. Well, almost none.

Stars PR director Bob Moore went into the locker room about 90 minutes after the game. Everyone had left except Mills, who was still getting dressed. Moore went over to congratulate him.

"Sam, great game," said Moore. "I bet you're happy the season's finally over."

"No, Bob. It's not over yet," Mills said. "We've still got to play Tampa Bay."

"Yeah, I know. But that one doesn't count."

"They all count, Bob," Sam said. "Every game counts."

The trip to London was a fiasco. Very few of the players wanted to go. They had just won the league championship, and they didn't want to get on a plane and fly seven hours to play a meaningless game. To make matters worse, there was a major scheduling snafu. The team was unable to get a charter flight and had to fly commercial to London.

Players were cramped into seats. Some didn't bring any money. The team ended up sending several players home shortly after arriving.

But Mills had a great time. Moore still has a picture of Sam and Melanie riding horses through London's Hyde Park.

"They took in all the sights," says Moore. "They did all the touristy stuff over there while other guys were bitching about the trip and wanting to go home. That was Sam. The whole time I knew him, I never heard him complain about anything."

More than 40 years later, Melanie Mills vividly remembers that London trip.

"Sam didn't mind at all going over there," she says. "When you loved the game as much as he did, what was another game? It was exciting for us. I had never been out of the country before."

14

When history is written, we'll remember who kicked butt in the spring.

—John Pease, Stars defensive line coach

A MONTH AFTER THE Stars won the USFL title in 1984, Donald Trump got his wish when 15 of the league's other 17 owners agreed to his proposal to move to the fall. Because of their television agreement with ABC, they would play one more season in the spring in '85 and then move to the fall in '86. Or at least that was the plan.

The lone two owners who opposed a fall move were the Stars' Myles Tanenbaum and the Michigan Panthers' Alfred Taubman.

Trump might not have been able to get the votes for a fall move had Tampa Bay Bandits owner John Bassett not taken ill. Bassett was one of the USFL's most influential and respected owners. He was vehemently against Trump's plan to move to the fall. But he was diagnosed with brain cancer early in '84 and died in May of '86 at the age of 47. When Bassett got sick, most of the opposition to Trump's move-to-the-fall plan withered. Most of the owners were desperate for a way to stop the financial bleeding.

Trump's plan was still to try and force a merger with the NFL, much like the American Football League had successfully done in the late '60s. But he insisted that wasn't the case.

"We're not looking for a merger," Trump said. "We're looking for a fight."

Actually, he was looking for a fight that would lead to either a merger or a big payday. Two months after the fall announcement, the USFL took its fight to federal district court in Manhattan, filing a $1.3 billion antitrust suit against the NFL.

Immediately after the August vote to move to the fall in '86, the Stars' Tanenbaum announced that he would be moving his team from Philadelphia to Baltimore. "We cannot compete with the Phillies and the Eagles in the same stadium [in the fall]," he said.

The Stars could've stayed in Philly for the '85 season and played their games at the Vet for one more spring. But with the NFL's Colts having bolted from Baltimore to Indianapolis in the middle of the night four months earlier, Tanenbaum saw no reason to wait. He wanted to get down to Baltimore and get a head start on marketing his team there for the move to the fall, even if he wasn't totally convinced that would ever happen.

The city of Baltimore had agreed to let the Stars play their home games at Memorial Stadium, where the Colts had played and where the city's Major League Baseball team, the Orioles, also played.

Memorial Stadium was located on E. 33rd Street and Ellerslie Avenue in Baltimore's Venable Park neighborhood. Known as "The Old Gray Lady," it hosted six World Series and the 1958 NFL Championship Game between the Colts and the New York Giants, which the Colts won 23–17.

But the Orioles objected to letting the Stars play their '85 spring home games there, which forced the Stars to find a contingency plan.

They explored the possibility of playing their games in '85 at the Naval Academy in Annapolis, Maryland. But the school nixed the idea. The only other real option was Byrd Stadium at the University of Maryland in College Park, which was 30 miles south of Baltimore.

Philadelphia had become home for the Stars. With the Eagles struggling—they had won a total of eight games in 1982–83—the city's football fans had embraced the Stars, who had won 36 of 42 games in their first two seasons. They averaged more than 30,000 fans per game on their way to the league title in '84. A post-championship rally in Center City drew more than 50,000 people. For a two-year-old team in a new league, that was impressive.

The players and coaches had enjoyed the two years they spent playing and living there and weren't anxious to relocate. Neither was Mora, who had bought a home in South Jersey. His youngest son, Steve, was going to be a high school senior.

The city of Baltimore had offered the Stars the use of the Colts' old training facility in Owings Mills, a suburb northwest of Baltimore. But Mora told Tanenbaum he preferred to keep the team in Philadelphia for the '85 season, and practice and train there, even if it meant dealing with a three-hour drive down I-95 to Byrd Stadium for home games. Tanenbaum acquiesced to Mora's wishes.

Baltimore barely paid attention to the Stars. It was still mourning the loss of the Colts. The city loved their Orioles and weren't really in the mood to get very interested in a spring football team, especially one that played its games closer to Washington, DC, than Baltimore. At Byrd Stadium, the Stars averaged just 14,000 fans per game in '85. Three of their last four home games there failed to draw 8,000 people.

Mora wanted to continue using Veterans Stadium as the Stars' training and practice base during the '85 season. But after they returned to Philly from training camp in Florida in late February, the city unceremoniously evicted them, giving them 24 hours to get all of their equipment and belongings out of Veterans Stadium. The city even confiscated the team's chalkboards.

The Stars suspected that the city had finally given in to pressure from the Eagles' Tose. The Eagles were coming off their third straight losing season, and Tose had become very sensitive to suggestions in the newspapers and on the local radio sports talk shows that the Eagles were the city's second-best professional football team, which probably was true. Tose would end up selling the team that April.

When the Stars left their locker room in the basement of the Vet for the last time after being evicted, Jim Mora wrote a six-word message with a Sharpie on the wall near the locker room door underneath the Stars' logo.

It said simply: "They kicked the wrong team out."

Several Stars players lingered outside the locker room.

Finally, safety Scott Woerner said, "Fuck it. I've been thrown out of much better places than this."

Scrambling to find a place in Philly to practice, Tanenbaum, who was a member of the University of Pennsylvania's board of trustees, persuaded the school to rent space on campus to the Stars during the '85 season. The school provided them with office and locker room space in the ROTC building and gave them use of a practice field about 50 yards off the busy—and noisy—Schuylkill Expressway. The only thing separating the practice field from the traffic was a six-foot-high chain-link fence. The coaches had to yell to be heard by the players during practice.

The team's offices were scattered around the ROTC building. Bill Kuharich remembers that his office was right next to a chemistry lab.

"At a certain point, there is a certain ludicrousness to things you deal with in your life," says Mike Johnson. "That '85 season was about as ludicrous as it gets. I mean, practicing and living in Philly and then getting on a bus or in your car and driving three hours for our *home* games. You have to make a decision how you are going to deal with it."

The Stars dealt with it by laughing about it and accepting it as another challenge. They nicknamed themselves "The Traveling All-Stars" that season, after the popular 1976 baseball movie with Richard Pryor, *The Bingo Long Traveling All-Stars & Motor Kings.*

"You either throw in the towel and say *I quit,* or you decide to make the best of it," says Johnson. "That's what we did. We made the best of it. It did make it harder to play. But being a Mora team, he was a former Marine. So, he was like, *Alright, so what? You looking for excuses?* There still was an expectation."

It also helped having a leader like Mills. Given everything he had been through in his career, this was small potatoes. He told his teammates there *were* no excuses. They still had to be good.

"It's hard to complain when your fearless leader isn't saying a negative word," says Johnson.

It was a weird—and certainly not ideal—situation. Mora would take the train to Baltimore every Tuesday morning during the season for a sparsely attended press conference, often accompanied by team leader Mills, and then return to Philly right after.

The team would practice all week at Penn. On Saturdays before their nine home games, the coaches, players, and staff would bus or drive down I-95 and gather at a Holiday Inn on Route 1 not far from Byrd Stadium. They would hold their Saturday meetings there for the next day's game. They got to know every inch of that stretch of I-95 that season.

"We found a way to deal with it," Duck Riley says.

Offensive lineman Chuck Commiskey remembers one bus trip down to College Park for a game. He looked out the window of the team bus and saw Bill Dugan, a backup offensive lineman for the Stars, behind the wheel of his Datsun truck with a little camper attached to the back of it. Dugan's mother was in the camper waving.

"The whole thing was bizarre," Commiskey says.

Mills, Jamison, Johnson, Conwell, Fuller, and many other Stars players went on to successful careers in the NFL. But in early 1985, they didn't know what their futures held. They only knew that they had a chance to win a second straight USFL title, albeit for a city they didn't live, practice, or play in.

Looking back on that season 40 years later, the players are unanimous about one thing: Were it not for Sam Mills, that season would've been an absolute disaster.

"When we had those tough times in '85, Sam had his feet on the ground," says Conwell. "He was steady. He was still asking you how you were feeling, asking you about yourself.

"I don't remember any big pep talks from him that year. But when we needed a kick in the ass or were lethargic, which happened from time to time that season, he would go around and say, 'Hey, it's not over. We can still do this.' It was a get-your-head-out-of-your-ass type of thing."

In their first two seasons, the Stars won 31 of 36 regular-season games. The '85 season was very different. Kelvin Bryant got hurt early in the year and missed four games. The Stars won just one of their first five games. Twelve weeks into the season, they were 5–6–1 and on the brink of not even making the playoffs. Mills and the defense were keeping them in games, but the offense was struggling, averaging just 16.9 points per game in the first 12 games.

The Stars lost to Trump's Generals up in the Meadowlands, 10–3, for their sixth loss. Their offense struggled mightily in that game. Bryant was held to 52 yards on 17 carries. Chuck Fusina had one of the worst performances of his career, completing just 10 of 25 passes for 99 yards.

The Doghouse Defense had kept the Stars in the game. Until it didn't. With the score tied 3–3, Generals quarterback Doug Flutie engineered an 81-yard fourth-quarter drive. He completed a 44-yard pass to tight end Sam Bowers with two minutes left that gave the Generals a first down at the Stars' 4.

Flutie handed the ball off to Herschel Walker, who had again led the USFL in rushing with 2,411 yards in '85, over a thousand more than the runner-up, Jacksonville's Mike Rozier. As was the case so many times when these teams played, Walker was met in the hole by Mills, who tackled him for a one-yard loss. On the next play, Flutie wisely ran away from Mills and took the ball into the end zone himself for the game-winning score.

But something happened after that loss. A football team that looked like it was ready for Last Rites got up off its deathbed and played its best football of the season. Bryant and the offense finally got their act together, and the Stars reeled off five wins in their last six games and made the playoffs with a 10–7–1 record. They outscored their last six regular-season opponents 165–77.

In the first round of the playoffs, they once again faced Walker and the Generals at the Meadowlands. But the Generals were without Flutie, who had broken his collarbone a few weeks earlier. His replacement, Ron Reeves, threw a first-quarter interception that Stars cornerback Garcia Lane returned 91 yards for a touchdown. Mills and the Doghouse Defense again shut down Walker, holding him to 66 yards on 25 carries. The Stars ended up winning the game 20–17.

A week later, in the semifinals, the Stars beat the Eastern Conference-champion Birmingham Stallions 28–14. Mills & Co. held '84 league rushing champ Joe Cribbs to a minuscule 13 yards on nine carries.

The Stars' late-season resurrection caught everyone off guard, including Mora. When his team dropped to 5–6–1, he thought any chance at making the playoffs had slipped away.

He told his players as much before their playoff game against Birmingham. Tearing up, he told them how proud he was of them for what they had overcome and said they had nothing more to prove. He finished by telling them that if they somehow managed to beat the Stallions, there would be no more padded practices or hitting the blocking sled.

"We go out and beat Birmingham to make the championship game," Commiskey says. "The next thing we know [offensive line coach Jim] Erkenbeck comes in and says, 'Hey, guys. I know this is going to piss you off. But in the drills tomorrow, we're going in pads and we're going to hit the five-man sled.' We're like, *you've got to be fucking kidding me.*"

The Stars' opponent in the '85 championship game, which was played at the Meadowlands, was the Oakland Invaders, who had merged with the Michigan Panthers following the '84 season. Nearly 50,000 fans attended the game despite an early hard rain.

The Stars held a 21–14 lead at the half, but they fell behind in the third quarter 24–21. With eight minutes left in the game, Kelvin Bryant, who would rush for 103 yards, scored on a seven-yard run to put the Stars back in front.

Late in the fourth quarter, the Invaders drove down to the Stars' 5-yard line. But a personal foul call on third-and-two pushed Oakland back to the 20. After a pair of passes into the end zone by Invaders quarterback Bobby Hebert fell incomplete, the resilient Stars won their second straight championship.

"Never say die," a giddy Myles Tanenbaum said after the game.

"We stayed together through thick and thin," Chuck Fusina said.

They did.

Leaders like Fusina and Mills were the reason the Stars somehow managed to weather what they had to endure that season.

"Sam's attitude transcended to the rest of the team," says defensive back Antonio Gibson. "When you look back on that, as tough as that could have been, I don't know if a lot of guys, especially those close to Sam, ever said anything about it. We still felt like we were playing for Philadelphia even though we really weren't. We were able to deal with that because of guys like Sam."

15

The guys on that team were some of the best guys I ever met. I played in the NFL for 10 years after we disbanded. I loved those 10 years. But it wasn't the same experience.

—Mike Johnson

THE STARS HAD won their second straight championship and Mills earned his third straight All-USFL nod, recording 190-plus tackles for the third straight year, along with 5 ½ sacks and three interceptions. But no one was sure what was going to happen next.

The USFL owners had voted to move to the fall in '86, but there was considerable skepticism that it would ever happen.

While the league had an agreement with six-year-old ESPN to televise their games in the fall of '86, they needed a major network partner if they were going to go head-to-head with the NFL. Fox was still a few years away from getting into the sports broadcasting business, and ABC, NBC, and CBS were already televising NFL games in the fall, which gave some credence to the league's claim that the NFL was a monopoly. But until the lawsuit was settled or there was a favorable verdict for the spring league, everything was up in the air.

The USFL's cash-strapped owners let several of their top players out of their contracts so they could sign with the NFL and play immediately—Steve Young signed with the Tampa Bay Buccaneers, Reggie White with the Eagles, Mike Rozier with the Houston Oilers, and Bobby Hebert with the New Orleans Saints. Stars center Bart

Oates left to play for Bill Parcells and the Giants, but only after the Giants agreed to pay the Stars $100,000 to let him out of his contract.

Most of the USFL players, including Mills, bided their time and waited to see what was going to happen. In January 1984, shortly before the USFL's second season, the NFL held a special "supplemental" or "dispersal" draft of USFL players in the event the spring league went belly-up. Eighty-four USFL players were drafted by NFL teams, including nine players from the Stars. Interestingly, Mills wasn't among them. Even after his impressive performance with the Stars in '83, NFL teams *still* weren't convinced a 5'9" linebacker could play in their league.

One of the reasons Tanenbaum had reluctantly moved to Baltimore besides needing a place to play if the league actually played in the fall of '86 was he felt that, with the Colts having left and the NFL wanting to put another team in Baltimore, their presence there might increase their chances of moving to the NFL if any of the USFL teams were absorbed by the NFL in a settlement.

Stars players like Duck Riley and Glenn Howard were realists. They knew a merger, as unlikely as it was, was probably the only way they were going to be able to extend their playing careers. They knew their chances of getting picked up by an NFL team if the USFL folded weren't very good.

Many of the team's players, including Mills, remained in the Philly area after the '85 season. They got jobs to help pay the bills—Sam was still working at the Roosevelt Paper Co., as well as with a local construction company. He and Melanie and the kids bounced between Long Branch and a house they were renting in South Jersey. After a few months, Sam, Chuck Fusina, and Duck Riley organized regular workouts for the players who were still living in the Philly area in the unlikely event the USFL played another season.

As time passed, it started to become more evident that they weren't going to be playing another season together. At least not with the Stars. That December, Norman Braman, who had bought the Eagles from Leonard Tose eight months earlier, fired his head coach, Marion Campbell. Braman, who was from West Philly but lived in South Florida, where he had a string of car dealerships, initially expressed interest in David Shula, the 26-year-old son of Miami Dolphins coach Don Shula. Shula, just four years out of Dartmouth, was his dad's wide receivers coach at the time.

Even Shula realized he wasn't ready to be an NFL head coach. He shot for the moon and asked Braman for a 10-year contract that quickly put an end to the negotiations. Shula eventually got an NFL head-coaching opportunity six years later when he was hired by the Cincinnati Bengals. He spent four seasons there and never made the playoffs. He never even had a winning record.

Braman's next target was Jim Mora. Because of the uncertainty with the USFL, Tanenbaum had given his coaches and front-office staff the green light to leave and take other jobs if they wanted. Mora was now a hot commodity. The St. Louis Cardinals had already offered him their head-coaching job, but he had turned it down.

Jim Finks, who had been hired as the general manager of the hapless New Orleans Saints a couple of weeks earlier, met with Mora at a hotel at the Philadelphia airport and offered him the Saints' head-coaching job. Mora immediately felt comfortable with Finks, an ex-NFL quarterback who had turned the Minnesota Vikings into one of the NFL's top franchises in the early '70s. But he was reluctant to leave Philly. It had become home. Or as close to a home as a gypsy pro football coach can have.

The Saints, who entered the league as an expansion team in 1967, were still looking for their first winning season. After a 5–11 finish in '85, owner Tom Benson, who had bought the team from the franchise's original owner, John Mecom, the previous spring, cleaned house, firing Bum Phillips, who had been both head coach and general manager, and Pat Peppler, the team's director of football operations. He hired Finks to try to turn things around.

All things being equal, staying in Philadelphia and coaching the Eagles, who had fallen on hard times since making the Super Bowl in 1980, was Mora's first choice.

But all things weren't equal. After meeting a few times with Braman, Mora had become increasingly concerned with the tone of negotiations. There was a reason the media would nickname the Eagles owner "Bottom-Line Braman." He cared more about what he liked to call "fiscal sanity" than he did about winning.

He quibbled over every dollar in Mora's contract during their negotiations. When he wanted to include the money Mora would make from a weekly coach's radio show as part of his total salary and pay him less out of his own pocket, Mora realized he could never be comfortable working for the guy. He turned the job down and immediately called Finks and accepted the Saints job.

"One of the things I liked about the Saints job was they hadn't had success for a long time," Mora says. "I felt like if we could go in there and win, that it would be big for the city, big for the organization. It'd be something that you'd be proud of, that I would be proud of."

Mills was disappointed when Mora turned down the Eagles' head-coaching job. If Mora had taken the job, Mills would have eagerly signed with the Eagles.

The linebacker loved playing in Philly. The football fans there had embraced him. He also loved the proximity of the city to his hometown of Long Branch, which was just an hour and change from Veterans Stadium. His family and friends had driven down from North Jersey for many of his games during the two years he played at the Vet before the Stars moved to Baltimore. The Long Branch-to-Philly caravan would have only gotten bigger if he had played for the Eagles.

Mora accepted the Saints job in late January of '86. Most of his coaching staff went with him to New Orleans, including Carl Smith (offensive coordinator), Jim Skipper (running backs), Jim Erkenbeck (offensive line), John Pease (defensive line), Dom Capers (defensive backs), Vic Fangio (linebackers), and Joe Marciano (special teams). Bill Kuharich, who had been the Stars' assistant general manager, was hired by the Saints as the team's director of player personnel.

Vince Tobin was also expected to go to New Orleans. But after Mora turned down the Eagles' head-coaching job, Braman hired Chicago Bears defensive coordinator Buddy Ryan, which created an opening on Mike Ditka's staff in Chicago.

The Bears had just won the Super Bowl, crushing the New England Patriots 46–10. The team's player personnel director at the time was Bill Tobin, Vince's older brother. On Bill's recommendation, Ditka offered Vince the Bears' defensive coordinator job. The opportunity to work in the same organization with his brother was very appealing, as was coaching a Super Bowl-champion defense that had led the NFL in fewest points allowed (12.4) and takeaways (54) the previous year.

Vince also had two young children at the time, and he didn't think New Orleans would provide the best family environment for them. He had reservations about the crime rate and the city's school system. So he went to Chicago.

After Tobin took the Bears job, Mora hired Steve Sidwell as his defensive coordinator in New Orleans. Sidwell and Mora had coached together on Eddie Crowder's staff at the University of Colorado in the late '60s and early '70s, and then again in '82 with the New England Patriots before Mora took the Stars job.

Mora's Saints were beginning to take shape, and that shape would soon include Sam Mills.

16

I liked Sam a lot. But to all of a sudden make the leap of faith that he was going to be a great player in the NFL, as much as I liked him with the Stars, I wasn't ready to make that kind of commitment to him.

—Jim Mora

THE TRIAL IN the USFL's antitrust suit against the NFL began on May 19 in the federal courthouse in lower Manhattan. It lasted 11 weeks. The parade of witnesses included NFL Commissioner Pete Rozelle, Los Angeles Raiders owner Al Davis, New York Jets owner Leon Hess, ABC broadcaster Howard Cosell, Donald Trump, and a litany of television executives.

The gist of the USFL's case: The NFL had pressured and coerced the three major television networks at the time—NBC, CBS, and ABC—not to televise USFL games in the fall of 1986.

Before the trial started, USFL Commissioner Harry Usher had said that the league would play that fall regardless of the trial outcome, though few people actually believed that. During the trial, Trump even testified that the USFL's future was "dependent upon the outcome of this trial."

The USFL had several owners who would have made sympathetic witnesses in the trial, owners who had lost millions and were having difficulty meeting their payroll and paying their bills. But the league's lead counsel, Harvey Myerson, a hotshot New York lawyer who Trump had brought in, and whose fall from grace would later include spending four years in federal prison for fraud, elected to have just one owner testify: his buddy Trump. And Donald came off as anything but sympathetic.

"I was part of the problem," Trump admitted in his 1987 book *Trump: The Art of the Deal.* "As a witness, I was well-spoken and professional, I think. But that probably played into the NFL's hands. From day one, they painted me as a vicious, greedy, Machiavellian billionaire, intent only on serving my selfish ends at everyone's expense."

It didn't take much paint.

Steve Ehrhart, the USFL's former executive director, said he learned later that the NFL had conducted a mock trial before the actual trial. In the mock trial, the USFL won a huge verdict. That prompted the NFL to change its whole strategy.

Rather than attempt to defend some of their individual predatory practices, which included commissioning a Harvard Business School study about how to kill the USFL, it set its sights on Trump. They made him the face of the league, portraying him as a rich, brash opportunist trying to extort money from the just-trying-to-mind-its-own-business NFL.

Before the verdict was announced, the NFL was still concerned enough about a possible negative trial outcome to discuss a merger with the USFL. The NFL proposed the possibility of absorbing two teams from the spring league, one of which almost certainly would've been the Stars because the NFL wanted a team back in Baltimore. But an overconfident Trump and Myerson wanted at least four—and possibly as many as six—teams from the spring league to join the NFL. The NFL told them that was never going to happen.

Testimony in the trial finally ended on July 23. Six days later, after 31 hours of deliberation, the six-person jury handed down its verdict.

Technically, the USFL won the trial. The jury found that the NFL had indeed used its monopoly power to damage the younger league in an attempt to retain control of the pro football market. That was the good news for the USFL. The bad news: The six jurors found Trump and the spring league so unsympathetic that they awarded them only a symbolic $1 in damages.

"We decided that there was a monopoly and that the NFL had tried to maintain it, but that the USFL mostly had damaged themselves," Margaret Lilienfeld, one of the six jurors, later told reporters.

"All the jury said was what I had testified," Rozelle said afterward. "That we are a natural monopoly. In my view, all professional sports leagues are that and have been since before the turn of the century. Now we can go back to playing football."

The USFL still might have had a chance to survive if it had gone ahead and played in the fall of '86. The league was down to eight teams at that point. Just two of them—Trump's Generals and the Tampa Bay Bandits—were in NFL markets. They still had a cable deal with ESPN for the '86 season. But the embarrassing $1 verdict—treble damages actually brought it to $3—had broken any will that the USFL owners had left to soldier on. Plus, their legal counsel, Myerson, told them that *not* playing in '86 while they appealed the damage award actually was a smarter legal strategy. Two years later, in March 1988, a federal appeals court would uphold the original July '86 verdict and the $1 damage award.

Six days after the jury verdict, USFL Commissioner Harry Usher announced that the USFL would not play in '86. Three days after that, on August 8, the league informed the 300-plus players still under contract, including Mills, that they were released from their USFL contracts and free to sign with another professional football league, including the NFL.

NFL training camps had already opened, but NFL teams wasted little time signing players from the spring league. Nearly 20 players from the Stars were gobbled up by various NFL teams. Mills' linebacker buddies Mike Johnson and George Jamison signed with the

Cleveland Browns and Detroit Lions. William Fuller signed with the Houston Oilers, Irv Eatman with the Kansas City Chiefs, safety Mike Lush with the Indianapolis Colts, Kelvin Bryant with the Washington Redskins, and Joe Conwell with the Eagles. Pete Kugler went back to San Francisco. All-USFL punter Sean Landeta joined Bart Oates in North Jersey with the Giants.

George Cooper had a workout scheduled with the Steelers, who had cut him in 1982 before he signed with the Stars. But he injured his hamstring and didn't get signed. Glenn Howard worked out for the Giants and Jets. He signed with the Jets, but they found bone chips in his knee and cut him.

With the possible exception of fellow future Hall of Famer Reggie White, there had been no more dominant defensive player in the three-year existence of the USFL than Sam Mills. Since Mills hadn't been selected in the NFL's supplemental draft of USFL players in January of '84, he was an unrestricted free agent after the USFL folded. Anyone could have made him an offer. Yet, even after the incredible success he had in the USFL, the only two teams that contacted him were Mora's Saints and the Super Bowl-champion Bears, where Vince Tobin was the new defensive coordinator.

Even now, all everyone else could see was 5'9".

Jim Finks picked Kuharich and Mora's brains about all of the available USFL players, including the ones Mora had coached in Philly. Mora had been a witness in the USFL–NFL trial. He had already been hired by the Saints at that point. One of the things the NFL's lead counsel, Frank Rothman, had asked Mora when he was on the stand was whether he thought the Stars, who clearly were the best team in the USFL, could've beaten an NFL team. Any NFL team. Much to the dismay of his former players, he said no.

Mora had been very wary of going too far out on a limb in any assessment of the spring league or its players. He knew he was being viewed as "that USFL coach," even though he had been a well-regarded NFL assistant for five years before taking the Stars job.

He knew his new players in New Orleans were going to be watching to see how many of his former players he brought in. And even today he readily admits that he just wasn't sure how a player's success in the USFL would translate to the NFL.

That included Mills.

Mora had watched as Mills became one of the USFL's very best players, but he still wasn't sure how good he was going to be in the NFL. Sam was the main reason the Stars won two USFL championships, but he hadn't grown any taller in the league's three years of existence, and Mora still had doubts about whether a 5'9" inside linebacker could thrive in the NFL.

"There just weren't many linebackers in the NFL that size," he says. "Probably none."

When Jim Finks asked Mora whether any of his players in Philadelphia could help the Saints, he mentioned Mills' name along with a few others. But he wasn't "100 percent sold" yet that Mills could be a starter and make the Saints better.

"I told Jim I thought Sam was a really good player in the USFL," he says. "And I thought he deserved a chance with our team and that we should sign him. That was it basically."

The biggest thing the USFL did for Mills was give him the opportunity to play and improve his skills. If the spring league had lasted just one year instead of three, Kuharich isn't sure Mills would've ever become the player he did.

As was the case early on with the Stars, Tobin didn't have the same reservations about Sam's size that Mora did after the USFL folded. He believed unequivocally that Sam could excel in the NFL and badly wanted to bring him to Chicago with him.

But the Bears already had the league's most dominant defense. It featured four future Hall of Famers—middle linebacker Mike

Singletary and defensive linemen Richard Dent, Dan Hampton, and Steve McMichael.

The Bears had played a 4–3 scheme under Buddy Ryan, with Singletary, a seven-time All-Pro and 10-time Pro Bowler, in the middle, flanked by outside linebackers Wilber Marshall and Otis Wilson, who also were Pro Bowlers. But Tobin believed they could be even better with Mills.

Tobin was prepared to talk to Ditka about switching to a 3–4 and putting Mills inside alongside Singletary.

"I would've found a place to put him and I fought like hell to get him," Tobin said. "But in the end, I think he felt he wouldn't have quite the same opportunity in Chicago that he'd get in New Orleans with Jim."

Even without Mills, Tobin ended up playing a lot of 3–4. He frequently had Dent line up as an outside linebacker.

Tobin's willingness to change up a defense as great as the Bears' to make room for Mills tells you all you need to know about how highly he thought of Sam.

Ultimately, the Saints were a much better fit for Mills. He would be playing in the very same defensive scheme he had played for three years in Philadelphia. He wouldn't have to worry about fitting into a Super Bowl-winning defense whose coordinator was going to adjust the scheme just for him.

He had existing relationships with Mora and much of his staff, including Mora's young linebackers coach, Vic Fangio, who had been a defensive assistant in 1984 and 1985 with the Stars.

While the Bears and the Saints were the only two teams with any interest in Mills, his good friend, Stars defensive back Antonio Gibson, had several interested suitors after the USFL folded. His agent, Mike Corbi, had arranged visits for him with the Los Angeles Raiders and the San Diego Chargers.

Just before Gibson and Corbi were scheduled to leave for the West Coast to talk to the Raiders and Chargers, Kuharich called and asked them to fly down to Louisiana and meet with the Saints first.

As it happened, Mills and his agent, Grasella Oliphant, were on the same plane as Gibson and Corbi. The Saints were a couple of weeks into training camp at that point. Mora held his first two training camps with the Saints at Southeastern Louisiana University in Hammond, which is about 60 miles northwest of New Orleans. After flying to New Orleans, Mills and Gibson and their agents drove up to Hammond together.

After arriving in Hammond, they spoke with Mora and the other Saints coaches and watched practice. After that, they met with Finks and talked contract. Mills and Oliphant were underwhelmed by what the Saints offered and ended up leaving and returning to New Jersey. Gibson stuck around.

The Saints were playing their first preseason game that weekend. They asked Gibson to stay in Hammond until they got back. They eventually offered him "a lot more" money than he was making in the USFL. He signed with them and never made it to the West Coast for his visits with the Raiders and Chargers.

Despite all of Mills' USFL accolades, the Saints curiously offered Gibson a better contract. "Think about that," Gibson says. "Sam had been the best player in the USFL, and they were offering me more money."

After Mills left, Gibson assumed Sam would probably end up in Chicago with Tobin. But a day after Gibson signed, Mills reappeared in Hammond. The Saints had wisely agreed to sweeten their offer.

Gibson was "really excited" to be able to keep playing with Mills. He knew he was going to a team that had lost 11 games the previous year, to a team that had never had a winning season in its 19 years of existence. But it gave him confidence knowing Mills was there. He had seen firsthand the impact he could have on a defense.

The Saints were a backward organization before Finks and Mora got there. They didn't just lack talent; they lacked the organizational structure and know-how to even assemble and develop that talent.

Before Finks arrived, they didn't even have a pro personnel department. There was one pro scout, a couple of college scouts, a scouting director, Joe Woolley, and that was it.

As Mora and Kuharich began *evaluating* the Saints' roster, they compared it to the Stars' roster and quickly realized that many of the Stars' starters would be better backups than many of the current Saints backups. But Mora was wary of bringing in players from the USFL unless he was convinced that they could make an immediate difference. He didn't want to create an "us versus them" atmosphere. He didn't want to send a message to the players who were already there that their new coach didn't think they were good enough, even if that was pretty much the way he felt about a lot of them.

"We felt [the Stars] could've been competitive with 50 percent of the NFL," says Stars offensive lineman Chuck Commiskey, who also signed with the Saints.

The Saints ended up signing 12 USFL players that first summer. Eight made the team, including four of Mora's players from the Stars—Mills, Gibson, Commiskey, and wide receiver Herbert Harris. The other four USFL alums on the Saints' '86 roster were linebacker Vaughan Johnson (Jacksonville Jaguars), fullbacks Buford Jordan (New Orleans/Portland Breakers) and John Williams (Michigan Panthers), and running back/kick returner Mel Gray (Los Angeles Express).

One player from the Stars that Mora elected not to bring with him to New Orleans was his quarterback, Chuck Fusina. Fusina had been a key part of the Stars' success. He had a 41–12–1 record as a starter for Mora. He had thrown for more than 10,000 yards and 66 touchdowns.

But the Saints already had a quarterback with USFL roots in Bobby Hebert, who had played against the Stars in the 1983 and 1985 USFL Championship Games for the Michigan Panthers and Oakland Invaders.

Hebert was a Louisiana native with a big arm who had played his college ball at Northwestern (Louisiana) State in Natchitoches and grew up about an hour from New Orleans. That made him very popular with Saints fans.

Mora had great regard for Fusina, but he was concerned about how it would look if he brought Fusina in to compete against Hebert. That turned out to be a big mistake. Fusina didn't have Hebert's natural ability, but as Joe Paterno had told Carl Peterson a few years earlier, he knew how to win. Hebert didn't.

Hebert was one of those quarterbacks you remember more for the natural talent he possessed rather than the results he got with it. He would play for eight years with the Saints. He helped get Mora's teams to the playoffs four times, but he always came up small under the bright lights of the postseason. He would lose all three of his playoff starts with the Saints, throwing seven interceptions and just three TD passes and completing only 56.9 percent of his passes in those three defeats.

Fusina was initially disappointed that Mora didn't bring him to the Saints. He spoke with some of Mora's offensive assistants, who assured him he was good enough to play for the Saints. He reluctantly understood Mora's hesitation as a new coach to bring him in and pit him against a popular player like Hebert.

"If Hebert hadn't already been there, I'm pretty sure Jim would've brought me in," Fusina says. "But the organization had put a lot of money into Bobby when they signed him a year earlier. He was going to be the guy."

Mora acknowledged that if Hebert hadn't already been there, he more than likely would've wanted Fusina.

Fusina would eventually sign with the Green Bay Packers, where he backed up mediocre Randy Wright on a team that lost as many games that season (12) as Fusina had in three years in the USFL.

17

We used to joke with Sam and call him Mora's son. Sam would get all embarrassed by it and say, 'I wish you wouldn't say that kind of stuff.' But Jim clearly loved him.

—SAINTS OFFENSIVE LINEMAN CHUCK COMMISKEY

JIM MORA HAD a well-earned reputation for pushing his players to the limit. That was particularly true in August 1986 in his first training camp with the Saints at Southeastern Louisiana University in Hammond. Louisiana summers are miserable, and this one was worse than most. The temperature was in the mid-90s and the humidity would've made the devil sweat. The Saints only stayed at Hammond for two summers. In 1988, they moved their camp to a much cooler climate—La Crosse, Wisconsin. The Kansas City Chiefs and Jacksonville Jaguars also moved their camps to Wisconsin. Along with the Green Bay Packers and the Minnesota Vikings, the six teams formed what became known as the Cheese League.

By his own admission, Mora was a hard-ass. Even as an assistant coach earlier in his career, his approach was always to be extra-tough, extra-demanding early on. Basically, he wanted to let his players know who was boss.

Mora had the Saints practicing *three times a day* in Hammond. The third practice was only a special teams practice, but that was little consolation to the players, who still had to go out on the field and bake in the sun. And Mora didn't concern himself with scheduling the practices early in the morning or late in the evening when the temperatures might be a bit cooler or the humidity a shade lower. He would post the schedule, temperatures and humidity be damned.

"We're about a week and a half into training camp and I'm killing our football team, working the hell out of them," Mora remembers with an even mixture of sympathy and pride. "I was working the dog out of that team in the worst heat and humidity I've ever coached in. It was my first year, and I wanted to set a good standard, a good example. I was gonna push the hell out of them."

It was a different time back then. Heat stroke received no more consideration in the NFL in the '80s than concussions, which was to say none at all. The NFL didn't have any rules limiting the length of time players could be on the field or the number of full-contact practices a team could have during training camp. If somebody collapsed from fatigue or heat prostration, the training staff just carted him off, and he was replaced by another warm body. That would change in 2001 after Minnesota Vikings offensive lineman Korey Stringer died of exertional heat stroke during a training camp practice. Stringer's death led to league-wide heat-related illness protocols.

Looking back, Mora realizes how lucky he was that somebody didn't collapse and die during one of those practices in Hammond.

The Saints had been in pads in that oppressive Louisiana heat for six straight days when the team finally signed Sam Mills. Safety Brett Maxie was one of the first players to meet Mills when he walked into the locker room at Southeastern Louisiana. As he shook Sam's hand, Maxie's first thought was that the guy had some "big paws." His second thought: *Damn, he's so short. He's supposed to be our middle linebacker? Are they serious?*

He wasn't the only one wondering that. Mills' small size became even more striking to his new teammates as he walked down the hill to the practice field alongside the team's other new inside linebacker from the USFL, 6'3½", 240-pound Vaughan Johnson. Johnson looked like a Greek god. Sam, well, maybe a mini-me Greek god.

They looked like Mutt & Jeff. The Saints players knew of Mills, knew he had played for Mora in the USFL. But this wasn't the USFL. It was the NFL. As they looked at him, it seemed to justify their belief that their new sadistic coach had no freaking idea what he was doing.

Dom Capers, Mora's defensive backs coach, watched the players' reaction when Mills arrived at the practice field. He was standing near the offensive line group and saw a few of them elbowing one another and snickering, saying, "That must be Mora's boy."

The Saints were doing nine-on-seven work when Mills and Johnson arrived. Nine offensive players—five offensive linemen, a tight end, a running back, a fullback, and the quarterback—running the ball between the tackles against seven defensive players—three down linemen and four linebackers. Everybody was in full pads.

"It wasn't really *live* live," Mora recalls. "But it was as close to live as you can get."

As soon as Mills got there, Mora told him to put on his helmet and sent him in at one of the inside linebacker spots. The Saints had some pretty good defensive linemen on that '86 team. Jumpy Geathers, Frank Warren, Bruce Clark, and Jim Wilks. Rickey Jackson, who had been to three straight Pro Bowls, was out there at one of the outside linebacker spots.

As Sam stood next to those guys, all of Mora's doubts about Sam's size came rushing back.

"He looked short, *really* short," Mora says. "I'm standing there and I know what the other players are thinking. They're thinking, *Holy shit. This stupid damn USFL coach brings this little guy in from the USFL and expects him to play? Is he nuts?*"

The offense called a play and Mora stood there, bent over with his hands on his knees, talking to himself and muttering, "C'mon, Sam. Do it for me, baby. Show 'em what you got."

“I was praying, hoping that he was going to step in there and play like I’d seen him play in the USFL,” says Mora.

Mills didn’t disappoint his coach.

Sam highlighted that nine-on-seven drill. He had big 320-pound guards towering over him. They would run right at him, and he would step up with his short body, get under their pads, use that six-inch punch of his to knock them back, then slip away from them and make the tackle. He did it three or four times in a row.

Everybody’s eyes lit up. A wide smile formed on Mora’s relieved face. From that moment forward, Mills would never look short to him again. He looked like he belonged out there with the defense. With one practice performance, Sam won over the majority of his new teammates and gained their respect.

Vic Fangio remembers making eye contact with Mora during that drill.

“We weren’t standing next to each other,” he says. “We were about 15 yards away from each other. And we both smiled.”

There wasn’t a big learning curve for Mills and Antonio Gibson as far as the defense the Saints were running. Vince Tobin was in Chicago, but Mora’s new defensive lieutenant, Steve Sidwell, also was running a 3–4 that featured most of the same concepts as the defense Tobin and Mora had run with the Stars.

“Steve Sidwell had coached with Jim before,” Gibson said. “So the defense was pretty similar. In the beginning, we weren’t as aggressive as we had been with the Stars as far as blitzing and stuff. But that eventually changed.”

The environment that Mills and Gibson walked into in the summer of ’86 was much different than the one they had left with the Stars. They went from an ultra-successful team that had won two league championships to the hapless Saints, or, as many of their paper-bag-wearing fans called them back then, the *Aints*.

The additions of Mills, Gibson, Commiskey, and Vaughan Johnson from the USFL improved the Saints' talent level. So did the '86 draft. Finks and Kuharich were both excellent talent evaluators. They selected offensive tackle Jim Dombrowski of Virginia with the sixth overall pick and added two running backs, Dalton Hilliard of Louisiana State in the second round and Rueben Mayes of Washington State in the third round. They also drafted linebacker Pat Swilling from Georgia Tech in the third round.

Hilliard and Mayes became the Saints' 1–2 rushing punch for Mora's ground-based offense in the late '80s. Swilling would join Mills, Johnson, and Rickey Jackson to form what would become arguably the best linebacking quartet in NFL history.

Two of the Saints' first three picks in the draft the year before Finks, Mora, and Kuharich arrived were inside linebackers. They had taken Alvin Toles of Tennessee in the first round with the 24th overall pick, and then selected Jack Del Rio, a cocky 6'4", 248-pounder out of Southern Cal, in the third round.

The Saints had started six different players at the two inside linebacker spots the year before Mora arrived. Glen Redd, a five-year veteran out of BYU, started all 16 games at one of the spots. Veterans Scott Pelluer, Jim Kovach, and Dirt Winston started eight games at the other inside spot. Toles also got one start. Head coach Bum Phillips' son Wade, who was the team's defensive coordinator, eventually settled on Del Rio, who started nine games as a rookie, six at inside linebacker alongside Redd and three at one of the outside spots. Del Rio tied the franchise record for fumble recoveries with five and made the NFL's All-Rookie team. Jack was feeling pretty good about himself heading into the '86 season.

Del Rio was a good player, but he was as self-centered as they came. For a guy who would later spend a dozen years as an NFL head coach, he was never much of a team player.

Del Rio never bought into Mora's program and didn't buy into the players he brought in. He viewed both Mills and Vaughan Johnson as threats to him the minute they stepped onto the practice field. And rightfully so. He quickly realized that both of them were much better players than he was.

Mora treaded carefully. He knew Del Rio and the other players were watching him, but he also knew many of them weren't going to be around for much longer as he and Finks and Kuharich rebuilt the team.

Del Rio and Redd were the two starting inside 'backers against the Atlanta Falcons in the '86 season opener. Mills and Johnson backed them up and played on special teams. The Saints got destroyed in that game, 31–10. The Falcons racked up 442 total yards, including 245 on the ground, much of it at the expense of Del Rio and Redd.

That game was Del Rio's last start for the Saints. He was replaced the next week by Toles and got traded the following summer to the Kansas City Chiefs for a fifth-round draft pick.

It raised a lot of eyebrows when Mora benched Del Rio. But the bottom line was he just wasn't as good as either Mills or Johnson. That eventually became obvious as the pair would develop into the best inside linebacker tandem in the league.

After the Saints lost to San Francisco in Week 3 of the '86 season to drop to 1–2, Mora decided the time had come to insert both Sam and Antonio Gibson into the starting lineup. Gibson, like Mills, had been used primarily on special teams in the Saints' first three games. Gibson replaced Russell Gary at strong safety. Mills replaced Redd at left inside linebacker. Mills and Alvin Toles would be the Saints' two starting inside linebackers for the rest of the '86 season. While Vaughan Johnson played a lot, Mora wouldn't make him a starter until the following season.

Mills' first start for the Saints was a New Jersey homecoming up in the Meadowlands against Bill Parcells' Giants. More than 300 friends and family members made the pilgrimage to Giants Stadium to root on Long Branch's favorite son.

With Mills and Gibson in the lineup, the Saints held the Giants, who would lose just two games that year and win the Super Bowl, to a touchdown under their season average, losing by three, 20–17. Sam had eight tackles in the game as the defense held the Giants' running backs to three yards per carry and intercepted Phil Simms three times.

The Saints wasted another terrific defensive performance the following week when they lost to the Washington Redskins, 14–6. But they would rebound to win five of their next six, including impressive back-to-back November wins over the playoff-bound San Francisco 49ers and LA Rams. They finished the season with a 7–9 record.

Their offense wasn't very good. Hebert missed a big chunk of the season with a broken foot and would start just three games. The Saints scored more than 24 points only twice the entire season and finished 19th in the 28-team league in scoring (18 points per game). They were 26th in touchdown passes (a mere 13) and turned the ball over an astounding 43 times.

But the defense kept them in games. With the additions of Mills, Gibson, Johnson, and Swilling, they improved from 22nd in points allowed in '85 (25.1 per game) to seventh (17.9) in '86. They jumped from 22nd in yards allowed per play (5.4) to third (4.6).

Their run defense was one of the best in the league. They finished first in opponent rush average (3.2) after finishing 23rd the previous season (4.3), and they improved from 19th to fourth in rushing yards allowed per game (97.4).

Mills finished second on the team in tackles that year with 92. Rickey Jackson had a team-high 114 to go with nine sacks and a career-high six forced fumbles. Jackson made the Pro Bowl for the fourth straight year and earned his third straight All-Pro selection.

Mills quickly impressed his new Saints teammates with both his work habits and uncanny ability to read offenses and tip off the rest of the defense to what was coming. It gave the Saints' defense a massive advantage.

"Sam would prepare in the film room almost like he was an assistant coach," Gibson says. "When I went to New Orleans with him, to see him walk into that huddle during a game and to see those squinty eyes and call the play. . . if it was third down, Sam was already telling guys in the huddle what to watch for on that play.

"We break the huddle and line up, and right away, Joe Montana or whomever we were playing against would be getting behind center and looking the defense over. Sam would already be hollering out what to look for based on the [offensive] set.

"And he hardly ever was wrong."

18

We ended up with four damn good linebackers. Some people believe they're one of the best sets of linebackers ever. We had great defenses there for a while with those guys.

—Jim Mora

THE YEAR BEFORE Jim Mora and Sam Mills arrived in New Orleans, the Saints' defense wasn't very good. They had a handful of good players. Defensive linemen Frank Warren and Jim Wilks were both products of the Saints' 1981 draft. Warren was taken in the third round out of Auburn. Wilks was a 12th-round afterthought out of San Diego State. Both ended up playing important roles in Mora's defense. Warren spent 14 years with the Saints, starting 83 games for them. Wilks played 13 years in New Orleans and started 154 games. Both players are in the team's Hall of Fame.

Cornerback Dave Waymer was also already there when Mora was hired. Waymer, a 1980 second-round pick out of Notre Dame, started 155 games for the Saints. He was selected to the Pro Bowl in '87. Like Warren and Wilks, he's in the Saints Hall of Fame.

Far and away the best player that Mora inherited, though, was Rickey Jackson. Like Warren and Wilks, the 6'2", 243-pound Jackson was a product of the Saints' '81 draft. He was their second-round pick that year out of the University of Pittsburgh.

Jackson was born and raised in Pahokee, Florida, a dirt-poor town of 5,500 people on the shores of Lake Okeechobee in South Florida.

Despite its small size, Pahokee has produced more than a dozen NFL players over the years, including wide receiver Anquan Boldin, running back Fred Taylor, and cornerback Janoris Jenkins.

Jackson played his college ball on a talent-rich Pitt team coached by Jackie Sherrill that had more than a half dozen other future NFL players, including fellow linebacker Hugh Green, offensive linemen Russ Grimm and Jimbo Covert, defensive tackle Bill Maas, and Hall of Fame quarterback Dan Marino.

Jackson was a complete linebacker. He could play the run and drop into coverage. But what he did best was rush the passer. He probably had the best "get-off" in the NFL in the '80s and early '90s.

He had eight sacks as a rookie in '81 for a Saints team that won just four games. He notched 12 in both '83 and '84, and 11 in Bum Phillips' last season as coach in '85 when the Saints lost 11 games. He made the Pro Bowl four straight years from '83 to '86. He was a second-team All-Pro in '84, '85, and '86.

During his last two years at Pitt, the Panthers had back-to-back 11–1 seasons. But as he entered his sixth NFL season with the Saints in '86, Jackson still hadn't played on a winning team in New Orleans. The Saints managed to go 8–8 in '83, then went backward, finishing 7–9 in '84 and 5–11 in '85.

Everything changed in '86 with the arrivals of Sam Mills, Vaughan Johnson, and Pat Swilling.

Credit Bum Phillips and his director of football operations, Pat Peppler, for Johnson ending up with the Saints. They selected him in the '84 supplemental draft of USFL players, which was held midway through Johnson's first season with the Jacksonville Bulls. The Saints' scouting report on Johnson was based primarily on his college career at North Carolina State, where he had 384 tackles and was a first-team All-America selection in 1983 by *The Sporting News.*

Johnson was a vicious hitter who once said that when he hit somebody, "I like to see their eyes glaze over and roll back [in their head]."

Swilling, like Jackson, had elite pass-rushing skills. He set the single-season sack record at Georgia Tech with 15. He had seven in one game against North Carolina State.

Johnson and Swilling both played quite a bit in '86 but weren't starters yet. Alvin Toles started alongside Mills inside, and James Haynes started at right outside linebacker, opposite Jackson.

Swilling was used primarily as a nickel pass rusher as a rookie. He had four sacks that year, two more than Haynes, who was more of a run defender than a pass rusher. Mills had become a starter in Week 4 but would initially get replaced on passing downs. They would take him out, move Jackson inside, and add a fifth defensive back.

Sidwell and Mora initially had concerns about tight ends beating Mills down the seam and quarterbacks throwing over the top of him.

Mills was more than a little frustrated that Mora still wasn't convinced he could be an every-down linebacker in the NFL. He had spent three years with him in the USFL. He had been the best linebacker in that league; a three-time first-team All-USFL player. No, the USFL wasn't the NFL. But he felt he had certainly proven that his size wasn't a liability in pass coverage.

But sulking wasn't in Mills' mental makeup. His attitude was that if they still had doubts, then he would erase them. He rolled up his sleeves and went out and proved to them that he was an every-down linebacker. He stayed after practice every day that first year and caught balls on the JUGS machine. He'd have a quarterback stay out on the field with him and try to loop balls over his head.

After a few games, Mora and Sidwell realized that it really made no sense to take their best linebacker off the field. They kept Jackson outside as an edge rusher and left Sam inside. By 1987, when Johnson became a full-time starter, all four of the Saints' linebackers were every-down players. Third-and-one or third-and-12, it didn't matter. All four stayed on the field.

In seven seasons from '87 through '93, the Saints' defense finished in the top six in passing yards allowed six times. They were second in '91 and first in '92 and '93. No one would ever again suggest that Mills was a coverage liability.

In Mills' first seven years in New Orleans, the Saints finished in the top eight in points allowed six times, including back-to-back No. 1 finishes in 1991 and 1992.

From 1987 to 1992, the Saints held opponents to 16.4 points per game in the regular season. That was the second-best average in the league over that period. Most significantly, their 62 regular-season wins in those six years were the third most in the NFL, behind only Buffalo and San Francisco (72).

The straw that stirred the drink for Mora's defense was Mills, Jackson, Johnson, and Swilling. They became known as the "Dome Patrol" after posing for a promotional poster in front of the Superdome. The poster became a bestseller, and the nickname became one of the most popular in professional sports.

"We were pretty damn good with those four guys," says Fangio. "We also had good defensive linemen in front of them who protected them and kept blockers off of them."

Mills, Johnson, Jackson, and Swilling would be selected to a combined 20 Pro Bowls during their careers, 18 while playing together with the Saints. In 1992, all four were selected to the Pro Bowl. It's the only time in NFL history that four linebackers from the same team have ever been selected to the Pro Bowl in the same season.

The Saints would finish in the top seven in the league in opponent rush average in five of Mills and Johnson's first six years together in New Orleans.

Much like he had so many times against Herschel Walker in the USFL, Mills had a knack for making the critical goal-line and short-yardage stops. He did it so often that it was a surprise when he didn't do it.

"It was weird," his son Sam III says. "It would be third-and-one or fourth-and-one and I'd be thinking, *I don't think the other team is going to get this.* It's usually the other way around, but my dad and Vaughan and the rest of that defense was so good at stopping teams in short-yardage situations that you just expected them to do it."

The Saints' ability to stop the run set up a multitude of second- and third-and-longs for Jackson and Swilling to tee off on opposing quarterbacks, and they capitalized. Jackson's 128 career sacks would be the 16th most in NFL history. Swilling is 31st with 107 ½. In the six-season period from '87 through '92, the pair would combine for 127 ½ sacks. That's more than *21 per year!*

Mora was never a big offensive risk-taker. He was a charter member of the live-to-fight-another-down club. Go for it on fourth down? It wasn't in his DNA. The aggressive analytics-motivated play-calling in today's game gives him acid reflux.

That was especially the case in New Orleans, where he had one of the league's very best defenses. His attitude: Why take risks on offense when your defense is going to get you the ball back?

He also had one of the best kickers in NFL history. Morten Andersen's 565 career field goals are the second most in league history. He was a seven-time Pro Bowler, and a five-time All-Pro, and he was inducted into the Pro Football Hall of Fame in 2017.

"Once we got inside the other team's 35, we knew we were guaranteed three points if we didn't turn the ball over," says Jim Skipper, who was Mora's running backs coach for 13 years in Philadelphia and New Orleans.

"Everybody always jumped on [offensive coordinator] Carl Smith and used him as a scapegoat when we lost. But we were doing the best thing we could with the people we had to win games. Everybody said we were so conservative. We were. We were a defensive team that could run the ball and had the best kicker in the history of football."

Mills was the Dome Patrol's maestro. He conducted the beautiful music the quartet made during their seven years together. He made all the defensive calls. Any audibles that needed to be made at the line of scrimmage, he made them.

"Sam was the unquestioned leader of the group on the field—mentally, spiritually, and schematically," says Fangio.

Of the other three linebackers, Mills was closest with Johnson. They roomed together on the road. Mills' oldest son, Sam III, says Johnson particularly appreciated his father's football mind. He was grateful there were certain things he didn't have to worry about because Sam would take care of them and tell the rest of the defense what was coming so they could play fast.

Like the rest of the team, Rickey Jackson initially had some reservations about Mills when he first signed with the Saints due to his size. But he quickly came around after watching him play and getting to know him. They, too, became close friends.

One year, both Sam and Rickey were negotiating new deals with the Saints. Sam had replaced his original agent, Grassella Oliphant, with Brett Senior, a respected NFL adviser who was more experienced in tax matters and financial planning than Oliphant. Senior represented several Saints players.

The Saints had moved their training camp to Wisconsin by then. Brett Senior flew up to La Crosse to meet with Finks and finish up some things on a new deal for Mills.

Finks was also trying to get a new deal done with Jackson, who didn't have an agent. He wanted to negotiate his own deal, which was slowing the whole process. Finks had a good relationship with Senior and asked him if he could talk to Rickey and help him understand that the offer the Saints were making was fair.

Senior put together the salary numbers on all the league's top edge rushers. He and Mills then met with Jackson. Mills was silent as Senior ran down the numbers for Jackson of what the Saints were offering him and what other edge rushers around the league were making. He showed him the incentives in the Saints' offer and pointed out that they were very attainable and that he had a good chance to be the highest-paid edge rusher in the league.

After Senior got done, Mills finally spoke.

"Rickey, you know how important it is for you to be on that practice field with us," Mills told him.

After a few seconds of silence, Jackson looked at Mills.

"Okay, I'll do it," he said. "But I want you to come with me when I sign it."

"Rickey," Mills said, "if Brett is telling you it's a good deal, it's a good deal."

"I know," Jackson said. "But I still want you there."

"Okay," Mills replied.

Mills accompanied Jackson to Finks' training camp office at the University of Wisconsin-La Crosse. Rickey signed his new deal, and everybody lived happily ever after. Most of the time.

Jackson and Swilling were both "high-maintenance" players. They had big egos that occasionally needed massaging, especially Swilling. He arrived in New Orleans with a giant chip on his shoulder because he thought he should've been a first-round pick.

"That's not necessarily a bad thing with athletes," says Bill Kuharich. "But Pat always thought he was better than the other three. He wasn't interested in doing any of the dirty work. In his mind, it was sacks that got you the big bucks, and that's all he cared about. He wanted to redo his contract every year. He was a pain in the ass. He was a pain in the ass from day one."

That pain in the ass did have his upside. Swilling had one of the fastest first steps in the game. When offensive tackles would overcompensate for his tremendous edge speed, he would counter with an outstanding spin move that he had developed. From 1989 through 1992, Swilling recorded 55 sacks. No defensive player in the league had more sacks over that four-year period. Reggie White, who is considered one of the three or four best defensive players in NFL history, had 54. Swilling made four straight Pro Bowls in those four years. In 1991, he had a league-high 17 ½ sacks and was named the NFL Defensive Player of the Year.

After the '92 season, which ended with a hugely disappointing playoff loss to the Philadelphia Eagles, both Finks and Mora felt it was time to part ways with Swilling. Coming off a 10 ½-sack season and his second straight All-Pro selection, his stock was never going to be higher.

The Saints put the word out before the '93 draft that Swilling could be had for the right price. When the Detroit Lions offered them multiple picks, including their first-round pick, which happened to be the eighth overall selection, the Saints jumped at it. The Saints would end up using that No. 8 pick on Hall of Fame offensive tackle Willie Roaf.

Swilling played two years for the Lions after the trade, and then two more with the Oakland Raiders. He would have just one more double-digit sack season after he left the Saints (13 with the Raiders in '95).

"Pat never understood the importance of the other three guys to his own success," Kuharich said. "They fed off each other. That never occurred to him."

Mills was a godsend to Vic Fangio early on. Fangio was just 28 when Mora brought him along from the Stars. He was just three years removed from being a graduate assistant at the University of North Carolina, four years removed from coaching high school. It was his very first time in charge of a position group at *any* level. Even Jim Finks initially had some major reservations about Fangio's lack of experience. But Mora believed in Fangio and convinced Finks that

Vic was the right man for the job. And Mills always had Vic's back. The other linebackers took their cue from Sam.

"I'm sure Rickey had his questions [about me] early on," Fangio said. "But we forged a good relationship early and it's lasted all these years. Having Sam there helped a lot as far as Rickey learning to trust me. He was the leader. He was the trusted voice. All of those guys trusted Sam."

Mills was effectively a coach his entire career, both on the field and off. He counseled teammates. If a young player was struggling or dealing with something, Sam could sense it and often would bunk with him in training camp so that he had somebody to talk to and help guide him.

"He was the elder statesman," says Brett Senior. "Keep in mind, he already was 27 when he got to New Orleans. He became the guy everyone looked to. They saw the way he practiced and studied and looked at film and acted in the community, and they followed his lead."

19

You'll never confuse football players with the Bolshevik revolutionaries who stormed the Winter Palace.

—TONY AGNONE, LONGTIME NFL PLAYER AGENT

SAM MILLS' BIOLOGICAL clock was already ticking when he signed with the Saints at 27. Besides his size, his age was one more reason no other teams besides the Saints and Bears had shown any interest in him after the USFL went belly-up.

He was trying to make the most of his late NFL start. Every minute, every practice, every game counted. So, imagine how he felt when the league's players went out on strike in '87 for the second time in six years.

In '82, while Mills was debating whether to take a chance on a new spring league, the NFL players struck for 57 days. The work stoppage wiped out seven weeks of the season and forced the league to slash its regular-season schedule from 16 to nine games. The shortened season cost the NFL owners tens of millions of dollars.

When the players went on strike again two weeks into the '87 season, the owners were ready.

"You guys are cattle and we're the ranchers," Dallas Cowboys President Tex Schramm arrogantly told NFL Players Association chief Gene Upshaw during their labor negotiations. "We can always get more cattle."

The owners brought in "replacement" players so they could continue playing games. The strike lasted just 24 days, during which the

Sam's parents – Juanita and Sam Sr. Sam was the third youngest of 12 children born to Juanita. She died in July of 2003, three weeks before her son was diagnosed with cancer. *Mills family*

Long Branch High School in 1977. *Long Branch High School*

Sam's senior picture at Long Branch High School. *Long Branch High School*

Mills played fullback as a freshman at Long Branch and wore No. 37. He moved to linebacker and offensive guard as a sophomore and wore 51, which also would be his jersey number with the Saints and Panthers. *Long Branch High School*

Sam's high school coach, Frank Glazier, had a huge influence on his career. He taught him how to watch film and read offensive tendencies and to believe in himself. *Long Branch High School*

Even as a high school player, Mills already had perfect tackling form. Here he wraps up an opposing running back his senior year. *Long Branch High School*

Mills was an outstanding wrestler at Long Branch High School, winning two district titles and finishing as the New Jersey state runnerup in 1977. He missed his high school graduation because he was late getting back from a wrestling tournament in West Germany. *Long Branch High School*

Montclair coach Fred Hill was worried that Sam might transfer when Frank Glazier got the William Paterson job in 1978. But Sam told him he had made a commitment to him and was going to keep it.
Montclair State University

Montclair only lost a total of five games in Sam's last three years at the school. He recorded 501 tackles in four years there, which remains a school record. He was a two-time Kodak All-American.
Montclair State University

Jim Garrett's house on Ocean Ave. in Monmouth Beach, NJ, was called the Whale House because of the huge wooden whale that hung on the side of the house. Garrett worked out Mills and other players in his oversized yard before he signed with the Cleveland Browns. Even after getting cut by the Browns, Sam often worked out at the Garrett house. Jim was influential in convincing Mills to sign with the Philadelphia Stars. *Paul Domowitch*

Sam's eyes are focused on the running back as he pursues the play and closes in for the tackle. *Bob Moore*

Jim Mora initially wanted to cut Mills, but eventually came to believe in him. They were together for 12 years in Philadelphia and New Orleans. He has called Sam the best player he ever coached. *Bob Moore*

Missed tackles wasn't yet a statistic when Mills played for the Stars. But it was rare when anyone got away from him. He was one of the surest tacklers in the game. *Bob Moore*

Sam directs the Stars defense from his inside linebacker position in Jim Mora's 3-4 defense. *Bob Moore*

The Stars appeared in all three USFL championship games and won two of them. Jim Mora, owner Myles Tanenbaum, and general manager Carl Peterson are shown holding the 1984 championship trophy during a city celebration in Philadelphia. *Bob Moore*

Sam and Melanie on their wedding day in 1983. *Mills family*

Sam makes a tackle on Arizona Wranglers running back Kevin Long in the 1984 USFL championship game, which the Stars won. *Bob Moore*

Herschel Walker was the USFL's most prolific running back, but he seldom fared well against Sam and the Stars' defense. *Bob Moore*

Donald Trump, who owned the USFL's New Jersey Generals and is shown here with Herschel Walker, was largely responsible for the demise of the spring league after just three seasons. *Dave Pickoff, AP Photo*

The Dome Patrol – Pat Swilling, Rickey Jackson, Sam, and Vaughan Johnson – were one of the best linebacker units in NFL history. They were together for seven years. *New Orleans Saints*

The Saints had one of the NFL's best run defenses in the seven years that the Dome Patrol was together. They finished in the top eight in rushing yards allowed six times. *New Orleans Saints*

In 1992, all four of the Saints' starting linebackers made the Pro Bowl. Swilling, Johnson, Sam, and Jackson pose together before a practice. It's the only time in history that four linebackers from the same team have been selected. In their seven years together, the quartet made 14 Pro Bowl appearances. *Brett Senior*

Sam and Mel enjoy an evening in Oahu during one of Sam's five Pro Bowl trips to Hawaii. He earned his first invitation in 1987, in his second season with the Saints. *Mills family*

Sam Mills had an exceptional relationship with the media everywhere he played. Reporters flocked to his locker after games, and he was a frequent guest on local TV and radio shows. Here he is on a radio show on WTIX-AM with New Orleans sportscaster Ken Trahan (far left) in the late '80s. *Mills Family*

Sam's coaches have said he was never fooled and never took a wrong step on the field. Here he plants his left leg and heads toward the point of attack. *Carolina Panthers*

A pre-snap shot of Sam against quarterback Elvis Grbac and the San Francisco 49ers in a 1995 game. The Panthers won that game, 13-7, but the Niners were a thorn in Mills' side during his career. His teams were 8-16 against San Francisco during his career. *Carolina Panthers*

Sam returns an interception in a 1996 game against the St. Louis Rams. He was a first-team All Pro selection that season at the age of 37. *Carolina Panthers*

Vic Fangio and Sam were together for 15 years, including all three seasons that Mills played for the Panthers and another when they coached together there. *Carolina Panthers*

When Dom Capers was named the head coach of the Panthers, he urged GM Bill Polian to sign Sam. *Carolina Panthers*

Sam's understanding of the Capers-Fangio defense was invaluable to the rest of the Panthers' young defense. Here he directs pre-snap traffic and makes sure everyone is in position. *Carolina Panthers*

When Sam flew to California to get measured for his statue, the sculptor's neighbor had a pet panther. Sam reluctantly agreed to get his picture taken petting the panther. *Todd Andrews*

Carolina Panthers owner Jerry Richardson and Mills stand next to each other on the sideline during a game. Richardson had a special place in his heart for the 5-9 linebacker, who led the expansion team to the NFC Championship in its second year of existence. *Carolina Panthers*

Kevin Steele, shown talking to Sam, had never coached in the NFL before he was hired as Carolina's inside linebackers coach in 1995. He said Sam taught him more about being a pro coach than anybody else. *Carolina Panthers*

While the Carolina offense is on the field, Mills talks in-game strategy with his linebackers. *Carolina Panthers*

Owner Jerry Richardson was so appreciative of what Mills had meant to the Panthers in their first three years of existence that he had a statue of Sam erected on the east side of the stadium shortly after he retired in 1997. At the base of the statue, sculpture Todd Andrews inscribed: "*Sam Mills – Leader and Gentleman.*" *Carolina Panthers*

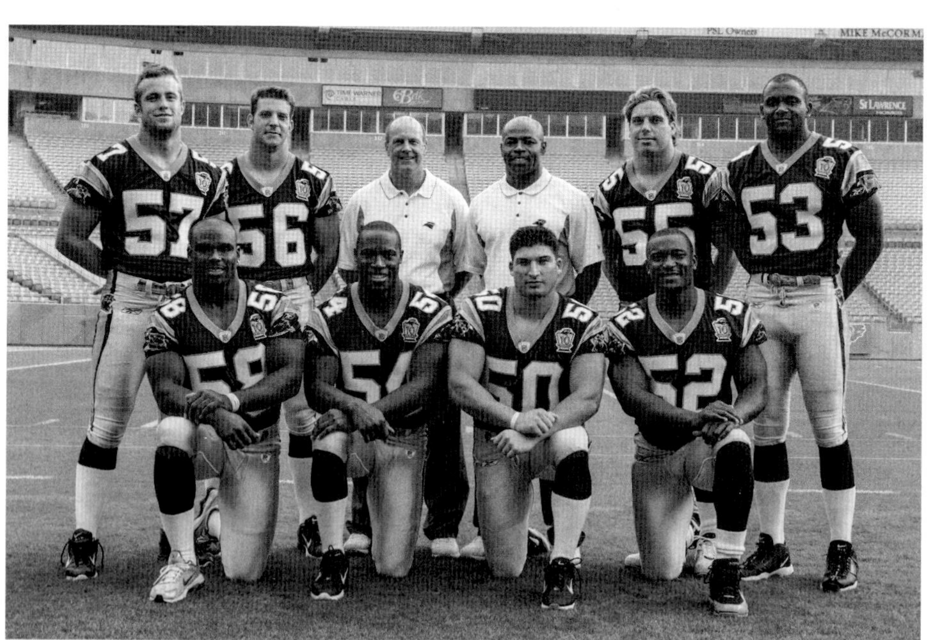

After Sam was diagnosed with cancer prior to the 2003 season, head coach John Fox had Ken Flajole (to Sam's immediate left) help Sam coach linebackers. Dan Morgan (55, to Sam's immediate right), later the Panthers' general manager, would occasionally accompany Sam to his chemo treatments. *Carolina Panthers*

The Mills family in 1999 when Sam was in his second year as an assistant coach with the Panthers. From left to right: Larissa, Melanie, Marcus, Sam, and Sam III, with baby Sierra being held by her mom and dad. *Mills family*

Sam never pushed football on either of his sons (Marcus on Sam's left and Sam III on his right). But they both embraced the game. Marcus played at Penn State and Sam III played at his father's alma mater, Montclair. Sam III, who spent 17 years as an NFL assistant, later became the defensive line coach at the University of Alabama-Birmingham. Marcus runs a consulting business but also became an assistant at Charlotte Latin High School, where he went to school. *Mills family*

Sam's son Marcus poses in front of his dad's statue with his three children: Eden, Addison, and Marcus Jr. *Mills family*

In his memorable address to the Panthers players before their 2003 playoff win over the Dallas Cowboys, Sam said his approach to fighting his cancer was to "keep pounding." He told the players to do the same. Sam's *Keep Pounding* mantra resonates in Carolina to this day. In the photo, two of Sam and Mel's children – Sierra and Marcus, bang the team's *Keep Pounding* drum before a game at Bank of America Stadium. *Carolina Panthers*

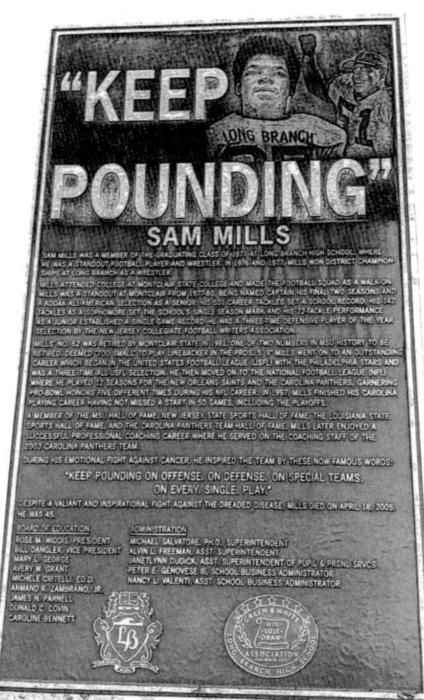

A plaque honoring Sam stands next to Long Branch High School's football field.
Paul Domowitch

Three generations of Mills men in front of Sam's statue at Bank of America Stadium. From left to right: Sam Sr., Sam Jr., Sam III and Leon. *Mills family*

Sam's widow Melanie and Jim Mora unveil his bronze bust in 2022 when Sam was inducted into the Pro Football Hall of Fame. *Kirby Lee, via Imagn Images*

Several of Sam's former Long Branch High School teammates and coaches were among the hundreds who made the trip to Canton in 2022 for his posthumous induction into the Hall of Fame. *Ed Balina*

Tributes to Sam can be found all over Long Branch High School. Just beyond the front door of the school is a trophy case with memorabilia including his jerseys from Long Branch and the Saints and Panthers. *Paul Domowitch*

Sam's locker at the Pro Football Hall of Fame includes helmets from both NFL teams he played for, an All-Madden team jacket and the 1996 TV Guide cover he appeared on with Panthers teammate Kerry Collins. *Ed Balina*

Sam's agent, Brett Senior (center) is flanked by Pat Swilling (second from left) and Rickey Jackson (second from right) during the after-party following Sam's posthumous induction into the Pro Football Hall of Fame in 2022. *Brett Senior*

Sam's gravestone at Monmouth Memorial Park in Tinton Falls, NJ, fittingly includes a football. *Mills family*

league played three weeks of games with rosters filled with guys most fans had never heard of and never would hear about again.

Upshaw did a lot for the players in the quarter-century he spent as the executive director of the players' union. But the '87 strike wasn't his finest moment. Aside from free agency, which baseball players had had since 1970 and NFL players still had no chance of getting, it wasn't clear what the union was really after.

It wasn't clear to many of the players either, which is why nearly 15 percent of the league's 1,600 players crossed the picket line during the strike. Some did so immediately. Others crossed later when it became clear that the owners were going to play as many games as they had to with the replacements.

Upshaw and the players would eventually get free agency, but they got it in a courtroom, not on the picket line. In February 1989, the league unilaterally created "Plan B" free agency, which allowed teams to protect 37 of the top 47 players on their roster, with the other 10 able to become unrestricted free agents. The owners hoped that would protect them from a court challenge. It didn't.

In November of '89, the NFL Players Association decertified as a union, which allowed them to sue the league in federal court.

Three and a half years later, a federal jury in Minneapolis ruled that Plan B violated federal antitrust laws. A year after that, in 1993, the owners and players agreed to a free agency system that included a salary cap.

The owners had repeatedly claimed for years that free agency would be the death of pro football. They claimed it would destroy competitive balance, turning the league into haves and have-nots. It was suggested that, despite revenue-sharing, small-market teams wouldn't be able to compete.

Nothing could have been further from the truth. Thirty-plus years after the advent of free agency, pro football is more popular and more profitable than ever, for both the owners and the players, for big markets and small. An NFL franchise was worth about $130 million in the early '90s, prior to free agency. Today, the value of NFL teams varies from $5.2 *billion* (Cincinnati Bengals) to $11 *billion* (Dallas Cowboys).

Just three NFL teams—the Philadelphia Eagles, Washington Redskins, and Minnesota Vikings—didn't have any veteran players cross the picket line during the '87 strike. All of the others had various levels of defections. The Saints had nine players cross, including six starters—wide receiver Eric Martin, left tackle Daren Gilbert, center Steve Korte, defensive end Bruce Clark, nose tackle Tony Elliott, and safety Antonio Gibson.

The fact that so many NFL players, including the likes of future Hall of Famers such as Joe Montana, Randy White, and Tony Dorsett, crossed the line during the '87 strike wasn't a big surprise. The NFL Players Association wasn't exactly United Steelworkers or the Teamsters. They were highly paid professional athletes.

The Saints' Gibson crossed the line about a week into the strike. Sam Mills didn't join him. Gibson's decision to cross could have destroyed their relationship, but it didn't.

"We didn't talk about it," Gibson says. "It was a decision I made on my own. No one from the union ever came in and talked to us and said, 'This is what we're striking for.' When you're young and single like I was at the time, maybe you don't look at stuff like benefits and everything else like some of the older guys like Sam did. Not that it wasn't important, but it wasn't the first thing that came to my mind. It wasn't a big priority for me.

"Everybody was talking about free agency, which I obviously was for. But at the same time, it didn't seem like we had any chance of getting true free agency, no matter how long we held out. And I was right. My biggest thing was, what are we striking for?"

Gibson played in all three of the Saints' 1987 replacement games, two of which they won. He and Mills spoke often during the 24-day strike. Sam never judged him for crossing the picket line. Mills' upbringing almost certainly had a lot to do with why he never rushed to judgment on people and respected others' opinions.

"When you grew up with so many brothers and sisters and aunts and uncles and different family coming in and trying to make ends meet, I think it's easier to understand that while your walk isn't my walk, I can still respect you," Sam III says of his father.

Sam's relationship with Gibson remained strong through the strike and after. In fact, a year and a half later, their relationship would go to another level after Gibson's mother passed away. Gibson, who was single at the time, took in his teenage brother, James Williams. Sam and Melanie helped Gibson adjust to the responsibilities of being a caretaker.

"My relationship with Sam helped me solidify my ability to suddenly be a positive big brother/father figure," Gibson says. "Sam always had been a big brother/mentor to me from the first time I met him with the Stars. Our trust in each other allowed our families to grow healthy bonds."

During the '87 strike, Mills and Bobby Hebert organized workouts at the Mike Miley playground just across the street from the Saints' practice facility in the New Orleans suburb of Metairie.

The strike ended on October 15, mainly because players all over the league were poised to return if Upshaw didn't call a ceasefire.

Not everything went back to normal right away. There were some lingering hard feelings in the Saints' locker room. Running back Rueben Mayes, who had rushed for 1,353 yards as a rookie in '86 and 917 more in '87, bought his offensive linemen personally engraved shotguns for Christmas that year, but he didn't get any for the three offensive linemen who had crossed the picket line—Gilbert, Korte, and rookie center James Campen. Players who had crossed the picket line were also left off invitation lists to a couple of Christmas parties. But in the big scheme of labor upheaval, that was kids' stuff.

"Maybe it was different on some other teams," Gibson says. "But we weren't a team with a lot of veteran players who had been together for a long time. That first year when Sam and I got there, we had something like 35 new guys on the team, including a lot of guys from the USFL."

Jim Finks wasn't very concerned about locker room resentment against the players who had crossed the line impacting the team's on-field performance after the strike.

"Anytime you have a bunch of football players, they're not all going to be Boy Scouts and they're not all going to love each other," said Finks, who played quarterback for the Pittsburgh Steelers from 1949 to 1955. "As I said during the strike, people who made excuses about the strike dividing them . . . were just setting themselves up for failure. Whether the players love each other is not an issue at all. Time heals all wounds."

The Saints had split their first two games before the strike, beating Marty Schottenheimer's Cleveland Browns at home but losing to Buddy Ryan's Philadelphia Eagles on the road. Mills had a good game against the Eagles, recording seven tackles. But the Saints' offense turned the ball over five times, including three interceptions, two of them by Hebert.

After the Saints won two of their three replacement games during the strike, they had a 3–2 record coming out of the strike. Their first game after the strike was against the 49ers, their NFC West archnemesis.

The Niners had won all three games during the strike, including two with Montana, running back Roger Craig, and wide receiver Dwight Clark and several other veterans who had crossed the picket line.

The Saints took a 19–17 lead early in the fourth quarter when Van Jakes blocked a Max Runager punt and Alvin Toles returned it 11 yards for a touchdown. But Montana brought San Francisco right back, hitting Mike Wilson with a 14-yard touchdown pass to put his team up by five.

The Saints drove to the San Francisco 20 but had to settle for Morton Andersen's fifth field goal of the game to cut the lead to 24–22. With time running out, the Saints had a first down at the San Francisco 43, but they decided to let yet another Andersen field goal attempt decide the game. Carl Smith called three run plays with Rueben Mayes, which gained just eight yards, then Andersen came on to try a 52-yard field goal with seven seconds left. His attempt sailed wide left.

After the game, Mora was furious with his offense for coming up short so many times and settling for Andersen field goals. He was also more than a little ticked off with the New Orleans media, who had been so used to watching the Saints stink up the place that they seemed overly impressed by the fact that the Saints had come so close to beating the powerful 49ers.

"We got stuffed every time we got down to the goal," Mora said after the game. "I'm tired of coming close. I'm tired of *shoulda, woulda*. The bottom line is who gets the W and who gets the L. The Saints aren't good enough, and you [media] guys writing about us being a playoff team and all that is bull. That's malarkey.

"We've got a long way to go, a lot of work to do. We're close, but close ain't worth shit and you can put that on TV for me. For people to even think we're a playoff team is ridiculous. If we were a playoff team, we would've beaten San Francisco today."

Mora's blunt message definitely made an impression on his players. They didn't lose again the rest of the regular season. They reeled off nine straight wins, including a rematch with the 49ers at Candlestick Park three weeks later.

Gibson said Mora's postgame comments that day hit their mark.

"He was right," he says. "It was after that that we started saying, 'Hey, we're as good as they are. We've got good players too. We can and should be beating them.'"

The Niners had a two-game lead over the Saints going into the Week 10 rematch. They were 7–1. New Orleans was 5–3. Niners coach Bill Walsh was effusive in his praise of the Saints in the days leading up to the rematch. He said their defense had "stopped everybody dead in their tracks." He said the Saints coaching staff was "among the best in football."

Mora called bullshit.

"He's trying to stroke us," he said of Walsh. "He wants our guys thinking we're so good. And it makes him look even better if they beat us."

The 49ers took a 24–23 lead with 2:54 left on a 29-yard touchdown pass from Montana to tight end Ron Heller. Hebert completed a 23-yard pass to Lonzell Hill and a 31-yarder to Eric Martin to give the Saints a first down at the San Francisco 24 just before the two-minute warning. Two Dalton Hilliard runs gained one yard. After a third-and-nine incompletion by Hebert, Andersen attempted a 40-yard field goal into a stiff Candlestick wind with 1:06 left. The kick barely made it over the crossbar and was only inches inside the right upright. But it went through and gave the Saints the lead, 24–22.

The Niners still had more than a minute to work with, which, for Montana, was an eternity. He got them to the Saints' 40 with 25 seconds left, but they were still out of kicker Ray Wersching's range. Two passes went incomplete. Then, on third down, with no timeouts left, Montana had one of the few brain farts of his career. Unable to find an open receiver, he took off and ran. He gained nine yards but was unable to get out of bounds and stop the clock. Time ran out before Wersching and the Niners' field goal team could get on the field.

Two weeks after the win over San Francisco, the Saints made history. They beat the Pittsburgh Steelers on the road, 20–16, to improve to 8–3. The '87 regular season had been reduced from 16 to 15 games because of the strike. So their eight wins clinched the Saints' first winning season in franchise history.

Mills had a big game against the Steelers. He had a team-high seven tackles and a big fumble recovery early in the third quarter after a strip sack by Pat Swilling. It was one of six takeaways by the Saints in the game. They would finish fifth in the NFL that year in takeaways with 45.

Andersen, who had a league-high 36 field goal attempts that season, put the Saints up 20–14 with six minutes left. But the Steelers drove down to the New Orleans 1. On third down, the Steelers called a pass play. Running back Frank Pollard was wide open in the end zone, but Rickey Jackson deflected Mark Malone's pass, and it fell incomplete.

On fourth-and-one, Mills thought the Steelers would try to run it. After seeing their alignment, he was sure of it and called it out to the rest of the defense. It was a power toss to the left side with Pollard. Vaughn Johnson and defensive end Jim Wilks took away the outside and turned the play in. Mills and safety Brett Maxie were there to stop Pollard and prevent a go-ahead score.

"I made the initial hit and then Sam just finished the guy off," says Maxie. "We went into the locker room and you would've thought we had won the Super Bowl. There were guys on that team that had been there for years. A lot of lean years. The bags [over fans' heads] were coming out. Then Jim Mora comes and we have our first winning season ever."

Mills' ability to decipher alignments and tendencies was uncanny. After the game, he said he knew a power team like the Steelers would run the ball on fourth down. He credited Wilks and Johnson with preventing Pollard from getting outside. "They did a great job of forcing him back [inside] to the strength of our run defense," he said. "My job basically is to come and clean up and make sure he doesn't fall forward. If he keeps his feet driving, I have to make sure he doesn't get that extra push. I was unblocked and got a good shot at him."

You might think clinching a winning season wouldn't be a particularly big deal in pro sports. But this was the Saints. Futility had been their middle name. Twenty seasons in the league and 20 seasons without a winning record. Beating the Steelers to go 8–3 was a huge deal for both the players and Saints fans.

More than 2,500 fans greeted the team at the New Orleans airport that night when they returned from Pittsburgh. They carried signs that read “Bag Heads No More” and, quoting Mora, “Shoulda, Woulda: The Saints Did It.”

The Saints kept rolling after the win over the Steelers. They won their last four games by a combined 50 points. They put up 142 points in those four games as Hebert and the Saints’ offense finally seemed to find its stride. They finished second in the league in scoring in ’87, averaging 28.1 points per game.

The Saints finished with a 12–3 record, which was the second-best record in the league. Unfortunately, the team with the best record was the damn 49ers, who finished 13–2.

As a result, the Niners got a first-round bye, while the Saints had to play the Minnesota Vikings in a wildcard round game at the Superdome. It would be the franchise’s first-ever playoff game.

The Vikings had finished second behind the Bears in the NFC Central with an 8–7 record and weren’t going into the game with much momentum. They had lost three of their final four regular-season games, including a 27–24 loss to Washington a week earlier in which they had blown a 10-point lead with five minutes to go.

The Saints were seven-point favorites against Minnesota. If they disposed of the Vikings, they would face San Francisco again in the divisional round.

A Swilling strip sack of Vikings quarterback Tommy Kramer set up an early Saints touchdown on a 10-yard touchdown pass from Hebert to Eric Martin that gave New Orleans a 7–0 lead. But that TD turned out to be about the only sign of life the entire day from Hebert and the New Orleans offense.

Maybe they were looking ahead to a rematch with the 49ers when they faced Minnesota. Maybe they were just overdue for a bad game after winning nine in a row. Whatever it was, they got their heads handed to them by the Vikings, 44–10.

The Saints would score just three more points after that early touchdown—on a 40-yard Morten Andersen field goal in the second quarter. The offense finished with just nine first downs and 149 total yards and turned the ball over six times, including four interceptions.

A muffed punt by Mel Gray set up a Minnesota field goal to make it 7–3. Then, later in the first quarter, the Vikings' Anthony Carter, a former USFL teammate of Hebert's, returned a punt 84 yards for a touchdown to give Minnesota a 10–7 lead. The Vikings never looked back after that.

With three seconds left in the first half and already up 24–10, the Vikings had a third-and-24 at the New Orleans 49. Vikings coach Jerry Burns was going to just have his quarterback take a knee. But the Saints were penalized for having 12 men on the field, which moved the line of scrimmage up to the Saints' 44. Instead of a kneel-down, Burns had Wade Wilson throw a Hail Mary into the end zone. Wide receiver Hassan Jones jumped up and caught the ball for a 44-yard touchdown. Any chance of a second-half Saints comeback went down the drain with that score.

Hebert completed just nine of 19 passes for 84 yards and threw two interceptions before leaving the game in the third quarter after getting his eye gouged at the bottom of a pile by Vikings defensive tackle Henry Thomas.

Hebert was replaced by Dave Wilson, who completed just two of 12 passes for 20 yards and threw two more interceptions.

"They fumbled on the first play of the game and we score and then Morten kicks a field goal early in the second quarter to put us up 10–3, and it looks like we're going to cruise. Then all hell broke loose," remembers Kuharich. "It was ugly. I think a lot of it was inexperience. [A lack of] playoff experience. We didn't have a single player on that team who ever had played in the [NFL] postseason before. Not one.

"We went 12–3 and didn't even get a bye because the 49ers went 13–2. That became a common theme for us. We had to play in the wildcard every year because we were in the same damn division as those guys. The four years Jim's teams were in the playoffs, we had a good enough record to win every division except the one we were playing in three of those four years."

That first playoff defeat hurt, but not as much as the three that would follow. They had gone 12–3. They were a young team with a great defense. They assumed the playoffs would be an annual occurrence and that it would be just a matter of time before they won a Super Bowl, or at least got to one.

The Saints' long-suffering fans were just happy to finally have a winning team to root for. Late in the game, with their team down by multiple touchdowns, the crowd rose to their feet and gave the Saints a standing ovation.

Antonio Gibson was stunned.

"I mean, we were getting blown out," he says. "I never would've expected that. But they hadn't ever won before. The fact that we were winning and had a new coach and new players like Sam to go with veterans like Rickey Jackson and others who were good guys and good players, everything was looking up."

Even Mora managed to be upbeat after the loss to the Vikings. There were no *shoulda-wouldas* in his postgame press conference. No *diddly-poos* or *malarkeys.*

"The loss was disappointing, but I'm not at all disappointed in our team," he told reporters. "We had the second-best record in the National Football League. We had a lot of good times, and we did some things for this organization and this city and this state that have never been done before. We just picked a bad day here to play poorly. We need to get better in some areas. If we continue to work in the offseason, we can be a good team again next year."

20

Nothing about my career so far has been likely. I came into this league too something, and I'll go out being too something. Too short, too old, too expensive, I've heard it all.

—Sam Mills

THE PLAYOFF LOSS to the Vikings was a disappointing end to a great season for Mills and the Saints. But their success had clearly changed the perception of the team around the league. They no longer were the *Aints*. They were now a playoff team on the rise. Five players from the Saints, including Mills, made the Pro Bowl after the '87 season, by far the most in franchise history.

Mills' first Pro Bowl invitation was a huge moment for someone who, when he was cut by the Browns just five years earlier, thought he might never get the opportunity to play in the NFL.

The other four Saints players who made the Pro Bowl that year were Morten Andersen, cornerback Dave Waymer, left guard Brad Edelman, and tight end Hoby Brenner. Sam was the only member of the Dome Patrol to get an invitation to Hawaii. Pat Swilling, who had 10 ½ sacks that year, and Rickey Jackson, who finished with 9 ½, were both snubbed.

The all-expenses-paid trip to Hawaii for the Pro Bowl was a huge thrill for Mills. He brought along Mel and the kids. Sam III was almost nine. Marcus was closing in on five.

The NFC team that year was coached by the Vikings' Jerry Burns, whose team had upended the Saints in the playoffs. In a twist of irony, the AFC team was coached by the Browns' Marty Schottenheimer, the guy who had cast the deciding vote to cut Mills when he was trying to earn a job with the Browns back in '81.

The game was a defensive struggle with the AFC beating Mills' NFC all-stars 15–6. Buffalo Bills quarterback Jim Kelly scored the game's only touchdown on a one-yard rollout. Sam played well, forcing an early fumble when he stripped the ball from Browns running back Kevin Mack and returned it 37 yards to set up the first of Andersen's two field goals.

After returning to New Orleans, Mills took a couple of weeks off, then returned to the weight room to begin preparing for the '88 season. Making the Pro Bowl had changed nothing for him. He still approached everything with the same one-bad-practice-away-from-getting-cut attitude. Mills worked out six days a week during the off-season, taking only Sundays off. Gibson usually would be his workout partner, whether he liked it or not.

"There were a lot of Saturdays I was hoping he wouldn't be knocking on my door," Gibson says. "But that never happened. He was always there."

They would go to a track, and Mills would tell Gibson that they were going to run eight sprints. Then they'd run 12.

"He would trick me into doing eight just to get me out there," Gibson says. "If we were going to run two miles, well, I could run to two miles all day. But Sam would show up with a stopwatch. If we were going to run two miles, it had to be in a certain time."

During the offseason, Mills also worked at one of Saints owner Tom Benson's car dealerships.

"Nobody worked [in the offseason]," Gibson says. "Guys might've gone back to college and gotten their degree or whatever. But nobody got a 9-to-5 job. Except Sam. It was just the way he was. He always had a plan. I guess a lot of that had to do with getting cut early on and not trusting the whole football thing."

At Benson's dealerships, Mills wanted to learn the whole operation. Keep in mind, this was a guy who had initially considered becoming an auto mechanic rather than going to college. He never worked on cars at Benson's dealerships. But he sold them, and he worked in the finance department. He put in the same kind of time and energy and focus into learning the car business that he did with football.

The city of New Orleans had fallen in love with Sam. He quickly became one of the team's most popular players: a leader on the field and a role model off it. But no matter how successful he became, he never forgot his roots. He never forgot those tough days growing up in Seaview Manor. If he saw someone on the street who was down on his luck, he'd get out of his car, talk to them, and see if there was anything he could do to help them.

One time, when he was driving home from the Saints complex, Mills saw a Pop Warner team practicing. It was obvious they were desperately short of equipment. Players were sharing helmets and shoulder pads. When one player went out, he'd have to give his equipment to another player. As soon as he got home, Sam called Brett Senior and instructed him to use an apparel deal he had recently signed with Reebok to donate equipment to the program. He told Senior that he didn't want anyone knowing that he was the one who had donated the equipment.

"Outside of maybe Reggie White, I never met anybody else like that or saw anybody else like that," Gibson says. "He never changed. His first year in the USFL, he was making nothing. He made more when he was with the Saints, but he was the same guy the whole time he was with the Saints as he was with the Stars. The only thing that changed was maybe the clothes he wore and the cars he drove. And even the cars he drove were never flashy."

After finishing with the second-best record in the league the year before, Mills and the Saints went into the 1988 season with high hopes. They had one of the league's best defenses. They had the NFL's No. 2 scoring offense in '87. The Super Bowl no longer seemed like a pipe dream for the franchise.

The '88 season opened on what would become a very familiar note over the next seven years—a close loss to the 49ers. A fourth-quarter fumble by Bobby Hebert set up a game-winning field goal in a 34–33 Niners win at the Superdome.

The Saints managed to rebound from that loss and win their next seven games. But then they lost back-to-back games to the Rams and Washington Redskins. They lost to the Rams at home 12–10. The Saints' defense didn't give up a touchdown. It held the Rams to four Mike Lansford field goals. Mills was all over the field making plays in that game. He had a team-high 11 tackles. You shouldn't lose games when you don't give up a touchdown. Ever.

But in what would become a familiar pattern during Sam's nine seasons with the Saints, the offense came up small. Despite spending their first-round pick that year on a running back—270-pound Craig "Ironhead" Heyward—the Saints were held to 33 rushing yards on 18 carries by the Rams. Hebert completed just 19 of 37 passes for 215 yards and one touchdown.

The Saints would average more than 22 points a game in just two of Mora's 11 seasons in New Orleans.

"We had a great defense and still lost games because we couldn't score," Bill Kuharich says. "Our wide receivers were very average. And our tight ends—John Tice and Hoby Brenner—were slower than slow. They were basically oversized tackles.

"Our backs caught a lot of passes. Hilliard, Mayes, Barry Word, Ironhead [Heyward]. But [wide receiver] Eric Martin would lead us in receptions every year and you wondered how. Because he couldn't get away from anybody.

"I'd say it's a shame we didn't have a difference-maker outside. But frankly, even if we did, I'm not sure we would have thrown him the ball more. It was really unfortunate that we never could be more explosive on offense."

It would be easy to dump all the blame for the Saints' offensive struggles during that period on Hebert. But it wouldn't be totally accurate.

"I know Bobby took a lot of the heat for our lack of production in the passing game," Kuharich says. "Some of it was deserved. But I watched him in the USFL when he had Anthony Carter and Derek Holloway and guys that could spread the field. He was good enough [to do that in the NFL]. The problem was that he never had a cast [of receivers] around him with us."

Even with their offensive shortcomings, the Saints headed into the final month of the '88 season with a 9–3 record and a good chance to make it back to the playoffs, until their offense failed them again. They averaged just 13 points a game in their final four games, losing three of them. They lost to the New York Giants at home 13–12. They were eviscerated on the road by the team that eliminated them from the '87 playoffs, the Vikings, 45–3. And then they lost for the second time that season to the 49ers, 30–17.

The Saints, 49ers, and Rams, who were also in the NFC West, all finished with 10–6 records. But the Niners and Rams both had better conference records than the Saints, so they qualified for the playoffs, while the Saints were the odd man out.

"We let things slip away from us," Rickey Jackson said of the Saints' late-season collapse that year. "It was our own fault."

Jackson and Swilling weren't nearly as dominating in '88 as they had been in '87. The Saints' sack total plummeted from 47 the previous year to just 31 in '88. Swilling and Jackson each had only seven sacks.

Mills had another outstanding year. He finished with 105 tackles, second only to Vaughan Johnson's 114, and had a team-high four fumble recoveries. He earned his second straight Pro Bowl invitation but was the only Saints defensive player to make it.

The '89 season ended up being more of the same. The Saints finished 9–7 but again missed the playoffs. Once again, they would lose both of their regular-season meetings against the 49ers, including a 31–13 pummeling at Candlestick Park. The 49ers went on to win their second straight Super Bowl that year, crushing the AFC-champion Denver Broncos.

Adding to the insult, the Super Bowl was played in the Saints' own house that year, the New Orleans Superdome.

When the NFL realigned its divisions after the 1970 merger with the American Football League, it clearly didn't make geography a priority. It stuck Atlanta and New Orleans in the NFC West with San Francisco and Los Angeles.

The league's decision to make the Saints and 49ers divisional neighbors would haunt Mora's tenure as coach, as Bill Walsh's 49ers became the NFL's most dominant team of the '80s and early '90s. In an 11-year span from 1984 through 1994, they won nine division titles and four Super Bowls.

From '87 through '94, the Saints lost 12 of their 16 twice-a-year meetings with the Niners. The lack of offensive production was usually the reason they would come up short. They scored more than 17 points in just five of those 12 losses. Ten of those 16 games were one-score affairs.

"I loved those games against the 49ers," Antonio Gibson says. "For us to be up and coming and knowing we had to go through them in that division, we always had good games with them. We didn't win enough of them, but we always had good, hard-nosed games against them."

Hebert was benched by Mora late in the '89 season and replaced by John Fourcade. Fourcade was another Louisiana boy. He grew up in Gretna, Louisiana, just five miles from the Superdome. He stepped in and led the Saints to three straight too-little-too-late season-ending wins.

After Fourcade's late-season success in '89, Hebert assumed he was going to be traded in the offseason. His contract was up, but the advent of NFL free agency was still three years away. So, he was at the mercy of Saints GM Jim Finks.

"The Saints offered me something around $700,000 [per year]," Hebert says. "I wanted the going rate for a quarterback at my level, which was around $1.2 million. I remember Mr. Finks telling me, 'We own you.'

"The offer they made me was one of those take-it-or-leave-it deals. They felt they held all the cards. They just wanted me to sit and rot. They thought I'd come around."

He didn't. When Finks didn't trade him, Hebert opted to sit out the entire 1990 season.

Hebert's holdout did not go over well with Saints fans. An indication of how unpopular he became: During the '90 season, thieves robbed a New Orleans clothing store and stole everything of value except a set of Hebert jerseys that he had personally autographed.

While Hebert stayed home, Fourcade opened the '90 season as the Saints' starting quarterback. Unfortunately, his impressive performances at the end of the '89 season didn't carry over into '90. After Mora named him his season-opening quarterback, Fourcade played horribly. The Saints scored just 15 points in losses to the 49ers (13–12) and Vikings (32–3). Mills and the defense played spectacularly against the Niners, holding them to 2.8 yards per carry and sacking Joe Montana six times. Mills had eight tackles and a sack against San Francisco. But the effort was wasted by the offense. Fourcade completed just 12 of 34 passes and threw three interceptions. The following week in the loss to Minnesota, he completed just nine of 23 passes and threw three more picks.

The Saints finally cracked the win column in Week 3, beating the hapless Phoenix Cardinals 28–7. Mills was all over the field as usual, notching nine tackles. Fourcade struggled again, completing just 11 of 23 passes and throwing his seventh interception in three games.

That was enough to convince Finks and Mora that Fourcade wasn't the answer at quarterback. The NFL had introduced bye weeks for teams in 1990. The Saints had theirs the week after their win over the Cardinals. During the bye week, they made a trade with the Dallas Cowboys, acquiring their backup quarterback, Steve Walsh, for three high draft picks.

The Cowboys had drafted both Walsh, who had played for head coach Jimmy Johnson at the University of Miami, and UCLA's Troy Aikman in 1989. Aikman, who would lead the Cowboys to three Super Bowl titles and go into the Pro Football Hall of Fame in 2006, quickly won the starting job, which made Walsh expendable.

While Walsh scrambled to learn the Saints' offense, Fourcade started the Saints' next game against the Atlanta Falcons. He played competently, completing 10 of 17 passes for 235 yards and two touchdowns. Mills & Co. held the Falcons to 2.8 yards per carry on the ground. But Falcons quarterback Chris Miller shredded their secondary, throwing for 366 yards and three TDs in a 28–27 Atlanta win.

The Saints would average just 17.1 points per game in '90, the fewest in Mora's 10 seasons in the Big Easy. Fourcade and Walsh would combine for just 15 touchdown passes, the sixth fewest in the league.

The Saints' defense was also missing a key player in '90. Their most talented defensive lineman, Frank Warren, was suspended by the NFL for the entire season for drug use. But Mills and the rest of the defense kept the Saints afloat. Opponents just couldn't run the ball against them. The Saints held opponents to just 17.2 points per game in '90, the eighth best average in the league. Mills and Vaughan Johnson spearheaded a run defense that held opponents to 97 yards per game. The pair combined for 215 tackles.

Meanwhile, Jackson and Swilling made life miserable for opposing quarterbacks. They had a combined 17 sacks. The Dome Patrol racked up 10 forced fumbles and nine fumble recoveries. Jackson had seven of those nine fumble recoveries and four of the 10 forced fumbles.

Swilling's 11 sacks earned him his second straight Pro Bowl nod and second straight second-team All-Pro selection.

Even after Walsh replaced Fourcade, the Saints' offense still couldn't get things going. The Saints managed to score more than 21 points in just three of their last 10 games. They never won more than two games in a row and limped into Candlestick Park in mid-December for their next-to-last regular season game with a 6–8 record.

Their playoff hopes were on life support. The 49ers had lost just one game all season. Walsh completed just nine of 25 passes and threw two interceptions against them, but Mills & Co. came to the rescue once again, holding the Niners to one touchdown as the Saints pulled out a 13–10 win to keep their season alive.

A week later, they beat the Rams 20–17. Walsh redeemed himself, completing a 34-yard pass to Eric Martin late in the fourth quarter to set up a game-winning 24-yard Morten Andersen field goal with two seconds left. Mills had another big game, recording nine tackles and recovering a second-quarter Rams fumble.

Despite their 8–8 record, the Saints managed to squeeze into the playoffs. Besides adding bye weeks in 1990, the NFL also increased the number of wildcard teams in each conference from two to three. The Saints qualified as the third wildcard team in the NFC. They had the distinction of becoming the first team in league history to make the playoffs in a non-strike year with a non-winning record.

"We didn't have Hebert or Frank Warren for the entire season," Mora says. "And we still went 8–8 and made the playoffs because our defense was so good. I was so proud of that team. We lost five of our first seven. Couldn't find the end zone to save our lives. But they never quit. Kept battling. That team fought their fool heads off without Hebert and Frank."

The Saints would face the Chicago Bears on the road in the wild-card round. The game reunited Mills with Vince Tobin, who was in his fifth year as the Bears' defensive coordinator. Mills played his butt off against the Bears, recording a team-high 12 tackles and helping hold Chicago's offense to one touchdown. But Tobin's defense muzzled the Saints' offense, holding it to 11 first downs and just 193 total yards. Walsh completed only six of 16 passes before injuring his shoulder in the second quarter and being replaced by Fourcade. Fourcade was five for 18 with two interceptions. The Saints' only points in the 16–6 loss came on a pair of Morten Andersen field goals.

It was another bitter playoff defeat, which was becoming a familiar refrain for the New Orleans Saints.

21

People have a short memory. True fans that know the game realize how good our defense was back then. But if you don't win a Super Bowl, it's kind of hard to be remembered or revered.

—Saints LB Vaughan Johnson

AFTER SITTING OUT the entire 1990 season, Bobby Hebert returned to the Saints in '91, signing a two-year deal with the team a month before the start of training camp. A shoulder injury limited him to nine starts that year, but the defense, led by Mills and the Dome Patrol, once again carried the team on its shoulders.

The Saints gave up the fewest points in the league (just 13.2 per game) and finished first in takeaways (48) and third in sacks (50). They gave up only 12 touchdown passes the entire season and had the league's second-best run defense, holding opponents to 75.8 yards per game. The defense allowed seven points or fewer in eight of their 16 regular-season games. They didn't give up a touchdown in six of their games.

Swilling had the best season of his career. He notched a league-high 17 sacks and six forced fumbles and was named the NFL's Defensive Player of the Year. Jackson added 11 ½ sacks and three forced fumbles.

Mills earned his third Pro Bowl invitation, received his first All-Pro nod (receiving first-team honors), and finished eighth in the Defensive Player of the Year voting. Vaughan Johnson earned his third Pro Bowl nod despite missing three games and parts of two others with injuries.

The Saints won their first seven games, with Mills and their suffocating defense allowing just 8.6 points a game in those wins. In a 26–0 Week 4 win over Minnesota, the Saints held the Vikings to six first downs and 151 total yards. Mills' longtime nemesis, Herschel Walker, who had been traded to the Vikings by the Dallas Cowboys, was held to 15 yards on 10 carries.

They took an 8–1 record into a Week 11 battle with San Francisco. The 49ers, who hadn't missed the playoffs in nine years, were without quarterback Joe Montana, who missed the entire '91 season with an elbow injury. They had a 4–5 record when they faced the Saints.

The Saints' offense had yet another dismal performance against the 49ers. Walsh, who was making his fourth start of the season for the injured Hebert, managed to complete just 10 of 25 passes. The Saints didn't have much better luck on the ground, where they were held to just 82 rushing yards.

But the defense forced three fumbles. The first, by Mills in the second quarter, set up the Saints' only touchdown. In the fourth quarter, the Niners threatened to tie the game, driving down to the New Orleans 29. But Swilling stripped the ball from quarterback Steve Bono, who had started in place of injured Steve Young, and Mills recovered it to kill the drive. The Saints hung on for a 10–3 win that improved their record to a league-best 9–1.

They lost their next four before finishing with wins over the LA Raiders and the Cardinals. Hebert returned and stopped the offensive bleeding, throwing for 320 yards in a 27–0 shutout of the Raiders. The defense had seven takeaways, including five interceptions, in a 27–3 win over the Cardinals.

The Saints' 11–5 record earned them their first division title in the franchise's 25-year history.

Their late-season four-game losing streak, however, had cost them a first-round bye. They ended up as the third seed in the NFC, which meant a wildcard-round game at home against one of their NFC West neighbors, Atlanta. They had split their two regular-season games with the Falcons, winning at home in Week 4 with Hebert, 27–6, and losing on the road in December without him, 23–20.

What had been a memorable season to that point once again ended in playoff heartbreak at the Superdome. The Saints sacked Falcons quarterback Chris Miller five times, including one by Mills. But the Falcons quarterback still managed to throw two TD passes against an injury-ravaged Saints secondary.

The Saints didn't blitz much during the Mora era. With Swilling and Jackson they didn't need to. But they had to play the Falcons without both of their starting corners, Toi Cook and Vince Buck, as well as their top backup corner, Calvin Nicholson.

With two and a half minutes remaining and the game tied 20–20, the Falcons had a second-and-nine at their own 39. Saints defensive coordinator Steve Sidwell, not totally trusting his secondary, decided to send both of his safeties after Miller and go for the knockout punch. The strategy blew up in his face. Miller managed to get the ball out quickly to wide receiver Michael Haynes, who ran 61 yards for the go-ahead score.

The Saints had one last chance to tie the game. They got as far as the Atlanta 35 with a little more than a minute left in the game. But Hebert forced a first-down pass for Eric Martin into tight coverage, and it was picked off by Falcons cornerback Tim McKyer.

Game over. Season over.

Mills was crestfallen after the loss. It was the most disappointing moment of his career aside from getting cut by the Browns. He had turned 32 the previous June. He was still at the top of his game, but he had felt the '91 team had a legitimate shot at making a Super Bowl run. Instead, the season ended with yet another first-round loss. Another first-round loss at home.

"It really hasn't hit me yet," Mills said after the game. "It'll probably hit me when I'm watching the Falcons on TV next week. That's when it will really eat away at me."

As it turned out, the Falcons got blown out the following week by Washington 24–7. Chris Miller threw four interceptions against the Redskins, who went on to win their second Super Bowl title in five years.

For a lot of reasons, the clock was ticking on Mora's Saints. What had been a young team when Mora arrived in the Big Easy in 1986 now had a lot of players on the other side of 30, including Rickey Jackson (34), Mills (32), and nose tackle Jim Wilks (34). Vaughan Johnson and Frank Warren were both 30.

The '92 season would be the Dome Patrol's seventh together. The talented quartet had helped turn around a hapless franchise, but for reasons largely beyond their control, they still didn't have a single playoff win to show for it.

The Saints opened the '92 season against the Philadelphia Eagles at Mills' old haunt, Veterans Stadium. It was a game that resembled so many others by the Saints back then: Mills and the defense played their asses off to keep them in the game, only to have the offense come up small.

Hebert completed just 12 of 30 passes and threw two interceptions. The ground game managed just 55 yards. The Saints scored their one and only touchdown with three minutes left in the game. Meanwhile, Herschel Walker, who had signed with the Eagles in the offseason, had one of the few productive games of his career against a Sam Mills-led defense, rushing for 114 yards on 26 carries. The Eagles won the game 15–13.

The Saints would lose just three more regular-season games that year, finishing 12–4. Predictably, two of the losses were to San Francisco, which cost them a chance at a second straight division title and a first-round playoff bye. With Joe Montana back, the 49ers finished with the league's best record, 14–2.

The Saints lost to the 49ers in Week 4 in the Superdome, 16–10, again scoring just one touchdown and turning the ball over five times, including three interceptions by Hebert, two in the second half. They lost another close one to them in Week 11 in San Fran, 21–20, when Steve Young hit Niners tight end Brent Jones for a game-winning touchdown with 46 seconds left.

Mills and the rest of the Saints' defense played even better in '92 than they did in '91. They led the league in points allowed (12.6) for the second year in a row. They had a league-high 57 sacks. The Dome Patrol forced 16 fumbles, including six by Jackson and four by Mills.

All four of the Saints linebackers made the Pro Bowl in '92. Sam had a team-high 130 tackles. Jackson, who had 13 ½ sacks to go with his six forced fumbles, earned his fourth All-Pro nod, and first Pro Bowl invitation in six years, and finished fifth in the Defensive Player of the Year voting. Swilling had 10 ½ sacks and was an All-Pro selection for the fourth straight year. Johnson earned his fourth Pro Bowl invitation. But his punishing style of play had begun to take its toll on his body. He battled injuries most of the season and had just 84 tackles, but didn't miss a game.

"Those four guys, our entire defense for that matter, certainly were good enough to enable us to go a long way in the playoffs, and we didn't," Bill Kuharich says. "That was a real shame."

The Saints made the playoffs for the third straight year and found themselves playing the Eagles, the team that had beaten them by two points in Week 1. The difference was that the rematch was in the Superdome in front of their own fans rather than at the Vet in Philadelphia, where the Eagles' rabid fans made it one of the toughest places to play in the NFL.

With 6 ½ minutes left in the third quarter, the Saints took a 20–7 lead following Morten Andersen's second field goal of the game. It looked like they were going to finally bring home the franchise's first-ever playoff win.

On the Saints' next possession, they went for the kill shot. Thinking the Eagles would be expecting them to play conservatively and keep the ball on the ground, Hebert uncorked a deep pass for wide receiver Quinn Early. But he overthrew Early and the pass was picked off by Eagles cornerback Eric Allen. The turnover triggered a massive momentum swing.

Hebert would throw two more interceptions, including another one that was picked off and returned for a touchdown by Allen, a future Hall of Famer. Hebert was also sacked in the end zone by Reggie White for a safety.

The Eagles would score 29 unanswered points and cruise to a 36–20 win.

It was an awful and embarrassing loss. After the game, a frustrated Mills was as critical of his teammates as he had ever been. "I don't like to think of this team as a team that chokes," he said. "But we played a horrible second half. That's why we didn't win."

The Saints wouldn't make it back to the playoffs for another eight years, long after Mills and the rest of the Dome Patrol were gone. Saints fans would go back to wearing bags over their heads.

22

When we started talking to the Saints about a new deal, their initial reaction was, 'Why don't you go see what the market is for you?' Sam was like, 'Wow, they're not even going to offer me a contract?'
—Brett Senior

THREE THINGS OCCURRED after the 1992 season that changed the course of the Saints' franchise and Sam Mills' career. In February of '93, just five months after a federal jury in Minneapolis had ruled that the NFL's Plan B free agency system violated antitrust laws, the league and the players agreed to a settlement that finally gave the players true free agency. However, unlike free agency in Major League Baseball, the NFL system was accompanied by a salary cap.

That April, the Saints broke up the Dome Patrol, trading four-time All-Pro and 1991 NFL Defensive Player of the Year Pat Swilling to the Detroit Lions.

Also that spring, General Manager Jim Finks, the architect of the Saints' turnaround from perennial joke to playoff contender, fell ill the day before the '93 draft. He attended the draft, but he had to be admitted to the hospital the next day. Finks, a two-pack-a-day smoker, was diagnosed with lung cancer. His condition improved enough at one point for him to return home. But he resigned in mid-July just before the start of training camp and died 10 months later at the age of 67.

Without Finks, the Saints were a rudderless ship. Owner Tom Benson thought he could step in and fill Finks' GM role, but he quickly discovered that he was in way over his head. Most of Finks' day-to-day duties were handled by Jim Miller, the team's vice president of administration, who Finks had hired in 1986.

Miller had spent five years working for the NFL Management Council prior to joining the Saints, serving as a liaison between the league office and the owners. He was also the owners' spokesperson during the league's 57-day players' strike in 1982. Kuharich, who was promoted from director of player personnel to vice president of football operations, shared the personnel duties with Mora.

"To be perfectly honest, after Finks got sick, we didn't know what we were doing," Kuharich admits. "The cap had just come in '93 and nobody had a clue how it operated.

"There were a handful of teams that knew how to manage the cap. And that was basically the teams that had people who had a hand in formulating the structure of the cap. They had an advantage because they knew the loopholes in it. Meanwhile, we were trying to play by the rules."

Once free agency came into existence, many of the Saints' veteran players began heading for the door. Quarterback Bobby Hebert signed with the Atlanta Falcons after the '92 season. Rickey Jackson and Vaughan Johnson left after the '93 season, signing with the 49ers and Eagles, respectively. Morten Andersen, like Hebert, signed with the Falcons after the '94 season.

"We just didn't do as well acquiring or keeping talent after Jim got sick," Mora says. "I'm part of that. I'll take some of the blame. We lost a lot of our top players to free agency. They were getting older and we didn't replace them. After Jim left, I made—we made—too many bad decisions."

Everything seemed to happen to the Saints simultaneously. Too many of their top players getting old. Finks getting sick. A new capped free agency system that they were painfully slow to get the hang of.

"Jim wanted to hang on to most of the veterans, like most coaches do," Kuharich says. "But he didn't understand the cap. Back then, a lot of people didn't understand the cap. You were trying to put 10 pounds of shit into a five-pound bag."

Mora wasn't the only person in the organization frustrated that the Saints were losing many of their top players. So was owner Tom Benson. He'd walk into Kuharich's office demanding answers.

"How the hell are the 49ers able to keep all of their guys and we can't?" an angry Tom Benson asked.

"They're cheating," Kuharich replied.

"How do you know they're cheating?" Benson said.

"Well, how else do you think they're keeping all their top guys?" said Kuharich. "They're putting contracts in drawers and paying players like Montana out of a car dealership."

Early on, there were a lot of loopholes in the salary cap rules. And 49ers President Carmen Policy knew better than anyone how to find them and exploit them to his advantage. There was a reason he became known as the "King of the Cap." San Francisco was masterful at front-loading contracts and manipulating bonuses and deferred payments. They were playing chess with the salary cap while most of the rest of the league, including the Saints, was playing checkers.

The 49ers had the highest payroll in the league prior to the advent of free agency and the salary cap. And yet, they seldom lost a veteran that they wanted to keep or were unable to add a free agent they really, really wanted, like Hall of Fame cornerback Deion Sanders or the Saints' Jackson, both of whom they signed after the '93 season.

Sometimes there's a fine line between cheating and being very creative. Jackson made $1.3 million in his final season with the Saints in '93. San Francisco signed him to a cap-friendly one-year, $167,000 deal that included nearly a million dollars in bonuses and incentives that didn't count against the Niners' cap. The Niners made it all the way to the NFC Championship Game in '93. A year later, they won their fifth Super Bowl title in 14 years.

The Saints would manage to win their first five games in '93, including a rare victory over San Francisco (16–13), and were an impressive 6–2 at midseason. But then the roof fell in on Mora's aging team. They lost eight of their next 10, finished 8–8, and missed the playoffs for the first time in four years.

"We scored more than 20 points just once in our last eight games and lost six of them, and that was all she wrote," says Kuharich.

For the first time since Mills arrived in New Orleans in '86, the defense struggled. After finishing first in points allowed in both '91 and '92, they finished 22nd in '93, giving up nearly 10 more points a game than the previous season. Jackson had signed with the 49ers. Johnson had left for Philadelphia. Swilling had been traded to the Lions. The remarkably durable Mills, who had missed just four games in his previous 11 pro seasons, missed seven games in '93 after needing surgery to repair an early-season knee injury. He somehow still managed to finish with 85 tackles.

The '94 season went even worse. The now 35-year-old Mills was the last Dome Patroler standing, and he played his heart out. He registered a career-high 155 tackles. But he just didn't have enough help. Without Jackson and Swilling harassing opposing quarterbacks, the Saints had just 31 sacks.

Without any pass-rush pressure, the pass defense suffered mightily. The Saints finished 26th (out of 28) in passing yards allowed and dead last in touchdown passes allowed. Offensively, they couldn't run the ball, averaging just 83.5 rushing yards per game in '94, the lowest since Mora arrived nine years earlier. The Saints finished 7–9 and again missed the playoffs. They lost both of their games against the 49ers by a combined 32 points.

The Saints' salary cap problems were suffocating them. They had lost a lot of key players to free agency and still somehow didn't have the cap space to sign anyone else. Mora was becoming increasingly frustrated.

"He was thinking, 'Hey, I'm coaching my ass off and there's nobody here directing the show,'" Kuharich says.

Before he died, Jim Finks advised Benson to hire another general manager. But Benson had visions of becoming the next Jerry Jones. Jones was the Dallas Cowboys owner who also served as his team's general manager. But Jones had an understanding of the game. He had played college ball at Arkansas. Benson didn't know enough about the game to handle that role.

"He said, 'We're going to do it this way,'" Kuharich says. "But *this way* didn't work."

The Saints were in freefall after the '94 season. Mills, who had given the last nine years of his life to the Saints franchise and had been with Mora his entire professional career, was now a 35-year-old free agent.

Sam wasn't looking to leave New Orleans, even though he could clearly see the Saints were struggling. He was still playing at a high level, but he knew the clock was ticking. He recognized that he probably only had a couple more years left before he would have to get on with the rest of his life.

Mills was very loyal. Even with all of the turmoil the Saints franchise was experiencing, he would've been content to finish out his career with them if they had made him a fair offer.

But they didn't make him any offer at all. At least not initially.

"By '94, they had kind of decided it was time to turn the team over," Brett Senior says. "They didn't even really reach out to Sam [about re-signing]. Then Carolina stepped up and made an offer to him."

The Saints weren't the 49ers, particularly in the way they treated their players. Niners owner Ed DeBartolo Jr. treated his players like kings. He didn't cut corners on anything. He put them up in five-star hotels on the road. He made sure their families were always taken care of. The Niners' team plane was second to none. The 49ers' training equipment was state-of-the-art. Tom Benson wasn't DeBartolo. The Louisiana car dealer had a reputation for being cheap. The reputation was well-deserved.

"Tom definitely was cheap," says Kuharich. "That wasn't a secret. Before he got sick, Finks had the final say on money. After he got sick, Tom had final say. I don't know how much was Tom telling [Jim] Miller, 'No, we're not going to spend this money.' But I'm pretty sure it was a lot."

Mills once told someone that he was like an elephant. When he was asked what he meant, he said, "Because [the Saints] pay me peanuts." He said it in a joking way, but Mills was a smart man. He knew exactly what other linebackers in the league were getting paid, and he knew what he was worth. In most cases, those other linebackers were getting more than Benson had ever paid him.

Mills was very frugal. For most of his nine seasons in New Orleans, he and Melanie and their four children rented a modest home in Kenner, a middle-class suburb just a stone's throw from the New Orleans airport. Their neighbors were normal folks, a teacher on one side and a police officer on the other. He didn't buy expensive clothes. He would hang on to a car until, as his son Marcus fondly says, "it was running like Fred Flintstone," jokingly meaning he was almost pedaling it with his own feet.

No matter how successful he became, Sam always felt he needed to have a contingency plan. A lot of it had to do with growing up poor in government housing in Seaview Manor and watching his mom struggle to put food on the table for her large family. But a lot of it also had to do with the rejection he suffered early in his career. He still felt one bad practice could end his career.

Sam remained driven by those early slights. One spring when he was playing for the Saints, the family was getting ready to go out to dinner. But the NFL draft was on TV. Sam told them he didn't want to leave until after the Saints made their first pick.

"Dad, who cares who they take?" Sam III said.

"I just want to make sure they're not picking somebody to replace me," his father said.

"Seriously? You just made the Pro Bowl," Sam III said incredulously.

"That was my dad," he says. "In his mind, you never turn it off. This was the opportunity you were given and you can't squander it."

One bad practice.

"Coming from the USFL, he wasn't paid very much," Marcus says. "His first contract with the Saints didn't pay him much either. His whole time in New Orleans, his thinking was: *At any time this could be taken away from me. This may not work out.* Even after he started making the Pro Bowl, nothing changed. We still lived in the same house in Kenner."

Sam loved everything Disney. He took Melanie and their four kids to Disney World almost every offseason. He took his two girls, Larissa and Sierra, on Disney cruises. When the boys got older, they accompanied their father to Disney World to golf and fish.

The first time Mills went to Disney World was in the late '80s when he was with the Saints. He had been invited to participate in The Goofy Games, a celebrity competition similar to ABC's popular *Superstars*, which debuted in the early '70s.

"I think he just liked the idea of us all being there together having fun," Sam III said. "He was a food guy. He loved eating all the different foods at Disney World. He could still get his workouts in there. There was golf."

Another thing Mills liked about Disney World was the anonymity. He was just another tourist there. He would occasionally get recognized. But he had a lot more privacy there than he did in New Orleans or on the Long Branch pier. He could spend time with his family and not have to stop and sign autographs every five minutes.

But if someone did ask for an autograph or a picture or just wanted to talk to him, Mills never, ever refused them.

"I don't remember a single time in his life that my dad was ever rude to someone," Sam III says. "We knew and understood that if anyone ever came up to him, we were going to be there for as long as that person wanted to talk. He never took it for granted. I think he always remembered being on the other side.

"I would have people tell me, 'I met your dad at the mall. He was looking for a belt and I was looking for a belt. We sat there and talked for 20 minutes.'"

Both of Sam's sons played college football—Sam III at his father's alma mater, Montclair State, and Marcus at Penn State. But he never pushed them into the sport.

"He really didn't care if we played sports," Marcus says. "He knew there were numerous paths that you could take and leave your mark. My brother and I both chose to play football. But he was just as excited to watch us run track. I played the sax. He was happy to come to my music concerts."

"He was just a normal dad, a great dad," Sam III says of his father. "We'd sit around the house and watch sitcoms together. We'd go bowling. I never felt any pressure football-wise. He never pushed us to play. It was our decision. For us, football never really was a part of the home. It was everything minus football."

A few years after signing with the Saints, Sam and Melanie bought a home in Manalapan, New Jersey, which is about 20 miles west of Long Branch. They would go up there during the offseason. Sam would take his two sons over to the Manalapan Rec Center. They would play basketball. Then Sam would go out and run some hills and do some bench jumps by himself.

"It wasn't until later that I realized how unique it was for someone to go off by themselves and do bench jumps," Marcus says. "But that was my dad."

For nine years, Sam Mills gave the New Orleans Saints everything he had. He understood the cold, hard business of professional football, but he was still hurt by the team's unwillingness to make him a contract offer until after he tested the free agent market. He knew he was near the end of his career. He wasn't trying to take the Saints to the cleaners. But he had been the heart and soul of their franchise for nearly a decade. He had led them out of the NFL darkness. He felt he deserved better treatment from them than he got.

After Mills got an offer from Carolina, the Saints did agree to match it. But it was too little too late. The damage had already been done.

"When the Saints told my dad to go shop around for an offer, I think he felt like, *Man, I still haven't made it. I still feel like I'm looking for a home, still looking to be accepted and told I'm good enough,*" Sam III says.

"It really hurt his feelings the way they treated him at the end," Melanie says. "He had played really well for them for a long time. He had been the perfect role model and team leader. After they did that, he wondered, *Where is the loyalty, if any?*"

Mora was furious when Mills signed with the Panthers. Kuharich remembers the coach coming into his office right after he found out.

"I've never seen anybody so mad in my life," he says. "He wasn't mad at anybody specifically. He was just mad that we had lost Sam on top of all these other guys.

"And a lot of them went to our division rivals. Sam went to Carolina, who they put in our division. Morten Andersen and Bobby Hebert went to the Falcons. And Rickey Jackson went to the 49ers. All teams we had to play twice a year."

Mora would leave less than two seasons later, resigning eight games into the '96 season. Ironically, the final straw would be a 19–7 loss to Mills and the Panthers. The listless Saints' offense managed just 174 total yards and 10 first downs in the game. Sam had a team-high 10 tackles and helped hold the Saints to 71 rushing yards on 20 carries. All of Mora's frustration came boiling over after the game in a memorable rant.

"We couldn't do diddly-poo offensively; we sucked," Mora said disgustedly to reporters after the loss. "We got our asses totally kicked in the second half [62 yards, two first downs]. That's what it boiled down to. It was a horseshit performance in the second half."

Mora quit the next day.

Mora had turned the Saints around. He took a franchise that had never known winning, and with the help of Mills and others, he transformed it into an annual playoff contender. Unfortunately for him, it's the four playoff one-and-dones in New Orleans that people remember.

"I was a shitty playoff coach," Mora says. "We went 7–1 in the playoffs in three years in the USFL. But in the NFL, I didn't do a good job."

23

He went to Carolina and they beat us with him. He played three years there and they built a statue of him. That's what people thought of Sam. That's an indication of what he meant to an organization.

—Jim Mora

IT WASN'T JUST players who were bolting New Orleans. The coaches were too.

In 1995, the NFL expanded for the first time in 19 years, adding a pair of franchises in Charlotte (Carolina Panthers) and Jacksonville (Jaguars). Dom Capers, who had been an assistant on Jim Mora's staffs in Philadelphia and New Orleans before leaving in 1992 to become Bill Cowher's defensive coordinator with the Pittsburgh Steelers, was named the Panthers' first head coach in January of '95. One of his first hires was Saints linebackers coach Vic Fangio, whom he brought in to be his defensive coordinator.

Unlike the Saints, the Panthers had no salary cap problems. They were a brand-new franchise without any players under contract. Mills was just a few months shy of his 36th birthday at the time. You wouldn't think an expansion team would've been all that interested in someone at the tail end of his career.

But the Panthers weren't your typical expansion team. Charlotte wasn't pro football country in 1995. It was NASCAR country. It was college basketball country. People weren't exactly rushing to buy the

PSLs (premium seat licenses) that the team was selling to help fund the construction of its new stadium.

The new stadium would be in Uptown, Charlotte's main business district, but it wasn't going to be finished in time for the Panthers' inaugural season. So, the Panthers would play their home games in '95 at Clemson University, which was a two-and-a-half-hour drive from Charlotte.

General Manager Bill Polian, who had been the architect of a Buffalo Bills team that went to four straight Super Bowls in the early '90s, knew that if his team was going to win Carolinians over, it had to do it quickly. Which meant bringing in established veteran players who could help the Panthers win right away.

Polian was from the Bronx and had spent the previous seven years with the Bills in western New York, where pro football was king. He didn't have an appreciation for how fanatical people in the South were about NASCAR. During the Panthers' first home game at Clemson, Polian happened to glance over at the stadium's huge Diamond Vision screen and noticed they were running the results of a NASCAR race on the crawl at the bottom of the screen.

"I kind of viewed [NASCAR] as competition," he says. "I didn't understand why we would be running their results during our games. So, the next day, I went to Charlie [Panthers Public Relations Director Charlie Dayton] and asked him why we were putting NASCAR results up there on the board. He said, 'Well, Bill. If we don't, we're liable to get run out of town.'"

Dayton, who spent 40 years as an NFL PR man, including more than two decades with the Panthers, was a North Carolina native who understood the team's audience.

"We were fighting for our niche early on," Dayton says. "It's not like it is today. The [NASCAR] races were on Sunday. We had a choice. We could either ignore them and risk that people might stay home and watch them rather than watch us at Clemson. Or run a crawl with how it was going. It was as simple as that."

Previous NFL expansion teams had typically struggled mightily early on. They were usually made up of inexperienced young players and bottom-of-the-roster veterans from other teams that they picked up in the league's expansion draft.

The Tampa Bay Buccaneers failed to win a game in their first season of existence in 1976 and won a total of seven games in their first three seasons. The Atlanta Falcons, who were founded in 1966, were 6–35 in their first three seasons. And the pathetic story of the expansion Saints was legendary. Their fans had to sit through 20 non-winning seasons before the clouds parted.

But that was all before free agency. Free agency gave an expansion team like the Panthers an opportunity to win sooner rather than later, which Polian felt was imperative. Three 3–13 seasons weren't going to cut it in Charlotte. They'd be playing in front of friends and family and no one else. So, signing an elder statesman and leader like Sam Mills who could teach the younger players how to win made perfect sense.

From the minute Fangio arrived in Charlotte, he had lobbied hard to sign Mills. They had been together for 11 years—nine in New Orleans and two in Philadelphia. They were good friends. Fangio knew the Saints were in a salary-cap bind and hadn't yet made an offer to Mills. He also knew better than anybody that Sam still had gas left in his tank. "To get a guy of Sam's stature and his ability and what he would bring to a new franchise, to me it was just a no-brainer," he says.

Capers, like Fangio, was all for bringing in Mills. He told Polian he couldn't think of a better guy to start a new franchise with.

Polian, who as a young scout with the Chiefs in 1981 had made the mistake of thinking Mills was too short to play in the NFL, long ago realized he had gotten that wrong. As soon as Capers brought up Sam's name, he contacted Brett Senior and offered Mills a two-year,

$2.8 million deal, which was pretty good money at the time. Senior reached out to his client, who happened to be at—where else—Disney World at the time with his family. Sam wasn't going to make the decision on his own. Everybody had a say. He and Mel and the kids held an impromptu meeting in their hotel room and voted unanimously to take the Panthers' offer.

"He asked us what we thought," said Marcus, who was 12 at the time. "His feelings about the way the Saints had treated him were pretty clear. We were all onboard for going to Charlotte. All I had ever known was New Orleans. I was excited to see what else was out there. I think my dad was too."

With the possible exception of Capers and Fangio, nobody was more excited to have Mills sign with the Panthers than Brett Maxie. Maxie and Mills had been teammates in New Orleans for eight seasons. They were also close friends.

Maxie, a safety who started 72 games for the Saints, had left New Orleans a year before Mills after suffering the second ACL tear of his career. He considered retirement, then signed with the Falcons in '94 before joining his old Saints position coach, Capers, in Carolina after he got the head-coaching job. Maxie signed with the Panthers a couple of weeks before Polian made the offer to Mills.

He was in Capers' office at the team's training facility at Winthrop University in Rock Hill, South Carolina, about 25 miles south of Charlotte, watching game film when the Panthers head coach told him they were going to try to sign Mills.

"We're going to make him an offer," Capers said. "I think he wants to come. But why don't you give him a call? It would help."

Maxie called Sam. He told Maxie he was excited about the prospect of playing for a new team.

"We're going to make it happen, Max," Mills told him. "I never thought I would ever be leaving New Orleans. But I think I have to."

For the second time in his career, Sam Mills was joining a startup franchise. He helped lead the first one, the Philadelphia Stars, to two USFL championships in three years. Now, at the age of 36, after four Pro Bowl appearances with the Saints, he was getting in on the ground floor of an NFL expansion team.

His signing with Carolina in early March of 1995 barely caused a ripple in the NFL free agency waters, even in Charlotte. The Dallas Cowboys' signing of Deion Sanders to a seven-year, $25 million deal got the biggest national headlines. Sanders had been the NFL's Defensive Player of the Year with San Francisco the season before. A week before signing Mills, the Panthers flexed their salary cap muscles by handing out a five-year, $13.8 million deal to 28-year-old pass-rushing linebacker Lamar Lathon.

Mills' signing flew well under the radar. He was just three months shy of his 36th birthday. Counting his three years in the USFL, he had played in nearly 250 professional football games. Besides Carolina and the Saints, no other teams had expressed any serious interest in signing him.

But the Panthers knew what they were getting. Mills would provide immediate leadership to a young expansion team. He would be a steadying force and a coach on the field.

"I had so much trust in him that I was going to listen to everything he said," Capers says. "It didn't take long for our players to feel the same way."

Much like he did in New Orleans, Mills mentored younger teammates and helped many of them deal with the pressures of professional football.

Lathon, who would record 21 ½ sacks in his first two seasons with Carolina, was an extraordinarily talented athlete. At 6'3" and 260 pounds, he was a physical freak and had incredible power, explosion, and range. But he was also high-strung and had a short fuse. Mills kept him focused and under control.

"The second Sam would see Lamar losing his cool and losing his concentration, he would settle him down," Capers says.

The Panthers won the coin flip with the league's other expansion team in '95, the Jacksonville Jaguars, so they had the first pick in the draft. Everyone thought they were going to take Penn State running back Ki-Jana Carter.

But Polian wanted a quarterback to build his new team around, much like he had done in Buffalo with Jim Kelly. He traded out of the top spot down to No. 5 and took Carter's Penn State teammate, Kerry Collins.

The 6'5", 247-pound Collins had a linebacker build like Kelly. He was a sturdy, strong-armed quarterback who would go on to play 17 years in the NFL and start 180 games. But the early part of that long career was, for lack of a better word, erratic.

When he arrived in Charlotte in '95, Collins was very immature and more interested in enjoying the celebrity perks of being a professional athlete rather than putting in the time to learn how to become a consistently productive NFL quarterback. "He went into the NFL thinking it was going to be one big party," his brother Pat said later.

Collins lasted just three seasons and a part of a fourth with the Panthers before they ran out of patience with his drinking, partying, immaturity, and inconsistent play, and released him. He would eventually get sober and turn his career around, but not in Carolina.

Mills tried unsuccessfully to get through to Collins. One time, Collins admitted to reporters that he was dealing with a lack of confidence. Mills sat him down and tried to talk him through it and give him some advice on how to deal with the media.

Another time, during training camp in Spartanburg, South Carolina, a drunk Collins was at a nightclub with some of his teammates and made a racist joke. He was an immature kid and was just trying to be funny and fit in. He thought his Black teammates would laugh. They didn't. The story got out and Collins found himself branded as a racist. He made a public apology, but the damage had been done.

"Sam sat me down and said, 'C'mon, man. You're better than this,'" Collins says. "It wasn't judgmental. He was trying to help me. I always appreciated that. Unfortunately, at the time, I was battling a lot of stuff and wasn't ready to be helped at that point. But I was always grateful to Sam that he took the time to try and help me."

Mills' leadership skills were off the charts. Hall of Fame coach Tony Dungy has a phrase he likes to use: *quiet strength*. It fit Mills to a tee. Sam wasn't a yeller or screamer. If he had something to say, it came from his soul. And the value of those words was multiplied by 100.

"Sam was a thermostat instead of a thermometer," Brett Maxie says. "You could see the room change when he walked into it. He was just the consummate pro and teammate because he was always doing the right thing, even when nobody saw it.

"It was how he challenged men to get better. A lot of great players would meet Sam for the first time and immediately feel like they had known him their whole lives because the impact he made on them was genuine."

The veteran Mills was the perfect fit for the inexperienced Panthers in so many ways in '95. Capers was a first-time head coach. Fangio was a first-time defensive coordinator. Kevin Steele, the team's inside linebackers coach, came from the college ranks and had never worked in the NFL before. Bill Davis, who was the team's outside linebackers coach, had been a defensive assistant under Capers in Pittsburgh but had never been in charge of a position group before.

Mondays and Tuesdays are typically off-days for players in pro football. But never for Mills. He called them his "advantage days." Those were the days when he got to be the coach and do the work. He would get an early look at the defensive game plan from Fangio. He would have Sam III or Marcus quiz him on it. By Wednesday, when the coaching staff would be giving the rest of the team the game plan for that week, Mills had already committed it to memory and would help his teammates learn it.

"The biggest piece for a defensive player is [figuring out] if it's going to be run or pass," Bill Davis says. "You have a run assignment to execute and a pass assignment. That's hard. But when Sam gives you the answer to the test before the play, well, now your chances for success go through the roof. That's what Sam brought to a young team. It was a hidden value that he brought to every practice and every game."

Kevin Steele had spent 14 years as a college assistant at Tennessee, New Mexico State, Oklahoma State, and Nebraska before Capers hired him. The Panthers were his first NFL job. Steele was a very good coach, but there's a significant learning curve when you go from college to the NFL, whether you're a player or a coach. Mills helped Steele navigate that learning curve.

"Many of the coaches on that staff had an impact on me as I made the transition," Steele says. "But to be quite frank with you, Sam taught me more about being a pro coach than anybody else, and it wasn't even close."

Like Fangio, Steele was only a year older than Mills. He would ask him questions about the pro game and would even ask him questions about Fangio and Capers' defense since Sam knew it a lot better than he did.

"I tell people all the time, as a rookie coach in the NFL, coaching a guy that was pretty close to the same age as me, the transition was pretty easy because Sam didn't allow me to make mistakes," says Steele. "He was always there to make sure, in his coded way, to not let me make mistakes as a transitional coach."

Steele still remembers one memorable play during that first season. This was before the NFL allowed teams to put communication devices in helmets. Teams were still using hand signals to send in plays and alignments. Steele was the defensive signal coach for the Panthers.

Fangio made a call and Steele was supposed to signal it in to Mills and the rest of the defense. But he had a brain fart. His mind went blank. For a few painful moments, he couldn't remember the signal for that particular play.

As Mills stood in front of the defensive huddle, he turned toward Steele to get the play signal. As Steele struggled to remember it, Mills didn't panic. He just turned back toward the huddle and called the defense himself. It turned out to be the exact same defense that Fangio had called.

"Sam, you bailed me out on that," Steele said when Mills got back to the sideline.

"Don't worry about it," Mills said. "It happens. I kind of knew from the down-and-distance and the personnel what Vic was gonna call."

Another time, the Panthers were playing against Steve Young and the 49ers at Candlestick Park. Young was a dangerous dual-threat quarterback. On a third-and-seven play, Fangio signaled in a "man-under" defense, which involves playing man-to-man coverage underneath and zone coverage deep. The downside to playing man coverage against a running quarterback like Young is that the cover people turn their backs to the quarterback, which allows the quarterback to take off and run. Brett Maxie vehemently disagreed with the call.

He voiced his displeasure with the call to Mills.

"Max, that's the call that came in from the sideline and that's what we're playing," Mills said.

"Okay, okay," Maxie replied.

The 49ers snapped the ball, and Young saw Maxie and the rest of the Panthers' defensive backs turn their backs to him to play man coverage. He took off and ran for an easy first down.

An angry Maxie ran toward the sideline and pointed at Capers and Fangio and told them what he thought of the call. Mills immediately got in front of his angry teammate.

"Max, next play," Mills said to him. "Get back to the huddle."

"I'm over there worried about what should've been done and Sam is, *Hey, shit happens, man. We gotta move on to the next play,*" Maxie says. "That's how he was."

A defense needs a quarterback just like an offense does. Everywhere Mills played—from the asphalt "fields" in Seaview Manor to Long Branch High to Montclair to Philadelphia to New Orleans to Carolina, Mills was the defensive quarterback. He made all the checks. He got everybody lined up in the right place.

The Panthers' other inside linebacker was Carlton Bailey. Polian had drafted him in '88 when he was the GM in Buffalo. Bailey had been a college nose tackle at the University of North Carolina whom the Bills converted to linebacker.

He had played linebacker for both the Bills and the New York Giants before signing with the Panthers. But he struggled early on learning Fangio's defense. Enter Mills.

"Sam essentially coached Carlton into having a great couple of years for us," Polian says.

Mills would tell Bailey before the snap whether it was going to be a pass or run. He didn't need to know why. He could just go and play.

Bailey started 14 games alongside Mills in '95. In their first season of existence, the Carolina Panthers' defense finished eighth in points allowed, fifth in takeaways, and 10th against the run. Mills had career highs in interceptions (five) and forced fumbles (five), tied his career high in fumble recoveries (four), and had 4 ½ sacks, which was the most in his career to that point. He finished fourth in the NFL Defensive Player of the Year voting behind the Bills' Bryce Paup, the Steelers' Greg Lloyd, and the 49ers' Merton Hanks. *At the age of 36!*

24

There are some people that accumulate stats and then you look back at their career and you can't remember a single play they made. With Sam, I can name a dozen game-changing plays he made for the Panthers right off the top of my head.

—Charlie Dayton, Carolina Panthers PR director (1995–2015)

NFL EXPANSION TEAMS are a lot like babies. They have to crawl before they can walk and walk before they can run. But the Carolinas had never had a professional football team before, and many local sports fans weren't sure they really wanted one. This wasn't a starving fan base longing to be fed NFL football.

"Charlotte was a basketball and racing city," Bill Polian says. "The people there didn't understand pro football."

It was more about educating the fan base about pro football than selling them on it.

"All the people in the region had known was college football, college basketball, and NASCAR," says Charlie Dayton. "Simple things like the waiver process, people weren't familiar with it."

Polian was very aware that a five-year plan wasn't going to cut it in Charlotte. He knew his new team had to speed through the crawling phase and become competitive as quickly as possible.

"That first year, playing in Clemson because our stadium still was being built, was hard," Dayton says. "But looking back, we still averaged 48,000 or something like that. Which was really remarkable given how far Clemson was from Charlotte."

Clemson is a two-and-a-half-hour drive down I-85 from Charlotte. The Panthers had looked into playing their home games a little closer to home. They approached the University of South Carolina, which is in Columbia, about playing there, as Columbia was 40 miles closer to Charlotte than Clemson. But South Carolina's athletic director at the time, Mike McGee, found the thought of having a professional team playing on the Gamecocks' college campus unseemly.

"I might be overstating this, but if so, only slightly," Polian says. "It took us, with traffic, more time to get home to Charlotte after our *home* games at Clemson than it did to get back to Charlotte when we played in San Francisco."

Mills already had experience at playing an entire season on the road. He had done it in 1985 with the Philadelphia Stars, who commuted from Philadelphia to the University of Maryland in College Park for their home games that year. Ironically, the distance between Philly and College Park is exactly the same as the distance between Charlotte and Clemson: 134 miles.

Much like he did when the Stars moved to Baltimore, Mills helped the Panthers market their team to a cautious fan base. He was a dream come true for Dayton and his staff.

"From his first press conference after he signed, Sam was just different," Dayton says. "He just had that quality about him. People knew he was special. In addition to everything else, he was lovable. I can't prove this, but I always felt we had a disproportionate number of female fans compared to other teams. I think Sam had a lot to do with that because people just loved the guy. Kids loved him. The mothers loved him. I think it helped us in the beginning to draw families. Because it wasn't like the dads were saying, 'Hey, I'm going to go to the game with my buddies.' We had so many families coming to the game. And women drive that. The mom drives that."

In the leadup to the Panthers' first season, Mills was the go-to guy for Dayton and the PR and marketing departments when they needed a player to speak with the media or make a public appearance at a sporting goods store, mall, or Rotary Club function.

"It's not just that he agreed to do it," Dayton says. "He was great at it. Sam was just a good person. He didn't wish ill on anybody. And it came across. Then, when you make the plays [on Sunday], you're the guy people go to after every game."

The Panthers went into their first season in '95 with higher expectations than most expansion teams. In addition to Mills and Lathon, they had used their ample salary cap space to sign a slew of veteran free agents, including Maxie, defensive ends Gerald Williams and Mike Fox, quarterback Frank Reich, safety Bubba McDowell, linebacker Darion Conner, tight end Pete Metzelaars, and veteran kicker John Kasay.

After trading back in the draft, they ended up with four of the first 36 picks, selecting Collins, cornerback Tyrone Poole from Fort Valley State, left tackle Blake Brockermeyer from Texas, and defensive tackle Shawn King out of Northeast Louisiana. They also picked up several veterans in the expansion draft who helped them early on, including center Curtis Whitley, wide receiver Mark Carrier, cornerback Tim McTyer, and nose tackle Greg Kragen.

They opened the '95 season on the road against Atlanta and lost in overtime on a 35-yard walk-off field goal by Mills' former Saints teammate Morten Andersen. Reich, a 34-year-old career backup, started at quarterback for the Panthers and was sacked nine times.

The defense, led by Mills and Lathon, was the Panthers' strength, just as it had been when Sam played for the Saints. The offense was dreadful, particularly early on. Carolina finished 25th in scoring in '95, averaging just 18 points per game. Panthers quarterbacks threw the league's fifth-fewest passing touchdowns (16) and had a league-high 25 interceptions.

A week after their overtime loss to the Falcons, the Panthers got their heads handed to them by the Buffalo Bills in another road loss, 31–9. Reich, who had spent the previous nine seasons with the Bills, started again at quarterback and completed just six of 21 passes for 44 yards.

Their home opener against the St. Louis Rams in Week 3 drew 54,060 fans to Clemson Stadium. The Panthers got drubbed 31–10.

After a Week 4 bye, Capers gave Kerry Collins his first NFL start at home against the Tampa Bay Bucs. Collins threw for 234 yards, but the Panthers lost for the fourth straight time, 20–13. They faced the Bears on the road the next week. Mills and Carlton Bailey combined for 23 tackles, but the Panthers lost again, 31–27, to fall to 0–5.

So much for wooing the NASCAR crowd with a fast start.

"You get an influx of talent, but it takes time for everybody to blend together," Bill Davis says. "When you're putting together a team from scratch like we were in '95, that's literally what you're doing. We had a lot of talent, but it hadn't blended early on."

The New York Jets were probably the worst team in the league that season. When they arrived at Clemson Stadium to face the Panthers in Week 7, they had lost five of their first six games by an average of 21 points. If there was ever going to be an opportunity for Carolina to break into the win column, this was it. But with just 22 seconds left in the first half, the Panthers were trailing 12–6.

Their offense once again was flailing. Carolina's only points had come on a pair of John Kasay field goals. Then, Sam Mills made the play that changed everything for the franchise.

On a second-and-10 at his own 40, Jets quarterback Bubby Brister attempted a shovel pass to fullback Brad Baxter. Mills read Brister's eyes, came through the line, and stepped in front of the short toss. He picked it off and returned it 36 yards for a touchdown to put the Panthers ahead at halftime.

In the second half, Mills and the Panthers' defense went into shutdown mode. They held the Jets to three points, four first downs, and 52 total yards to help secure the franchise's first-ever win, 26–15.

"Sam made that play against the Jets and it all came together," says Davis. "As a coach, you know when you're getting close. With the techniques and the scheme, with the understanding and how they're communicating. But that was the moment that just ignited us and brought us together as a group of talented guys, and they started playing together."

"That's the play that everybody remembers from that first year because it turned our season around," Capers adds. "We started getting positive momentum going for us after that. What ends up happening, when you're 0–5 and an expansion team, everybody starts questioning themselves and losing their confidence. But because of guys like Sam, that didn't happen to us."

Melanie didn't see her husband's big interception. She was stuck in traffic trying to get into Clemson Stadium and could only listen to it on the car radio.

The win over the Jets ignited a four-game win streak. A week later, the Panthers whipped Mills' old team, the New Orleans Saints, at home, 20–3. Mills had a big game, recording eight tackles and another interception.

The Panthers rallied to win seven of their last 11 and finish that first season with a 7–9 record, which was more than good for a first-year team. They nearly finished 8–8 but lost their final game to the Washington Redskins by three points.

Mills made play after big play that year. In a 20–17 Week 9 overtime win over the New England Patriots, he had a key forced fumble that killed a potential New England scoring drive.

In a 21–17 come-from-behind win over the Falcons late in the season, Atlanta had the ball at the Carolina 7-yard line in the fourth quarter and was threatening to make it a two-score game when Mills picked off a pass intended for his former Saints teammate Ironhead

Heyward. Two plays later, Kerry Collins threw an 89-yard touchdown pass to Willie Green to put the Panthers ahead.

The Falcons got the ball back and drove from their own 13 to the Carolina 7. But on first down, Mills stoned Heyward for no gain and killed the Falcons' offensive momentum. Falcons quarterback Jeff George threw three straight incompletions after that, and the Panthers won the game.

"Sam not only made big plays; he made big plays at the right time," Dayton says. "It seemed that every time he made a huge play, it was at a big time in the game. It changed momentum or preserved a lead. It wasn't in the middle of the second quarter when the game was going back and forth. It was late in the fourth quarter in the red zone. He was uncanny with his ability to make big plays when they counted."

Given the Panthers' early, fragile relationship with their fans in '95, Polian shudders to think what might have happened had the Panthers lost that Week 7 game to the hapless Jets and not turned things around.

"The second half of the first year really changed everything," Polian says. "In a city that really hadn't embraced us, it was tough going. And then we start 0–5. The people there didn't understand that it was a long season. There still was consternation over us not drafting Ki-Jana Carter and things like that.

"We had all of these new guys. There were no holdover veterans. Sam's leadership and Sam's closeness and belief in Dom, and vice versa, did a great deal toward keeping us focused and on an even keel and believing that we would come out of it. And of course, we did. We made a good run down the stretch and almost had a winning season."

25

The first time I ever met Sam I gave him a big hug. Through the years, we had hugs of joy and hugs of disappointment. A few days before his passing, we gave each other a goodbye hug.

—Panthers owner Jerry Richardson (1995–2018)

THE NUMBER OF people who have played in the National Football League and have also owned one of its franchises is very small. Two to be exact. One is Chicago Bears founder George "Papa Bear" Halas, who was a player-coach for the Bears from 1920 to 1928.

The other is Jerry Richardson.

Richardson was a 13th-round pick of the Baltimore Colts in 1959 when the NFL had just 12 teams and a 30-round draft. Richardson, a wide receiver out of Wofford College in Spartanburg, South Carolina, made the Colts as a rookie and spent two years with them. He was the team's Rookie of the Year in '59 when the Colts won the NFL championship. He caught a touchdown pass from Johnny Unitas in their 31–16 title-game win over the New York Giants.

Richardson turned out to be an even better businessman than he was a football player. He used his bonus from that '59 championship win to open the first Hardee's hamburger franchise in Spartanburg, with his friend and former Wofford College teammate Charles Bradshaw. Richardson later cofounded Spartan Foods with Bradshaw, which was the first franchisee of Hardee's, and later was the CEO of Flagstar, which was the sixth largest food services company in the

United States. It controlled 2,500 restaurants and had more than 100,000 employees.

When the NFL decided to expand into the Carolinas and Jacksonville in 1993, Richardson, a native North Carolinian, was awarded the Charlotte franchise.

As a former player who understood the importance of veteran leadership, particularly on a young starting-from-scratch team, Richardson recognized right away what Sam Mills brought to the expansion Panthers, particularly after he met him.

"Jerry immediately developed a respect for Sam, for what he was and what he could mean to the franchise in its developmental years," Vic Fangio says. "He took a liking to him right away, and they developed a special bond that you just don't see very often between an owner and a player."

Richardson was able to relate to Mills' difficult journey to the NFL. He, like Mills, had grown up in poverty and been shunned by the big football schools coming out of high school. Like Mills, he had made the most of his small-school opportunity. More than 65 years later, his name is still on many of Wofford's all-time receiving records.

Like Mills, there were questions about whether Richardson was big enough to play professional football, which was a big reason why he lasted until the 13th round. At 6'3", he certainly was tall enough. But he weighed just 180 pounds soaking wet. His nickname as a player was "Razor" because he was as thin as one.

"They had great respect for each other," Dayton says. "They both had come up the hard way, beating the odds. They had a special bond, but it was very private."

"Jerry and Sam connected very early on," Melanie Mills says. "I don't know exactly what it was, but they bonded from the beginning. I think Jerry admired Sam, and Sam admired him for building his own empire. Jerry was happy to have Sam there and didn't hide it."

Mills always respected successful businessmen, particularly those like Richardson who had come from nothing and created his own success. He also respected the fact that Richardson wasn't just "dabbling" in sports. After he was awarded the Charlotte franchise in '93, he divested himself of all his other business interests and focused on running the Panthers.

Jackie Miles, who was the Panthers' equipment manager for 20 years, from 1995 until 2015, was a good friend of Sam's. He grew up at 26th and South Street in Philly, not far from the University of Pennsylvania. When he was just 23, the Philadelphia Stars hired him as their assistant equipment manager, where he met Mills.

When they were reunited in Carolina, Miles made sure that Mills got the same number, 51, that he had worn with the Saints (he had worn No. 54 with the Stars).

Miles remembers a conversation he had with Jerry Richardson during the Panthers' first training camp at Wofford.

"Who is your favorite player, Jackie?" Richardson asked.

"That's easy," Miles responded. "Sam Mills."

"Really?" Richardson said. "Why?"

"Because he's one of the finest human beings I've ever known, and one of the best players I've ever seen," said Miles. "Once you get to know him, you'll see what I mean."

Panthers Vice President of Communications Bruce Speight, who was a young assistant on Charlie Dayton's staff back then, will never forget a training room scene that underscored the close relationship between Mills and Richardson. Sam was getting stitched up by the team's trainer after a game for a cut he had suffered.

"Mr. Richardson stood there the whole time and held Sam's hand and didn't let go until they finished stitching him up," Speight says.

The Panthers' impressive finish in '95 generated much-needed interest in the team as they moved into brand-new 73,000-seat Ericsson Stadium in Uptown. Despite being a second-year expansion team, the Panthers went into '96 poised for a breakout season.

They still had more salary cap space than most of the rest of the league, which allowed them to again be aggressive in free agency. They signed three-time Pro Bowl pass-rushing linebacker Kevin Greene from the Steelers, All-Pro cornerback Eric Davis from the 49ers, and tight end Wesley Walls from the Saints.

Mills turned 37 six weeks before the start of training camp, but he was still showing very few signs of slippage. Any impact age was having on him was offset by experience and preparation. He was like a god in the locker room. All of his teammates revered him and followed his lead.

"Even a player like Kevin Greene, who had been in the league 11 years and was considered one of its premier pass rushers, the esteem he had for Sam was off the charts," Charlie Dayton says. "He had played with a lot of good players on a lot of good teams by the time he got to Carolina. And I don't think I'm exaggerating to say he revered Sam. Sam transcended everybody."

Dayton wasn't exaggerating.

"I called him Sam Rock," said Greene. "He was not only the physical rock of our team, but he was the spiritual rock and the emotional rock and the leadership rock."

Even after Greene's arrival, it was Mills who made the trains run on time for the '96 Panthers.

"Kevin Greene was the lynchpin that second year," Polian says. "From a football standpoint, he was the difference-maker because of the way he could disrupt a game. But from the standpoint of keeping everyone on an even keel and focused and believing that we could get it done, Sam was the guy that did that."

The '96 Panthers were built around Mills and Greene and the defense. They opened the '96 season by rolling over Atlanta 29–6.

Mills set the tone early in the Week 1 win with a devastating hit on his former Saints teammate Ironhead Heyward. "I remember coming off a block and hearing this noise and saying *what the hell was that*?" Kevin Greene said. "Heyward was a big dude and Sammy just stoned him."

The Panthers followed their season-opening win over the Falcons by beating the Saints, 22–20, and the 49ers, 23–7. But then they lost four of their next six, mainly because the offense couldn't get out of its own way. The Panthers failed to score more than 17 points in any of the four losses.

"We didn't have any speed on offense. None," says Joe Pendry, who was the Panthers' offensive coordinator from 1995 through 1997. "We had a running back from Notre Dame, Anthony Johnson. He was a solid runner, but probably couldn't run 4.7 downhill with the wind behind him.

"Kerry Collins was a young quarterback, and we didn't have a lot of speed on the outside. Our whole offensive plan was to never turn it over and don't put the defense in bad situations. Rely on the defense to get turnovers. And when they got them, we had to score. That's how we played that year."

Greene and Lamar Lathon created constant problems for opposing quarterbacks, much like Rickey Jackson and Pat Swilling had when Mills was with the Saints. They combined for 28 sacks in '96. Mills was asked by Fangio to do more in the passing game in Carolina than he did in New Orleans, including blitzing more frequently, which he was very good at. He had a career-high 5 ½ sacks that season. The defense got the offense the turnovers they needed, finishing fifth in takeaways with 38.

"Kevin and Lathon combined for a lot of sacks that year," Capers says. "But Sam was the glue of that defense. When we needed a big play, Sam always seemed to come up with one."

Mills and Greene were to the Panthers' defense what Mills and Jackson had been to the Saints' defense.

After a pair of back-to-back road losses to the Falcons and Eagles in late October and early November, the Panthers were just 5–4. But then the offense started to play a little better and the defense really flexed its muscles. The Panthers reeled off seven straight wins to finish 12–4 and win the NFC West title over the 49ers. The Niners also had finished 12–4, but Carolina had won both head-to-head meetings to win the tiebreaker.

Mills had another outstanding season. He finished with a team-high 122 tackles, including 90 solo tackles, to go with his 5 ½ sacks. He returned a fumble for a touchdown in a 31–6 win over the Houston Oilers. He was a first-team All-Pro selection and earned his fifth Pro Bowl invitation at the age of 37. Three of the top seven players in the NFL Defensive Player of the Year voting that season were Panthers. Greene finished second to the Bills' Bruce Smith. Mills finished fifth, and Lathon finished seventh.

The Panthers were red-hot heading into the '96 playoffs. They hadn't lost a game since early November. They had outscored their last seven opponents 177–90.

In just their second season of existence, the Panthers had finished the regular season with a 12–4 record, won a division title, earned a first-round playoff bye, and were about to host the defending Super Bowl-champion Dallas Cowboys for the chance to go to the NFC Championship Game.

Any indifference Charlotte and the Carolinas initially had toward the Panthers had vanished. A ticket for the Panthers-Cowboys playoff game was almost as hard to get as a front row seat at the ACC basketball tournament. Almost.

Mills and Greene and the rest of the defense kept the Cowboys' offense and their three future Hall of Famers—quarterback Troy Aikman, running back Emmitt Smith, and wide receiver Michael

Irvin—in check much of the game. They picked off Aikman three times and held Smith to 80 yards on 22 carries. Mills had a team-high 11 tackles.

John Kasay's third field goal of the game early in the fourth quarter put the Panthers up 23–14. The Cowboys then drove down to the Carolina 2 but couldn't punch it in and had to settle for a Chris Boniol field goal that got them within six.

A 32-yard field goal by Kasay with 1:48 left made it a two-score game, 26–17. Mills put the game away with a third-and-long interception of Aikman. He nearly scored on the play. His knee hit the ground at the 1-yard line.

Mills didn't care.

They had won and he was all about team success. The win over the Cowboys meant a lot to him personally. It was the first playoff win of his NFL career. His Philadelphia Stars had won two titles in the USFL. But he had been 0–4 with the Saints in the postseason.

The win over the Cowboys would be the extent of Mills' playoff success. A week later, they would play the Packers in the NFC Championship Game in frigid Green Bay. The Packers had homefield advantage by virtue of their 13–3 regular-season record. The temperature at Lambeau Field at kickoff for the NFC Championship Game was three degrees. The wind chill: –17.

Mills was all over the field. What's a –17 wind chill to a guy who grew up playing on concrete? The Panthers took a 7–0 lead late in the first quarter when Mills picked off a Brett Favre pass for Don Beebe at the Green Bay 12 and returned it to the Packers' 2. Two plays later, Kerry Collins found fullback Howard Griffith for a touchdown. Carolina trailed by just seven late in the third quarter, but then Favre and the Packers pulled away.

Mills finished with a team-high 14 tackles, but the Panthers' offense came up small. Offenses coming up small would be the story of Mills' NFL career. The Panthers had managed just 251 yards in total offense against the Packers. Running back Anthony Johnson was held to 31 yards on 11 carries. Collins was 19 for 37 with two interceptions.

The Panthers had managed to make it all the way to the NFC Championship Game in just their second season, an amazing accomplishment. But the loss hit Mills hard. He still hadn't decided whether he was going to come back for another season. And even if he did, he knew there was no guarantee the Panthers would make it back to the playoffs.

"He definitely was down more than normal after the Packers game," Sam III says. "All of those years in New Orleans, I would see him after every game. No matter how big the game was, no matter whether they had won or lost, he would put on his dad face.

"But after that game, he was as low as I ever remembered him being. Looking back, I wondered if he knew that not ever going to the Super Bowl would be his legacy. I wondered if he was thinking down the road and feeling that if he wanted to be remembered with the greats, he needed to go to a Super Bowl.

"And that that probably was his last chance."

26

Nobody was going to cut Sam Mills. If he had wanted to come back and stretch it out one or even two more years, he could have. And nobody would have said a word.

—Charlie Dayton

ONLY A VERY small number of professional athletes are fortunate enough to be able to decide on their own when to walk away from the game. Most have the decision taken out of their hands. They get released, or become a free agent, and the phone doesn't ring. No one else offers them a job.

After the Panthers' disappointing loss to the Packers in the '96 NFC Championship Game, Mills briefly considered retirement, but he decided he wasn't ready to ride off into the sunset quite yet.

He was closing in on his 38th birthday, but age seemed to be only a number with him. He was coming off another superb season that included his third All-Pro selection and his fifth Pro Bowl invitation. Despite his age, he had managed to remain remarkably healthy. More aches and pains certainly. More time in the training room after a game or practice. But the bottom line was he hadn't missed a game in four years.

If the Panthers had beaten the Packers and made it to the Super Bowl, maybe Sam would've given more consideration to walking away. Or maybe he still would've come back for one more season anyway.

"It's hard for an athlete to give up that dream," Melanie Mills says.

"It's hard for him to admit that he can only play the game for so long. It's all they ever wanted to do. It's all Sam ever wanted to do. They're thinking, *What else can I do that's going to provide for my family and that I also enjoy doing as much as playing football?*"

Because he was cut twice at the beginning of his career and wasn't even sure he'd ever get the opportunity to play professional football, because he and Melanie had Sam III when both of them were still teenagers, Sam had always spent a lot of time thinking about and planning for life after football.

Before he made it with the Philadelphia Stars, the backup career plan was teaching. When he was in New Orleans, he thought he might want to get into the car business like Tom Benson. Later, after signing with the Panthers, the insurance business piqued his interest.

Brett Maxie remembers playing in a golf tournament with Sam after the '96 season. Maxie had already made up his mind he was going to coach after he was done playing.

Sam told him he was thinking about getting into the insurance business.

"You know what, Sam?" Maxie told him. "You do kind of look like an insurance guy. Put those glasses of yours on with a collared shirt on underneath the sweater and you got that look, man. I don't know if you'd be any good at selling insurance. But you definitely got the look."

The Panthers couldn't catch lightning in a bottle in '97 as they had in '96. Several key players, including Kevin Greene and Maxie, would leave. Both of them signed with San Francisco.

Greene felt he had outperformed his contract with the Panthers in '96. He led the league in sacks but wasn't among the 20 highest-paid linebackers in the league. He told the Panthers he wanted to renegotiate his deal.

Bill Polian was an old-school GM. He despised most agents and had little tolerance for players who didn't want to honor the contract they had signed, regardless of how good they were. In Bill's mind, a contract was a contract.

Greene held out of training camp and missed the team's first three preseason games. Polian, who would be inducted into the Pro Football Hall of Fame in 2015, a year before Greene, ran out of patience with him and released him. San Francisco swooped him up. The 49ers ended up beating the Panthers twice that season with Greene and making it to the NFC Championship Game.

Mills spent most of the '97 season dealing with a nagging leg injury. He managed to play in all 16 games, but the injury clearly affected his play. His age also finally began to show. He finished with 99 tackles, his lowest total in a season in which he played 14 or more games since 1989. He also failed to register a quarterback sack for the first time since '88.

The defense that had carried the Panthers to the NFC Championship Game the season before wasn't nearly as effective. They finished 14th in points allowed, 26th in takeaways, 23rd in sacks, and 22nd against the run. Carolina lost four of its first six games and five of its last seven and finished out of the playoff hunt with a 7–9 record.

Mills knew he couldn't play forever. As the '97 season wore on, he could hear Father Time whispering in his ear. He could also hear Vic Fangio.

Fangio talked to him about an exit strategy early in the season. He had noticed a slight change in Sam's movement in training camp that year.

"He didn't really want to retire," Fangio says. "He was a competitor, and you were going to have to drag him off the field."

Fangio told Sam he was born to be a coach and encouraged him to join the Panthers' coaching staff following the '97 season.

"I think he just felt it was time," his son Marcus says. "It was time to do the next thing in his life. At the time, he didn't know what that was going to be. He was thinking, *Should I sell insurance, or should*

I stay in football? And if I stay in football, what should I do? He had a whole bunch of different ideas. He wanted to take control of the decision rather than have it dictated to him."

There were no trumpets or standing ovations at the end for Mills. No grand goodbye tour. He didn't want one.

He didn't even tell anyone he was going to retire until the very end.

Sam called his agent, Brett Senior, the Tuesday before the Panthers' final game of the '97 season. He asked him if he and his wife, Victoria, could come down to Charlotte for the game. Then he said matter-of-factly, "Oh, by the way, I'm going to announce my retirement after the game.'"

Mills finished his career in style. He racked up 13 tackles and forced a fumble in a 30–18 season-ending loss to the Rams. As he walked off the field after the game, none of the fans at Ericsson Stadium realized that one of the best linebackers in NFL history had just played his final game. It was classic Sam Mills.

None of the media that covered the team had any idea Sam was calling it quits either, although given his age, they knew it was a definite possibility. Dom Capers held his postgame press conference, then told the reporters in the room that Sam wanted to make a statement.

Two weeks earlier, Senior had asked Sam for one of his jerseys to auction off at a fundraiser for a cancer event. After Sam announced his retirement to the media, the two of them went back into the locker room.

Almost everyone was gone. There were a couple of equipment guys still in there, a player or two, and Sam and Brett Senior. As they were walking out after Sam had showered, Mills suddenly remembered the jersey his agent had asked him for.

He went back in and asked one of the equipment guys to give him his game jersey. He then gave it to Senior.

"Sam, this is the last jersey you ever wore as a professional player. I'm not taking this jersey," Senior said.

"No, no. It's an important cause. Take it," Mills responded.

Senior never put that jersey up for auction. He got another one and gave that one back to Sam.

"That was Sam," Senior said. "That was the type of guy he was. He had just announced his retirement, but he didn't forget that he promised to get me a jersey. Then he gives me the most important jersey of his career. The last one he ever wore."

After giving it some more thought, Mills wisely nixed the insurance executive idea. He might've looked the part of an insurance guy with his glasses on, but he agreed with the assessments of his wife and kids that his salesmanship skills left a lot to be desired.

He decided he wanted to stay in football. Jerry Richardson had basically told him to pick a job, any job, in the Panthers organization and it was his for as long as he wanted it. Both Capers and Fangio knew he would make a great coach. He literally had been one on the field his entire career.

Many great players don't make great coaches because they don't know how to relate to players who didn't play the game at the same level or with the same level of commitment as they did.

Capers didn't think that would be the case with Mills.

"I knew he'd be a great coach," Capers says. "I knew his leadership would carry right on over to coaching. Sam just commanded respect from everybody just because of the way he handled himself. He always kept his head. He was smart. He was cool under pressure and never panicked."

Brett Maxie also retired after spending the '97 season with the 49ers. He returned to Carolina and joined Capers' staff as a quality control and assistant defensive backs coach. But Sam still wasn't sure he wanted to get into coaching.

It's a major lifestyle commitment. The hours are long and you spend even more time away from your family than when you were a player. As a player, Mills could do a lot of his film work and game prep at home. As a coach, he would have to be in the office from early in the morning until late at night. Sixteen-hour workdays aren't at all uncommon for coaches during the season. The offseasons are hardly a walk in the park either.

Mills initially decided to take a job as an assistant in the Panthers' personnel department. But after only a few weeks, he realized that he preferred the hands-on aspect of coaching. He wanted to be on the field interacting with the players and doing whatever he could to make other players better.

Even during his short stint in personnel, Mills would sit in on the coaching staff's meetings.

"He was in the meeting rooms every day with us when he was working in the personnel department," Maxie said. "We'd be evaluating the scheme from the year before and he'd be in there. He never missed a morning coming in. He was trying to double-dip. Then he just made the decision: *Here [coaching] is where I need to be.* He wanted to be a head coach someday. And he would've been a damn good one."

About a month after taking the job in the Panthers' personnel department, he talked to Capers and Fangio and joined the coaching staff as a defensive assistant.

27

Jerry Richardson obviously didn't know Sam was going to die so young. But he loved Sam and wanted to honor what he meant to the franchise in those early years. He was our team leader.

—Jackie Miles

SAM MILLS HAD played with great distinction for the New Orleans Saints for nine years. He helped transform them from a laughingstock into a respected playoff contender. He had been the ringleader of their elite linebacker corps, and the leader of one of the league's best defenses of the late '80s and early '90s. He had been one of the best and most popular players in franchise history.

But the Saints organization would be painfully slow to honor Mills. It's possible that the delay in honoring him was simply an oversight by a tone-deaf organization. But many suspect it was more than that.

Tom Benson was a man who could hold a grudge. Former Saints coaches and executives said he was very angry when Sam signed with the Panthers. Never mind that the Saints refused to make him an offer until after Carolina did. Never mind that a lot of other veteran players left around the same time. For some reason, Benson seemed to take Sam's decision to leave personally. As if he was expected to stay with the organization out of some sense of gratitude because they had been willing to take a chance on him nine years earlier.

Benson died in 2018 at the age of 90. Three years later, his widow, Gayle Benson, who replaced him as the team's owner, finally green-lighted Mills' entry into the Saints' Ring of Honor, more than a quarter-century after he had played his last game for the Saints, and 16 years after his death.

Mills was put in three years *after* Benson and defensive end Will Smith. Smith, who played for the Saints from 2004 until 2013, was a very good player, but he wasn't Sam Mills. The fact that Smith was murdered in a 2016 road rage incident likely had something to do with the team fast-tracking his induction into the Ring of Honor. But many felt he never should have gone in before Sam.

Jerry Richardson was extraordinarily appreciative of Mills' contributions to the Panthers. Shortly after Sam announced his retirement, Richardson decided to show his gratitude for what Sam had done for the organization in the three short years he had played for it by erecting a statue of him on the east side of Ericsson Stadium.

When Richardson first broached the subject with Mills, Sam was equal parts honored and embarrassed. This was a man who had never sought the limelight, who was content to do his job and fly under the radar. And now they were going to put up a statue of him?

"He wasn't very comfortable with it in the beginning," Fangio says. "I think he might've even tried to talk Jerry out of it. But Jerry was the kind of guy, when he had his mind set on something, there was no way you were gonna talk him out of it. And he wanted to put up a statue of Sam. It's a helluva deal now. It's a lasting remembrance of Sam that is still felt every day in the Panthers organization."

Richardson commissioned renowned California sculptor Todd Andrews to make the statue of Mills. It took Andrews a little over six months to complete.

"I had done quite a few [statues] similar to the one I did of Sam," Andrews says. "But most of them were of people who had passed away. It was so nice to have been able to actually have him here. He was such a nice guy."

Jackie Miles, the Panthers' equipment manager and Sam's good friend, said Mills would stop by his office and talk to him about the statue when it was being made. Miles said Sam would laugh about having his own statue, but as it got closer to becoming a reality, he started to get excited.

"He would joke and tell me he wanted to make sure his guns [arms] looked good," says Miles.

Todd Andrews' studio was in Grass Valley, California, which is in the western foothills of the Sierra Nevada Mountain range, about 57 miles northeast of Sacramento and 90 miles west of Reno, Nevada. Mills had to fly out there to pose for photographs and provide measurements.

"He put on his uniform and posed for me," Andrews says. "I just recreated it. [The statue] is a little bigger than life-size. It's 1 ¼ life. When you make a sculpture, if you make it life-size and you put it outside, it always looks small. So, to make it life-size, you have to make it bigger than life."

Andrews owned a big dog at the time, a rottweiler. There wasn't a lot that scared Sam Mills. But dogs did. He'd rather try to tackle a speeding car than get up close and personal with a dog. Any dog.

"He was deathly afraid of them," his son Marcus says with a smile. "It didn't matter how big or small they were."

Andrews' dog was fairly big. It weighed about 110 pounds. But the sculptor described him as "a big sissy." That provided little comfort to Mills.

When Sam found out Andrews had a dog, he asked him to put it in his office while he was there and close the door. But when the sculptor went to take a phone call and opened the door, the dog came running out. Sam froze. "He wanted no part of my dog," Andrews says.

Grass Valley is a charming semi-rural community. Andrews had a neighbor who raised big cats. Their seven-year-old daughter had a black panther that the family would take for walks on a leash.

"It had claws and fangs and everything," Andrews says. "It was a regular panther. Sam hadn't gotten there yet, and I thought, *I bet Sam would love to have his picture taken with the panther.*

"I asked my friend before Sam got there if they could bring him over and we'd take some pictures. When Sam got there and I told him we were going to have a panther stop by, he didn't want to have anything to do with it. But the little girl already was on the way over. She got out of the car and she's pulling this panther around. Sam reluctantly sat down and we did get a picture. He even put his hand on it."

Mills was supposed to go out to California a second time as the statue got closer to completion. But he had another obligation and sent Melanie instead. The rottweiler and panther were probably contributing factors.

"Todd was asking me, 'Is that how his thigh looks?'" Melanie says. "I'm like, 'How am I supposed to answer that?' But he just wanted to make sure he got it right."

"His wife had the final say as far as whether it looked like Sam or not," Andrews said. "She patted the statue on the butt and said, 'Yep, that looks just like him.'"

At the base of the statue, Andrews inscribed: "Sam Mills, Leader and Gentleman."

Sam was just 39 years old when the statue was completed. Marcus was 15. Still too young to fully comprehend what it meant to have an NFL team erect a statue to honor his father.

"As a young boy, you don't realize the importance or the significance of something like that," he says. "But my dad understood it. I remember him talking about it. And then I remember people coming up and talking about how big of an honor it was. I mean, not many people get a statue when they're still alive, and even fewer when they're still young."

They unveiled Sam's statue on a Saturday in late September that year, then retired his jersey number 51 the following day at halftime of a game against the Green Bay Packers. His number remains the only one retired by the franchise in its 30-year history.

"I think it's a great statue," Marcus says. "There are a lot of bad statues out there. But not this one. It's really cool to take my kids out there and just see it."

Todd Andrews still remembers a 2005 game he attended in Charlotte. The Panthers were playing the Saints, the other NFL team Sam had played for. Sam had died a few months earlier.

The Saints won the game 23–20 on a 47-yard John Carney field goal with three seconds left. After it was over, some Saints fans stopped by Sam's statue and put some Mardi Gras beads around his neck.

A few Panthers fans, who either didn't realize Mills had once played for the Saints or thought Saints fans were trying to desecrate the statue, took offense to the beads and started pulling them off. Andrews saw what was happening, ran over, and intervened.

"I said, 'Hey, I'm the sculptor and those people are paying tribute to Sam,'" he says. "'They're not rubbing it in your face because they won. They love the guy just as much as you did.'"

Two years earlier, when the Panthers made the Super Bowl, Andrews flew to Houston for the game against the New England Patriots. Mills had signed one of his jerseys and sent it to the sculptor shortly after he finished the statue. Andrews wore it to the game.

"They put me right over the area where the Panthers ran out," he says. "I stood up and was cheering and hooting and hollering. A bunch of guys turned around and saluted me because I was wearing Sam's jersey. It was so cool. The hair was standing up on the back of my neck."

Two decades after his death, the statue continues to be a popular visiting spot for fans on gameday. It has helped keep Sam's legacy with the franchise very much alive.

"You go to a game and watch how many people are having their picture taken with the statue, it's amazing," Charlie Dayton says. "And they're not all older people who watched Sam play. There are fathers with their kids.

"At the end of my career with the Panthers, when I wasn't still in PR and I had a little more time on game days, I would walk around and look at things. I was always struck by that. Just how many people were still drawn to Sam's statue.

"It's stunning how relevant he still is nearly 30 years after he played his last game. Most players who are gone for that long, unless you're Joe Montana or somebody like that, you fade into the background. Sam never faded. And it's as much because of his character as it is because of football."

28

Sam didn't have to talk to me. I wasn't even on the same side of the ball. He didn't owe me anything. He didn't have to take an interest in me. But he went out of his way to make sure I was noticed.

—Former Panthers wide receiver Steve Smith

SAM MILLS' MOVE from player to coach was as seamless as Dom Capers and Vic Fangio expected it to be. Mills coached the very same way he led as a player on the field—with a quiet, analytical approach. He seldom yelled or berated players. Instead, he taught them. He encouraged them. And he made them better.

Mills joined Capers' staff in 1998 as a defensive assistant, helping Kevin Steele and Bill Davis coach the linebackers. Although, as Steele points out, when it came to linebackers, Mills wasn't anybody's assistant.

Bill Polian had done a marvelous job building the Panthers for quick success. With veteran players like Mills and Kevin Greene and others, they made it to the NFC Championship Game in just their second year of existence. Unfortunately, that get-good-fast approach wasn't conducive to sustainability. Many of the veterans who helped the Panthers make it to the conference title game soon grew old, and Carolina flamed out quickly.

Polian left after the '97 season to become president and general manager of the Indianapolis Colts. After going 7–9 in Mills' final year as a player in '97, the Panthers plummeted to 4–12 in '98. As happens when a team goes south, there are casualties. Jerry Richardson reluctantly fired Capers after the '98 season and replaced him with former San Francisco 49ers head coach George Seifert.

Seifert had succeeded Bill Walsh as the head coach in San Francisco in 1989, where he had been enormously successful. He spent nine seasons as the team's head coach. They made the playoffs eight times and won two Super Bowl titles. The Niners averaged 12-plus wins a season under Seifert.

But Seifert resigned after the '96 season when team president Carmen Policy declined to offer him a contract extension following two straight divisional-round playoff losses. Policy wanted to replace Seifert with offensive-minded Steve Mariucci, who was the head coach at Cal at the time.

Capers wound up in Jacksonville as the Jaguars' defensive coordinator. Vic Fangio was reunited with Jim Mora in Indianapolis as the Colts' new defensive coordinator. Mills could've gone to Indy with Fangio and Mora but opted to stay with the Panthers even though he didn't know Seifert very well. Charlotte had become home, and his family loved it there.

He was the only coach on Capers' staff who would be retained by Seifert. Richardson had made it clear to Seifert when he hired him that keeping Sam was nonnegotiable, which wasn't a problem for Seifert. He liked and respected Mills and promoted him to linebackers coach.

The Panthers climbed back to .500 in Seifert's first year in Charlotte, winning six of their last nine games. But that was as good as it got. They finished 7–9 the next year and then crashed and burned in '01, winning just one game. Seifert was fired at the end of that disastrous 1–15 campaign and was replaced by New York Giants defensive coordinator John Fox.

The NFL added another expansion team in 2002, the Houston Texans. Capers was hired as the Texans' first head coach. Fangio joined him as the team's defensive coordinator. Capers offered Sam a job on his staff. But as much as Sam loved the idea of being reunited with Fangio and Capers, he decided to stay in Charlotte.

"Sam liked living there," Capers says. "He was well-respected. He and his family had made a home in Charlotte. I completely understood when he said he didn't want to leave."

Fox retained eight assistants from Seifert's staff, which was an unusually large number for a new coach. Mills was one of them.

"When I got hired, I heard nothing but good things about Sam," Fox says. "He had a great knowledge of the game. He was an easy guy for me to have on our defensive staff. He had a great rapport with the players and they responded to him. That's a big part of being a successful coach."

A perfect example of that was Dan Morgan. The Panthers selected Morgan, a linebacker out of the University of Miami, with the 11th overall pick in the '01 draft. Morgan was the same age as Sam's oldest son. He had grown up in the Philly area and played Pop Warner ball there. Morgan's family moved to Coral Springs, Florida, after his freshman year in high school.

"When I got drafted, it really was the first time I had been away from home," says Morgan. "When I played at Miami, my family lived only about 40–45 minutes away. So, when I got drafted, it really was my first time being on my own.

"Sam kind of took notice of that and took me under his wing. He became a father figure in a way. We'd go eat together. We'd go bowling. We developed a really, really close relationship. I'll always be grateful for his guidance and leadership when I first got there."

Bowling was one of Mills' favorite non-football activities. He learned how to bowl while growing up in New Jersey. He and Morgan took it seriously. They both had their own shoes and balls.

"It would be just us," Morgan says. "We were serious bowlers. It was competitive, but we always had a good time. We'd talk life, talk football. Those are times that I will always cherish."

Mills and Morgan had disparate football backgrounds. Mills was an undersized linebacker who had to prove he belonged at every level he played. Morgan was a prototypical middle linebacker—6'2" and 245 pounds—with 4.5 speed. He got a scholarship to a Division I football factory. He was one of the first players taken in the NFL draft.

"We both respected each other right from the start," Morgan said. "I was a first-round pick, but he knew from my background that I was blue-collar, hardworking. Nothing was ever handed to me, just like nothing was ever handed to him.

"The only difference between us was that I was taller than he was and faster than he was. But aside from our physical makeup, we were very similar type guys and players. We both loved football. We both were passionate about the game. We both worked our butts off to get where we were. We developed a strong bond. Sam had that passion for the game. He brought it to coaching. He was just so dedicated to the game."

With Mills' help, Morgan developed into one of the league's top middle linebackers and helped quickly transform the Panthers' defense from one of the worst in the NFL into one of the best. In Morgan's second year in 2002, the Panthers finished second in total defense and fifth in points allowed.

The thing that players like Morgan liked most about Mills was he didn't overcoach. A lot of coaches have a tendency to correct every little thing players do out on the field. Sam would allow players to play "loose" and make mistakes out on the field. Then he would make the corrections later when he was watching the practice film with them.

"I always appreciated that about him," says Morgan. "He wasn't a yeller or screamer. But you knew he demanded the best out of you. If you dogged it or weren't hustling to the ball and kept making the same mistake, he would eventually call you out."

Ken Flajole joined John Fox's staff in Carolina as a defensive quality-control coach after the '02 season. Flajole was impressed by

Mills' ability to relate to and teach players at both ends of the talent spectrum—high-round picks like Morgan as well as low-round picks and undrafted free agents.

"When I went there, I had been around some other ex-professional players who had gone into coaching," Flajole said. "Some of them were good. Some of them were not so good. The thing that impressed me about Sam, he wasn't the biggest guy in the world. He played a position that is historically very physical. Here was a guy who had to rely on great technique and had to rely on the mental part of the game [to succeed].

"Well, his ability to impart that to his players was the thing that struck me the most when I worked with him. Here was a guy that was a good pro player that didn't tell guys just do it [this way] because that's the way I did it. He broke it down and he helped the guy who maybe wasn't a first-round draft choice get better. That was his calling card."

Morgan would play seven seasons for the Panthers before injuries cut his playing career short. He went to the Pro Bowl in 2004.

Two rounds after they selected Dan Morgan in the 2001 draft, the Panthers took an undersized wide receiver out of Utah named Steve Smith. As a rookie with the Panthers, the 5'9" Smith was a special teams standout, returning three kicks for touchdowns. But he had trouble getting on the field as a receiver. He had just 10 catches his first season.

Richard Williamson, the Panthers' receivers coach, was hard on Smith. The first week of training camp, the rookie didn't get a single rep at wide receiver. Smith was shattered. He was a third-round pick and didn't get on the field for even one play. After one of the practices that first week, a frustrated Smith broke down and cried. Mills coached the Panthers' linebackers, not the wide receivers. But he saw how emotional Smith was and went over and consoled him.

"Just keep working," Mills said.

Throughout the season, even though he wasn't Smith's position coach, Mills would saddle up to Smith on the practice field and offer him encouragement.

"I don't know what their problem is, but you keep showing up these guys," Mills would tell him. "Because you may not play a lot this year, but you're showing our DBs what kind of receiver you can be."

The encouragement from Mills was invaluable, because he wasn't getting any from Williamson.

"God rest his soul, I loved Richard," Smith said. "But he was very hard on me. He was always criticizing and critiquing me. He never would just say, 'Hey, good job.' It always was, 'Hey, you can do better than that.' Maybe that approach works with some players. It didn't work with me. I never felt I was gaining anywhere. I felt like I was always working, but I wasn't seeing any tangible results that allowed me to play offense except on the scout teams.

"But Sam was consistent. Even though he wasn't my position coach, even though he didn't even coach on my side of the ball, he gave me compliments and encouragement that kept me going when he could sense I was down."

Smith had 54 receptions in his second season and had a breakout year in his third year with 88 catches, 1,100 yards, and seven touchdowns. He credits Mills with keeping him focused and positive.

"Sam just put something in me when I was a young man that I needed," Smith says. "Because I was struggling emotionally. You're building something, you're chopping wood, and somebody keeps coming by and saying, 'Nope, not good enough.'

"Sam was that constant voice in my ear that said *keep going.*"

Mills had empathy for players like Smith, even if they happened to play on the other side of the ball. He had been in their shoes. He knew what it was like to play your ass off only to be dismissed by coaches because of your size.

"Sam had been through the journey," Smith says. "He had been cut so many times and had to prove himself in a new league before he ever got a chance to play in the NFL. Because of what he had gone through, he carried that on his sleeve. He carried that journey on his sleeve and coached his players with that journey on his mind.

"He helped me get where I am today."

29

I was in Houston when he got diagnosed with cancer. He called me. We were close and talked a lot, so him calling me wasn't anything unusual. I said, 'Hey, what's up, Sam?' He said, 'I got diagnosed with terminal cancer today. They're giving me three months to live.'

—Vic Fangio

THE PANTHERS MISSED the playoffs for the sixth straight year in 2002, finishing 7–9 in John Fox's first season as head coach. But they won four of their last five and entered the '03 season with a talented young roster. They were feeling pretty good about themselves.

Then, two days after their first preseason game against Washington, one of their best defensive players, linebacker Mark Fields, was hospitalized when a cut on his thumb hadn't healed. It became infected, but the infection turned out to be the least of Fields' problems. Tests revealed that he had Hodgkin's lymphoma, which is a form of cancer that strikes the lymph nodes and other organs that are part of the body's immune system.

Even in 2003, Hodgkin's wasn't a death sentence. The survival rate was relatively high, a little north of 80 percent (it's closer to 90 percent today). But it still was a huge blow to both the player and the organization. Fields, who led the team in tackles and had a franchise-record seven forced fumbles and 7½ sacks in '02, would miss the entire '03 season as he underwent treatment.

The Panthers barely had an opportunity to digest the news of Fields' cancer diagnosis when, a little more than a week later, Mills got sick.

Not sick exactly, but he was lacking energy, which was something Sam never lacked. A few days after that, the man who never, ever missed a workout, found himself too tired to go out for a run or hit the weight room.

He had a burrito for lunch and it didn't go down well. Fox told him to go home and rest. But he woke up in the middle of the night and was vomiting violently. He thought he might have food poisoning. The next day, still not feeling well, he went to the doctor and they ran some tests.

Jim Skipper was Mills' closest friend on the Panthers' coaching staff. They had known each other for 20 years, going back to their days with the Stars. Skipper had been the running backs coach on Jim Mora's staff in Philly when Mills played there. He also coached the Saints' running backs during Sam's nine seasons in New Orleans. They reunited in Carolina in 2002 when John Fox hired Skipper to be his running backs coach.

Skipper suspected something was wrong when Mills showed up late two mornings in a row for the coaches' staff meeting. "Sam was late, and that ain't Sam; that ain't Sam at all," Skipper said. "I was close to going up to him and saying, 'Hey, man. What's going on?' Because I knew something was out of whack. Then, on the third day, coach Fox told us what was going on.

"Sam had cancer."

They found it in Mills' small intestine. Unlike Mark Fields' Hodgkin's lymphoma, the survival rate for Sam's type of cancer wasn't good. Only about 20 percent in 2003. And that's if it was caught early on. Sam's wasn't. It was already pretty far along. The doctors sat him down and gave him the devastating news: The cancer was inoperable. He probably only had three or four months to live.

The news hit Mills like a vicious blindside block. Death wasn't something Mills had spent a lot of time dwelling on. Professional athletes, particularly pro football players, tend to have a sense of invulnerability. Mills had just turned 44 two months earlier. Five years after his retirement, he was still in playing shape. He ran every day. He worked out regularly. He had lived a healthy life. He didn't drink. He didn't smoke. He never did drugs.

It's difficult to pin down exactly how someone gets cancer. It can be caused by a number of different factors, including genetic (family history), lifestyle (tobacco use, obesity, poor diet and nutrition), and environmental (exposure to carcinogenic chemicals or materials).

Seaview Manor, the government housing project in Long Branch where Mills grew up, bordered a synthetic coal gasification plant that was operated by New Jersey Natural Gas. Coal gasification involves converting coal into a fuel gas called syngas. Syngas can be used for electricity generation or converted into fuels such as gasoline, diesel, and methanol.

The coal gasification process at the Long Branch plant generated a waste called coal tar and coal tar contaminants like PAHs (polycyclic aromatic hydrocarbons) and metals like arsenic and lead.

Coal tar is used medically for skin conditions like psoriasis and dandruff, as well as in industrial sealants. But it's also a known human carcinogen containing chemicals like benzene. There's an increased cancer risk from prolonged exposure. It is believed that many of the contaminants from the plant got into Troutman's Creek, a tributary of the Shrewsbury River, which flowed through the plant site and along Seaview Manor and two other nearby low-income housing projects.

A report released by the Department of Health and Human Services in 2004, less than a year after Mills' cancer diagnosis, determined that the manufacturing process at the New Jersey Natural Gas plant next to Seaview Manor emitted multiple contaminants into the air and soil, including benzene, ethylbenzene, xylene, vinyl chloride, cadmium, mercury, and lead.

The plant, or at least the coal gasification process, was phased out in the early '60s and converted into a liquid propane gas facility. But the contamination from the process remained in the soil, sediment, and groundwater for decades. The contamination wasn't discovered until the '80s, leading to extensive investigations and cleanup efforts by the NJNG. They implemented extensive soil excavation treatment and capping, with the New Jersey Department of Environmental Protection overseeing it.

Seaview Manor would finally be torn down not long after the '04 HHS report. A decade later, with the soil and nearby creek deemed safe by the DEP, the Long Branch Housing Authority would build new low-income housing on the site.

The gasification plant has been blamed for high cancer rates and a plethora of other serious illnesses and birth defects among residents of Seaview Manor and the other housing projects. A class-action lawsuit was filed against NJNG, which the company eventually settled.

"From those projects, if I had a minute to count all of the people we lost to cancer—neighbors and people that lived in that community—it was pretty crazy," Leon Mills said. "And a lot of it was linked to the contamination from the plant."

A 2013 article in *Jersey Voices Magazine* indicated that many people in the area were still having health problems caused by the pollution that had been buried under the ground there for years.

"After Sam got cancer, we had the conversation about whether growing up where he grew up might've been the reason [he got sick]," his agent, Brett Senior, says. "He said he would go out and play in the dirt and on the concrete at Seaview Manor.

"His parents were just trying to raise their kids and survive. All he would say about it was that it was God's decision. But you have to wonder."

Sam didn't question his cancer diagnosis. The results were the results. But he wasn't about to accept the prognosis of three or four months to live.

He had spent his entire life beating the odds. He was determined to prove the doctors wrong just as he had all of the football people who said he was too small to play in the NFL. He wasn't going to just sit around and wait to die.

"When you have a crisis like that, you just regroup," Mills said after receiving the diagnosis. "You say, 'Well, it's not time to feel bad [for yourself]. It is what it is and now I need to regroup and say, "What's next?"' I don't know if it took me more than 24 hours to regroup."

Mills' diagnosis on top of the news about Fields left the Panthers organization devastated.

"We all were just stunned, particularly with it coming on the heels of Mark's diagnosis," Dan Morgan says.

The Panthers issued a very short news release about Mills' cancer the day of their last preseason game against the Steelers. Unsurprisingly, there was no mention that the doctors were giving him only three months to live. A meaningless preseason game became even more meaningless.

Sam III was up at their home in New Jersey when his father was diagnosed. Mel called him with the news. Sam asked how bad it was.

"Bad," she said.

Her eldest son immediately flew home.

"I think I realized the severity of it when I got home and Mr. Richardson came to the house," Sam III said. "He talked to my father and I'm thinking, if he's here, this must be pretty bad."

Richardson assured Mills that he needn't worry about anything. *Anything.* He told him that the Panthers organization would support him in every way. If he wanted to keep coaching while he was getting chemotherapy, they would be on board with that and do everything to accommodate him. If he needed to fly someplace to see other doctors or get additional treatment, Richardson put his private plane at Sam's disposal.

Marcus Mills was a junior at Penn State at the time. His father delivered the news to him himself.

"It wasn't a long call," Marcus recalls. "He pretty much got to the point. He laid it out there. Said the doctor was giving him three months. He said, 'I'm going to fight this thing. Just keep on doing what you're doing. I'm going to figure out a plan.'

"Having kids of my own now, I can't imagine making that phone call to them [telling them he's dying]. I could tell it was difficult for him. But it was clear he had a game plan and was going to fight it. When you think of your dad, you don't think of them being vulnerable like that, especially my dad, who always seemed bigger than life.

"I got off that call sad, but with confidence that if he says he's going to beat it, then he's going to beat it. He's not going to lie down and give up. I mean, I definitely expected him to do better than what the doctor was giving him."

30

He just loved being around the team and the players and the sport. That's probably why he lived so long after the diagnosis. Just his will to be alive. His will to impact people.

—Panthers linebacker Dan Morgan

Sam Mills had no intention of going home, curling up into a ball, and waiting to die. He had no intention of surrendering to the cancer. If it was going to take him, he wouldn't make it easy. *Three months? Screw that.*

With Jerry Richardson's blessing, Sam went to John Fox and told him he wanted to continue to coach for as long as possible. The chemotherapy treatments obviously would require some scheduling adjustments. But if Fox and his defensive coordinator, Mike Trgovac, were okay with it, he wanted to do it.

During the 16 years he spent as an NFL head coach, Fox liked to hire quality-control coaches who were overqualified. That way, if something unexpected happened on his staff, he'd have capable people who could step in and help out.

One of those overqualified people was Flajole, whom Fox had hired a few months before Mills' cancer diagnosis. Flajole had spent the previous five years with the Seattle Seahawks, coaching the team's linebackers and defensive backs after spending 20 years coaching the same positions at the major college level.

But after the Seahawks missed the playoffs for the third straight year in '02, head coach Mike Holmgren fired several of his assistants, including Flajole. Fox quickly snatched him up.

Having Flajole on his staff turned out to be a blessing for Fox after Mills got sick. Flajole was able to help Mills with the linebackers and fill in when Sam was getting his chemo treatments or recovering from them.

Anyone who has ever undergone chemotherapy or been around someone who did knows what the poison does to your body as it tries to kill the cancer. It saps your strength, takes away your appetite, makes you nauseous. Walking to the bathroom turns into a nearly insurmountable journey. All you want to do is sleep.

Sam experienced all of that. But he soldiered on, fighting through it.

"That was his whole makeup," Jim Skipper says. "You talk about a guy being positive. There was no negativity in him. Zero. Not one ounce. He never asked, *Why me?* I was there with him until the end, coaching alongside him. And the only time it became obvious how sick he was was right at the end when he was getting ready to pass."

Despite the chemotherapy treatments, Mills never missed games and didn't even miss many practices during the '03 season. His brave battle inspired the Panthers players.

"He was impressive," Flajole says. "Because the stuff he was taking was some toxic stuff. For Sam to power through it and still be around [the team] was amazing. It was a great inspiration for our players. If they thought they were having a tough day at practice, all they needed to do was look at what Sam was dealing with."

Morgan accompanied Mills to his chemo treatments a few times, keeping him company while they injected the poison into his body.

"It was during the season, so we would mostly talk football," Morgan said. "I just wanted to be there for him and help him take his mind off what he was going through."

When Mills would get finished with his chemo, he would go back to the Panthers' facility and go out to practice. He was sick and exhausted but didn't let the players see it.

Mills would lift weights before every practice. He always would run out onto the field from the locker room. He never wanted to talk about what he was going through.

"He'd say, 'Hey, it is what it is. You can either give up or live your life and press on,'" Morgan says. "That's what he did. He was courageous until the moment he died."

Jerry Simmons, who was the Panthers' strength and conditioning coach from 1999 through 2010, would see Mills running the stadium steps on Sunday mornings before games. *While he was getting chemo!*

Unless you were there to notice the little things, you never would have known Mills was dying. He worked hard to keep his weight up and maintain his muscle definition. It was important to him that no one start mourning him while he was still alive.

He employed the same super-human work ethic dealing with the cancer as he had when he was playing. He tried to keep the missed coaching assignments to a minimum. He put a cot in his office so that if he got tired from the chemo, he could take a short nap without needing to go home.

"It doesn't compute that he could find the type of strength to do that and still be so positive about everybody else; not let any negativity bleed into everyone else's world," says his son Marcus. "But that's what he wanted to do. My dad never really had that [self-pity] gene. I think we all feel sorry for ourselves. That moment where you ask yourself, *Why me?* And I imagine he did at some point. But we never saw it.

"He wouldn't let us see it."

31

It was an emotional speech and it stuck. He was going through chemo. He was dying. He understood the reality of his situation. He just told the guys, 'Hey, look. No matter what the situation is, you've got to keep looking forward. You've got to keep fighting. You've got to keep on pounding.'

—Jim Skipper

NO ONE, AND I mean no one, had *NFC-champion Carolina Panthers* on their bingo card heading into the '03 season. Google the preseason Las Vegas odds for that year and you'll find that just four other NFL teams were given a slimmer chance of making it to the Super Bowl than the Panthers.

The Panthers were just two years removed from 1–15. They had improved their win total by six games in '02, which clearly was a promising sign. But heading into the '03 season, they didn't even know who their starting quarterback was going to be, and neither of the options—37-year-old journeyman Rodney Peete and inexperienced Jake Delhomme, who had spent the previous four years as the Saints' third-string quarterback—seemed all that enticing.

Sam and Mark Fields' cancer diagnoses were also weighing heavily on everyone's minds entering the season, both inside and outside the locker room.

Greg Favors, who was on his fourth team in six years, had been signed in the offseason to provide depth at linebacker behind Fields,

Dan Morgan, and second-year man Will Witherspoon. But Fields' illness changed everything, and Favors found himself as the next man up at strongside linebacker. He would start 12 games in '03 and do a remarkable job filling in for Fields on a defense that finished a very respectable 10th in points allowed and 11th against the run.

Fox settled on Delhomme as his starting quarterback. Delhomme was competent, throwing three more touchdown passes (19) than interceptions (16). But the Panthers' '03 offense under Dan Henning was more the old-school ground-and-pound than quarterback-driven.

They had signed former Washington Redskins running back Stephen Davis in the offseason. The 6'2", 230-pound Davis, who had averaged 1,244 rushing yards and 10 touchdowns the previous four seasons with Washington, would rush for a career-high 1,444 yards for the Panthers in '03.

Still, the Panthers were hardly an offensive juggernaut. They finished 15th in scoring. They managed to score just 21 more points than their opponents (325–304). They put up more than 24 points in a game just twice in the entire regular season—once in a 27–24 Week 10 win over Tampa Bay, and then again in a 37–24 win over the 4–12 New York Giants in their final regular-season game.

The Panthers won their first five games and eight of their first 10, including an unlikely 12–9 overtime win over the Bucs in Week 2. The Bucs scored with no time left in regulation to tie the game and needed only the extra point to win. But Panthers defensive tackle Kris Jenkins blocked Martin Grammatica's PAT to force overtime. Carolina won the game on a 47-yard field goal by John Kasay.

They would finish 11–5 and win their first division title since that magical '96 season. Most of those 11 wins were by very thin margins. Ten of the 11 were by seven points or less, and *seven* were by three points or less.

"Looking back, I do think that what happened to Sam and Mark was a big reason we were so centered that year," says John Fox. "What they were going through allowed us to keep things in perspective. It was, *Oh, you think you've got it bad? Look at them.* We could always bring it back to the two of them."

While his team gutted out wins, Mills relentlessly battled his cancer. He endured the chemo treatments and somehow found the strength to continue to coach. The doctors' three- to four-month survival prognosis came and went, and Sam was still standing strong.

"Sam already was held in high regard in that city long before he got sick," says Ken Flajole. "But when people saw how he fought and how he battled and the character that he showed and the spirit that he showed after he was diagnosed, it just emboldened the spirit of the team. Our players embraced it and embraced him. They loved him for the kind of guy he was."

Sam's oldest son, Sam III, joined Jackie Miles' equipment staff that season, which gave him the chance to spend more time with his father as he battled the cancer. He and his dad would ride to work together each morning. He would take his father to chemo treatments and sit and talk with him.

"I didn't know how much time my dad had left, but it meant a lot to be there with him," he says.

Carolina's 11–5 record was the third best in the NFC, which earned them a first-round home playoff game against the 10–6 Cowboys. The Cowboys had beaten the Panthers in Dallas in mid-November, 24–20.

The Carolina offense had struggled mightily in that game, with Delhomme completing just nine of 24 passes. Stephen Davis had been held to 2.3 yards per carry. The Panthers had converted just one of 11 third-down opportunities.

Before the Panthers hired him as their head coach, John Fox had spent five years as the defensive coordinator for the New York Giants. His boss there, Jim Fassel, had a tradition of picking a player or coach each week to address the team after its final walk-through practice the day before the game. Fox had brought that tradition with him to Carolina.

The morning before the Cowboys rematch, Fox approached Mills and asked him if he would address the team after practice.

"It was kind of spontaneous," Fox said. "There was nothing real planned or orchestrated about it. It was one of those situations where Sam was as healthy as he'd been in a while, if that makes sense. He hadn't been around a lot [because of the cancer treatments]. The team was very excited to even see him, let alone hear him speak to them."

Fox says he had no idea what Mills was going to say.

"No clue," he says. "I just knew it would be thoughtful and from the heart. And that's exactly what it was. Sam wasn't a big rah-rah guy. But oftentimes, those end up being your best leaders because when they do speak, it's very meaningful."

In Charlotte, it will forever be known as the *Keep Pounding* speech. After practice ended that morning, the team's players, coaches, and training staff gathered in the middle of the field behind Ericsson Stadium. You could hear a pin drop as Sam spoke.

"Everybody talks about how my cancer battle has been an inspiration to you guys," Sam said to them. "But the truth is, it's been you guys who have inspired me and taught me how to keep fighting, keep pounding.

"When I got diagnosed, the doctors told me that I probably only had three or four months to live. But I refused to accept that. In life or football or whatever you do, you can roll over or you can *keep pounding.*"

Mills referenced the improbable overtime win over the Bucs when Kris Jenkins blocked the PAT with no time left to send the game into overtime. He said that game was the turning point for him personally in his cancer battle.

"No one blocks extra points; it just doesn't happen," Mills said. "But you guys believed you could and you did it.

"Just like you did that day, I'm going to keep pounding. They gave me three months. Three months and I was supposed to be dead. But I'm still here, and it's because of you guys."

Safety Mike Minter, who had played with Mills as a rookie in '97 and spent 10 seasons with the Panthers, called it a "simple speech."

"But that was Sam," he says. "The great speeches aren't great moments until later. Everybody who left the field that day knew."

"Sam's address became a big part of our success," says John Fox. "It rallied the team. It rallied the whole city. I coached for more than 40 years, and I never saw anything like it."

Dan Morgan said he was fighting back tears by the end of Sam's speech. He wasn't alone.

There are some cynics who will tell you words can't inspire a team to play better. But none of the people who would say that were there that day. Less than 24 hours after Mills addressed the team, the Panthers would go out and play their best game of the season, manhandling the Cowboys 29–10.

The game was never close. The Panthers scored on seven of their 12 possessions. Stephen Davis, who had been silenced by the Cowboys back in November, rushed for 104 yards in the win-or-go-home rematch, including a 23-yard touchdown run in the second quarter that gave the Panthers a 13–0 lead.

Delhomme also came up big, completing 18 of 29 passes for 273 yards, including a 32-yard touchdown pass to Steve Smith in the third quarter that put the game away. Smith also had a 70-yard catch that set up another score.

Sam III wasn't on the field to hear his father's unforgettable address. He was in the equipment room working at the time. He didn't even know his father had addressed the team until the players returned to the locker room.

"They told me, 'Hey, man. Your dad spoke to us,'" he says. "You could tell they were moved. I mean, during the course of the season, you hear a lot of guys speak and say things. But *Keep Pounding* touched a chord."

Keep Pounding became the team's inspirational battle cry for the '03 postseason. But it would become much, much more than that. It would become a legacy to one of the most beloved players in Panthers history.

Walk into the team's locker room or weight room today more than two decades after that speech, and you will see *Keep Pounding* signs on the walls. A year after Sam's death, Nike embroidered *Keep Pounding* inside the neck of the Panthers' game jerseys. It's been there ever since.

There is a giant *Keep Pounding* drum on the sideline at Panthers home games. Right before kickoff of every game, a special guest bangs the drum four times. Sam's wife, Melanie, has done it. So have three of his children. There is a *Keep Pounding* cancer fund. There is an annual *Keep Pounding* 5K run in Charlotte. There is a *Keep Pounding* Blood Drive and a *Keep Pounding* Kids Program. Nearly $25 million has been raised under the *Keep Pounding* banner for cancer research.

The week after their wildcard win over the Cowboys, the Panthers defeated the St. Louis Rams in overtime, 29–23, on a 69-yard touchdown pass from Delhomme to Steve Smith.

That set up a rematch with the NFC's top seed, the Eagles, in the NFC Championship Game in Philly. The Panthers had lost to the Eagles at home in November, 25–16. But they went into Philly and beat the Birds 14–3 to earn their first-ever trip to the Super Bowl. Carolina's defense had four interceptions and five sacks in the win. Dan Morgan had a team-high 13 tackles.

As Jim Skipper was leaving the field after the game, he saw Sam sitting alone on the visitor's bench at Lincoln Financial Field. Two decades earlier, they both had started their pro careers in Philadelphia with the Stars. They had become close friends. Their families were close.

"He had tears in his eyes," Skipper says. "I didn't bother him. He wanted to be alone. He needed time to reflect on whatever he was reflecting on. That touched me big-time. I'll always remember that moment. It should've been one of the happiest times of my life. We were going to the Super Bowl. But I was a little subdued in the locker room thinking about Sam."

The Super Bowl that year was in Houston. The Panthers' opponent was Bill Belichick's New England Patriots. The team flew down the Monday before the game, but Mills had a chemo treatment on Tuesday and was going to fly down separately later in the week.

The chemo treatment sapped Sam's strength worse than usual. He had waited his whole life to get to the Super Bowl. And he could barely walk to the bathroom. He called Brett Senior.

"I can't believe it," he told him in a soft, raspy voice. "This is something I always dreamed about. Getting to the Super Bowl. And I don't have the energy to get up and walk right now."

Senior said the two of them prayed together over the phone for a few minutes. Before hanging up, Mills said, "Brett, I'm going to be there."

Somehow, someway, Mills made it to Houston. At 6 a.m. on the morning of the Super Bowl, Senior's phone rang.

It was Mills.

"I'm going out for a run," Mills told his agent. "I feel great."

"You do? Really?" Senior said in disbelief. "That's terrific."

"Now, I don't know if he actually felt great," Senior says now. "But he did go out for a two-mile run."

That night, Mills was on the sideline coaching against Tom Brady and the Patriots in Super Bowl XXXVIII. Trailing by seven in the fourth quarter, the Panthers drove 80 yards on seven plays to tie the game with 1:08 left on a 12-yard pass from Delhomme to Ricky Proehl. But John Kasay's ensuing kickoff went out of bounds, giving Brady the ball on his own 40-yard line. He drove the Patriots close enough for Adam Vinatieri to win the game with a 41-yard field goal, 32–29.

To this day, the players and coaches on that Panthers team are convinced that Mills' inspirational *Keep Pounding* address before the Dallas game was what propelled them to the Super Bowl.

"Did Sam's speech give us a little more juice in that playoff run?" Ken Flajole says. "No doubt about it. You like to think that when you finally get into the tournament, you should have enough juice.

"But I think the guys had a little something extra. Because they weren't only playing for themselves, and their families, and the organization. I think they felt they were playing for Sam.

"They wanted to win for Sam."

32

Sam called me two days before he passed away just to tell me how much he loved me, how much he appreciated me. But what did I do outside of being a friend? Having known Sam made me a better person. It made me a better father. I live every day knowing that spiritually, Sam is alive in me.

—Antonio Gibson

SAM MILLS WAS supposed to be dead by Thanksgiving. But he said God wasn't finished with him yet, and he would get to spend two more Christmases with his family and make one of the most inspirational speeches in NFL history, and coach in a Super Bowl.

If the cancer was going to kill him, Sam was going to go down fighting. He was going to keep pounding until the very end.

"That's the only way you have a chance," he said. "To keep on pounding."

Sam continued the chemo torture, spending two days every other week at the Blumenthal Cancer Center in Charlotte receiving treatment. At one point, Jerry Richardson lent him his plane so he could fly to Ohio and get looked at by the oncologists at the nationally renowned Cleveland Clinic. But they had no miracle cure to offer.

He continued to coach but wasn't around nearly as much during the 2004 season as he had been the year before. The Panthers kept pounding, but it wasn't the same.

The offense lost its top two weapons right out of the gate. Steve

Smith broke his leg in the '04 season opener against Green Bay. Stephen Davis, their 1,400-yard running back, injured his knee in the second game against Kansas City and didn't play again that season. The Panthers would finish 28th in rushing.

They would lose seven of their first eight games in '04 and finish 7–9.

By mid-October, the cancer had spread to Sam's stomach and liver. But you wouldn't have known it to look at him. He looked like he could still go out there on Sunday and rack up a dozen tackles. Sam knew the cancer was gaining on him but somehow managed to remain upbeat.

He was going to savor every moment he had left.

Being able to continue to coach and be around the players helped take his mind off what he was going through. He was able to focus on something else besides the fact that he was dying. He said a good deal of the time, he didn't "feel like I even have an illness." He said the times he was reminded of it were when he was sitting in the chair at the cancer center with an IV in his arm.

"Those are the days when you feel it," he said. "It drains you. Drains you every which way. You're just tired. All of your senses are affected. You don't really care to see much light or hear any noises. You can't talk very much. You just want to rest. But that's part of it. If that's what I need to do to keep on living, then that's what I've got to do."

"I feel so blessed to have been able to do what I've done and to have come as far as I've come," he said.

The man was handed a death sentence and he was talking about being blessed. That, in a nutshell, was the essence of Sam Mills.

"There's a reason for this," he said at the time. "You can't always figure it out, but there's a reason. I really believe that a part of what I need to do and am supposed to do is help other people who are going through this fight. Letting them know they aren't alone."

In January 2005, Sam made his last trip to Disney World with Melanie and their youngest daughter, Sierra, who had just turned six. They were joined by Brett Maxie and his wife and two daughters.

Mills told Maxie he was excited because he had read about a new cancer treatment out in Arizona. He was planning to fly out there.

"Max, I'm going to beat this," Sam said. "I know I am. I'm going to beat this thing."

"That was how he was," says Maxie. "He was so competitive. Nothing could really rattle him. He always had the mindset that failure was not an option.

"He was one of those dudes, man, that was just relentless. Because he was always behind the eight ball from birth. Not being very big. Playing a sport that is fit for giants, for lack of a better word. But he didn't care about that. He went down fighting. To the end, he remained optimistic."

As the cancer took hold and his body began to betray him, Mills finally had to give up coaching after the 2004 season. Flajole would take over as the team's linebackers coach, which had essentially been the case for much of the previous season. Sam would still drop by the Panthers' offices and locker room occasionally when he was up to it.

Even as he continued to explore other treatments, Mills began planning for the end. He compiled a long list of all the people he wanted to say goodbye to. He planned his funeral service in New Jersey and a memorial service in Charlotte.

He chose the speakers and the scripture he wanted to be read. He selected the flowers and the food and even designed memorial cards to hand out to mourners. He wanted the card to look like a football trading card. But instead of his career stats on the back of it, he put some of his favorite Bible verses.

Sam asked his former Montclair teammate Terrence Porter, who now was a Baptist minister in Red Bank, New Jersey, to officiate his funeral service.

By February, Sam's family could see the physical deterioration that the cancer was causing to his body. He was starting to lose weight. He was gaunt. He was getting weaker, which was even more noticeable in Sam, who wasn't a man who had ever looked weak or vulnerable.

"You could tell the end was near," Marcus said. "He knew it as well."

Yet, in late March, Sam still somehow summoned the strength to fly to Arizona for the experimental treatment that he had read about. The doctors in Charlotte had told him they couldn't keep zapping him with chemo because his body was no longer able to handle it.

Before flying out to Arizona, Sam stopped by the Panthers' training facility to talk to Jackie Miles. "He was trying to reassure me that he was going to be okay," says Miles. "Then he gave me a big hug."

"I'll see you in a couple of days," Mills said.

About an hour after Sam left, the Panthers' defensive coordinator, Mike Trgovac, came into the training room and asked Miles if he had heard about Sam.

"Well, yeah," Miles said. "He was just here. He's going out to Arizona for a treatment."

"Jackie," Trgovac said, "he's going out there to die. This is like some voodoo, last-ditch medicine."

It was right at that moment that Miles realized his longtime friend didn't have long to live.

The treatment in Arizona wasn't voodoo. It was some sort of holistic thing, which Sam III found more than a little ironic since his father's entire approach to life had been holistic. "I hate chicken because of him," he says with a laugh. "My mom would make baked chicken for him all the time."

Shortly after arriving in Arizona, Mills called Sammie and asked him to send his golf clubs out, which the son took as a sign that maybe his father was feeling a little better.

Jim Skipper had a house in the Phoenix area and was out there for a few days of R&R at the same time Sam was getting his cancer treatment. Skipper was headed out to play a round of golf when Mills called him and asked if he could join.

They got to the course and started their round. On the seventh hole, Sam smacked a long 280-yard drive. Skipper couldn't believe it, given Sam's condition.

"Sammie, there ain't nothing wrong with you," he said.

But a hole or two later, Mills started feeling ill and they had to leave.

The next day, Mills checked himself into a Phoenix hospital. Sammie flew out there on Jerry Richardson's jet to bring his dad home for what would be his final days.

Sam Mills got in all of his goodbyes before he passed. About six weeks before his death, he asked Bruce Speight to accompany him to Florence, South Carolina, where he was receiving an award. Florence is about a two-hour drive from Charlotte, giving them a good amount of time to talk.

"Looking back, I think that was his way of really saying goodbye," Speight says. "I saw him again after that. But that was the last time we had a moment. It meant a lot."

As friends and family stopped by toward the end to see him, Mills would stop taking his pain medication when he was expecting visitors so that he would be lucid.

"It's unimaginable to me," says his son Marcus. "But I'm thankful that he spent so much time at the end being lucid and not in that zombie state that those drugs put you in so that I could talk to him and spend time with him before he passed."

Mills' valiant cancer fight and his relentless *Keep Pounding* attitude inspired everyone around him, including the medical staff who tried to keep him alive.

One day, one of Sam's doctors came into his room to tell him there wasn't much else they could do for him. Marcus said the doctor was tearing up as he was telling him. That didn't surprise him.

"When you're dealing with a patient like my dad, who was fighting with everything he had, I think the medical staff felt they had to fight just as hard," says Marcus. "They felt a weight and responsibility to try and make a miracle happen, no matter how impossible the odds were."

Sam died on April 18, 2005, a month and a half shy of his 46th birthday. They had given him three months to live. He kept pounding for 20. He saw two Christmases he wasn't supposed to see. He said goodbye to everyone he wanted to say goodbye to and passed away peacefully at home with his family by his side.

They held his memorial service in Charlotte four days after his death at University Park Baptist Church, and then his funeral service at Tower Hill Presbyterian Church in Red Bank, New Jersey, four days later.

They had initially wanted to hold the funeral service at Terrence Porter's church, Pilgrim Baptist, which also was in Red Bank. But they needed a larger venue to hold all of the people.

Hundreds of mourners traveled from all over the country—former coaches, executives, teammates, and friends—to pay their respects to Sam.

The memorial service in Charlotte was held just two days before the 2005 NFL draft. Dom Capers, who was the head coach of the Houston Texans at the time, wasn't sure he'd be able to attend. But when Mike Bunkley, the Panthers' team chaplain, called him and told him that Mills had wanted him to be one of the speakers, draft preparation suddenly wasn't all that important. Capers packed a bag and flew to Charlotte and did what Sam had asked.

"I knew I had to be there," Capers said. "Sam was a special, special man. One of a kind."

Brett Maxie, who had made the final trip to Disney World with Sam and Mel and Sierra four months earlier, was one of the other speakers at the Charlotte memorial service.

"It was one of the greatest honors of my life," Maxie says.

His former Philadelphia Stars' teammates, George Cooper and George Jamison, drove nine hours from Michigan to attend his funeral service in New Jersey. Mills had been the best man at Cooper's wedding 21 years earlier. He read a Bible verse at the service that Sam had picked out. It was from Ecclesiastes, Chapter 3:

To everything there is a season and a purpose under heaven. A time to live and a time to die. A time to plant and a time to pluck up that which is planted. A time to laugh and a time to mourn.

Antonio Gibson and his family drove from their home in New Orleans to the memorial service in Charlotte, then drove up to New Jersey for the funeral service. He spoke at the service in Red Bank.

"I remember saying at the service that Sam was the greatest person I had ever met," says Gibson. "And I let them know that there were a lot of people in that audience, from Carl Peterson to Jim Mora to Dom Capers, who I had an incredible amount of respect for. So many administrators and coaches and teammates that I've met in my life that I can say were great people.

"But the best person I ever met, hands down, was Sam Mills."

After the funeral service in Red Bank ended, an unusual thing happened. Nobody left. They all wanted to stay and talk about Sam.

"People stayed around," says Reverend Porter. "I'm used to doing these [funerals] where people are transitioning after it's over. They leave and want to get back to the rest of their lives.

"In Sam's case, that didn't happen. We were there for quite some time before they actually took Sam to Monmouth Memorial Park [where he is buried]. It was amazing. I had never seen it before and have never seen it since. People were talking and remembering and laughing and crying. This was all after the service. It was a very impactful day.

"My brother made a difference."

EPILOGUE

SAM MILLS III was on his way to work that late January morning in 2022 when his cell phone began to buzz. The caller ID said: *Pro Football Hall of Fame*. Mills knew what it was about. What he didn't know was whether the news was going to be good or bad.

For the third straight year, his father had been one of 15 finalists for the Hall of Fame. The Hall's selection committee had met a week earlier to pick the newest class of inductees. While the names wouldn't be announced for a couple more weeks at Super Bowl LVI in Los Angeles, Sam III was about to find out whether his father had at long last made it to Canton.

The Mills family had been preparing themselves for bad news. Sam had failed to survive the initial 15-to-10 reduction vote each of the previous two years he had been a finalist. There really wasn't any good reason to believe this year would be any different.

This was Sam's 20th and final year as a modern-era candidate. He was down to his last out. If he didn't get in this time, he would fall into the senior abyss with hundreds of other veteran players who had been bypassed during their two decades of modern-era eligibility.

In the previous 42 years of voting, just two players had managed to make the Hall of Fame in their final year of modern-era eligibility—defensive lineman Carl Eller in 2004 and cornerback Roger Wehrli in 2007. And both Eller and Wehrli were still alive when they were voted in.

Mills had been dead for 17 years. Out of sight, out of mind.

"Not a lot of people got a chance to know my dad and see him," his younger son Marcus says, referring to the fact that his father had spent his entire NFL career with a pair of small-market teams—the New Orleans Saints and Carolina Panthers—and never got the chance to perform on the sport's biggest stage: the Super Bowl. "It might've been easier [for him to get into the Hall of Fame] if he had lived and was still around coaching in the league and was on people's radar. But he wasn't.

"All people knew about him was the *underdog* story. But there was more to it than that. A lot more. What made him the leader of every defense he ever played on? Why were so many people willing to sacrifice everything for this man and do whatever it took for him?"

The Pro Football Hall of Fame is a very difficult club to get into. The NFL was formed in 1920 as the American Professional Football Association. During the 105 years of its existence, more than 35,000 players have played in the league. Another 2,500 or so have been head coaches, general managers, or executives. Out of that massive number, only 382 have been immortalized with bronze busts in Canton.

The Hall's 50-member selection committee is made up of veteran writers and broadcasters, current and former league executives, and Hall of Fame players, coaches, and executives. The committee is given a preliminary list of approximately 125 to 130 nominees in the late summer. By January, they whittle it down through two separate votes in October and December to 15 finalists.

From the Hall's founding in 1963 until 2020, the selection committee met in person the day before the Super Bowl in the city where the game was being played. It would spend the better part of eight hours discussing each of the modern-era candidates in depth, as well as the coach, contributor, and senior finalists, then vote by secret ballot. The Hall would announce the new class later that day at a press conference.

Since the COVID outbreak in 2020, the selection committee meeting has been held remotely on Zoom about three weeks before the Super Bowl, with the new class being announced at the *NFL Honors* television show on the Thursday before the Super Bowl.

Until 2025, the committee would hold two reduction votes to get down from 15 to five modern-era finalists. There would then be a yes/no vote on the five players, with each of them needing 80 percent (40 of 50 votes) to make the Hall of Fame.

But the Hall became concerned about leaks during the three weeks between the vote and the announcement. There were also complaints from a handful of Hall of Famers, most notably Deion Sanders, that it was getting too easy to gain entry into their elite club.

So the Hall decided to change the voting system on a trial basis in 2025 for at least two years, switching the second 10-to-five reduction vote to 10-to-seven. After the number was reduced to seven, each selector would have to submit five names from the seven survivors. The threshold remained 80 percent of the vote to make the Hall of Fame, but the new voting setup guaranteed a more divided vote and smaller classes.

The 2025 class had just three modern-era inductees, the fewest since 2007. They also took the five coach, contributor, and senior nominees and lumped them into a single group and had each of the selectors vote for three of those five, with only those who received 80 percent of the vote making it. The new voting setup played a major role in the snubbings of coaches Mike Holmgren in 2025 and Bill Belichick in 2026.

Each finalist, including the coach, contributor, and senior nominees, has a "presenter"—one or more selectors who essentially make the sales pitch for the candidate to kick off a group-wide discussion on his Hall merits. Mills' presenters were Jeff Duncan, the respected football writer for *The Advocate/Times-Picayune*, and Darin Gantt, a writer for the Carolina Panthers website who has covered the NFL for more than a quarter century. Gantt had been a selector since 2010, Duncan since 2014.

Duncan, Gantt, and other Mills advocates on the selection committee had been extremely frustrated that Mills hadn't even been able to survive the initial 15-to-10 reduction vote the previous two years.

"I'm like, *Jesus, why don't these other people see what I see?*" said Gantt.

Hall observers believe there has long been a bias by the selectors toward players who have won a Super Bowl. Football is the ultimate team sport, but the Hall of Fame is top-heavy with players from championship teams. The Green Bay Packers teams of the '60s have 12 players in Canton. The Pittsburgh Steelers teams of the '70s have 10. The '70s Cowboys teams have seven. The Miami Dolphins, who won back-to-back Super Bowl titles in 1972 and 1973, have six from those two teams in the Hall.

The one thing seemingly missing from Sam Mills' Hall of Fame resume was a championship. He won two of them in the USFL with the Philadelphia Stars, but none in the NFL, neither with the Saints nor the Panthers, though he helped turn around a hapless Saints franchise while leading one of the best linebacker units in history, and he was instrumental in Carolina getting to the NFC Championship Game in just its second year of existence.

The lack of a Super Bowl ring seemed to be the primary reason why he was still waiting to get into the Hall of Fame in year 20, while Chicago Bears middle linebacker Mike Singletary made it in in his first year of eligibility in 1998, despite the fact that the man who coached both of them—Vince Tobin—believed Mills was a better player.

After Duncan and Gantt made their compelling presentations, something finally changed. There was a long-overdue realization among the selectors that Sam Mills' long wait to get into the Hall needed to end.

For the first time, he advanced to the final 10. Then, on the second reduction vote, he made it to the final five, along with Tony Boselli, Richard Seymour, LeRoy Butler, and Bryant Young.

Sam III hit the answer button on his phone.

"Hello."

"Hi, Sam. This is Jim Porter, the president of the Pro Football Hall of Fame. It is my honor and privilege to inform you that your dad has been selected to the Pro Football Hall of Fame's class of 2022. Congratulations."

Porter said a few more congratulatory things, but Sam never really heard them. All he could think about was that his father finally had made the Hall of Fame. His eyes began to water. He looked up toward the sky and said: *You made it, Dad. You made it.* He couldn't wait to get off the phone so he could call his mother and brother and give them the news.

"People used to come up to me after they found out my father played [pro] football," Sam III says. "They'd ask where he played, and I'd tell them. They'd ask how long he played for, and I'd tell them. And they'd say, 'Wow, he must've been pretty good, huh?' And I never quite knew how to answer that question.

"Ever since I got that call, it's the easiest answer ever now. It's: *Yeah, he's in the Hall of Fame.* That explains everything. For me and my family, that was the bow put on his career. The acceptance that he had played for, had been searching for, his entire life."

The Pro Football Hall of Fame Enshrinement Week in Canton, Ohio, every summer is one of the biggest events on the NFL calendar, behind only the Super Bowl and the April draft. The events are held over five days and include the Gold Jacket dinner, where each of the new inductees is presented their Hall of Fame sport coat in front of dozens of their gold-jacketed peers. There is the Grand Parade through the streets of Canton, and a concert, and a Fan Fest with autograph sessions, as well as the annual Hall of Fame Game.

But the main event is the Saturday afternoon induction ceremony, where the new class is introduced, and their bronze busts are unveiled.

Nearly 300 of Sam's former teammates, coaches, and friends made the trip to Canton from all over the country to celebrate his Hall of Fame induction. Ed Balina and nearly 20 of Sam's Long Branch High School football teammates made the trip, most of them driving the same route Sam had 41 years earlier on his way to Kent State to attend the Cleveland Browns training camp.

Montclair had a large contingent there, including Vinny DeMarinis and Terrence Porter. Sam's former teammates and coaches from all three of the pro teams he played for—the Stars, Saints, and Panthers—packed Tom Benson Stadium. (Yes, the stadium where the induction ceremony is held and the Hall of Fame Game is played bears the name of the late Saints owner.)

For obvious reasons, the August 6, 2022, ceremony was bittersweet for the Mills family. The man who had just wanted a chance to fail had at long last had his greatness validated. But sadly, he wasn't there to enjoy it.

"It would've been great to see him with all the guys who had played before him," Sammie says. "He was such a student of the game. He knew who all those [other Hall of Famers] were, and what they had accomplished, and respected the heck out of them."

Marcus said it would've been cool to see his dad "joking and telling war stories about sacking Troy Aikman and tackling Barry Sanders."

The family picked Jim Mora to be Sam's co-presenter along with Melanie.

"It was an easy choice," Mel says.

During his 12 seasons coaching Sam, Mora did a complete 180 on him. He went from wanting to cut the guy, to wondering whether the leap from the USFL to the NFL was a bridge too far, to calling him the best player he ever coached.

"I loved that guy," Mora says. "Absolutely loved him. I'm getting emotional just talking about him. I coached him for 12 years in Philly and New Orleans, and he was the best I've ever been around."

During her acceptance speech on behalf of her late husband, Melanie talked more about Sam the person than Sam the player. She left her husband's football accomplishments to Mora.

"Sam became a legendary athlete, but he never forgot he was just a man," she said. "He treated everyone with respect and dignity.

"He would ask you about your day and he would listen because he cared. If you were working hard at anything, Sam would let you know he appreciated your hard work. He would make you feel seen.

"He led by example, and people followed."

By any measure, Sam Mills was a great player and a great leader. He left an enduring mark on the franchises he played for, and the game itself during a transformational era for the linebacker position.

He not only made his teammates and the players he later coached better players, he also made them better men, which isn't an easy thing to do.

He inspired them with the way he worked, and the way he handled adversity, and the way he lived his life. But more importantly, he left a mark on every person in his life. That legacy endures to this day on every team he played for, in every place he lived, and with the people whose lives he touched.

AFTERMATH

THE MILLS FAMILY

Juanita Bennett

Sam's mother suffered a stroke in the early '90s when he was playing for the Saints, and was wheelchair-bound for the remainder of her life. Shortly after her stroke, Sam bought her a house on the bay in Monmouth Beach and made everything in the house wheelchair-accessible. Juanita had loved to crab and fish. While her disability prevented her from doing that any longer, she still enjoyed going out to the bulkhead and watching her children and grandchildren do it. She died in July 2003 at the age of 77, just two weeks before Sam was diagnosed with cancer.

Sam Mills Sr.

Sam had a good relationship with his father, but it was very different from the one he had with his mother. Sam Sr. passed away in 2019. He was 87.

Melanie Mills

Melanie lives in Charlotte, just two doors down from her son Marcus and his wife, Briana, which gives her an opportunity to spend a lot of time with their three children, Eden, Addison, and Marcus Jr. When Sam was debating whether to sign with the Philadelphia Stars after getting cut by the Browns and Toronto Argonauts, Melanie encouraged him to do it.

Wallace Shaw

Wally was the eldest of Juanita Bennett's 12 children. He was 20 years older than Sam. He served as another father figure for Sam. It was Wally who took Sam to practices and games and rooted him on from the stands. A lifelong resident of Long Branch, Wally worked for the city much of his adult life and also moonlighted as a bartender. He died in February 2025.

Sam Mills III

Sam, who like his dad played college ball at Montclair, was an assistant coach with the Carolina Panthers for 15 years (2005–19) and with Washington for three years (2020–22). Since 2025, he has been the defensive line coach at the University of Alabama-Birmingham. "One time, when I was in high school, we were working out together," Sammie says. "As he was getting older and slower, I was getting older and faster. He had me run some routes. The first time, I think I kind of surprised him with my speed and agility. The next time, I'm thinking: *I can get you.* I put a move on him thinking I'm going to kind of shake and stutter him, sit him down and go. Well, he put his hand in my chest. I remember buckling and thinking, *Oh, that's different.* That's not something kids my age can do."

Marcus Mills

Marcus, who was a defensive back at Penn State, lives in Charlotte,

North Carolina, with his wife, Briana, and their three children. He runs a consulting business that helps companies with operational efficiency. He's also an assistant football coach at his old high school, Charlotte Latin. He spent a year as a graduate assistant at Penn State after he got out of college, and he was also an assistant at Temple for a year. "Our dad was a natural teacher, and both me and my brother got that from him," Marcus says. "History has shown that most great players make terrible coaches. But my dad was a coach first and then a player. Which is crazy since he's in the Hall of Fame as a player. But he would've been a Hall of Fame–caliber coach too, if he had lived."

Leon Mills

Sam's younger brother was one of the top high school running backs in Monmouth County. "They were hoping they were getting another Sam," Leon says. "I was a smaller version." He joined the army after graduating from Long Branch High and spent four years in the military. He later spent almost two decades working with incarcerated youths in central Jersey. Leon lives in Ocean Township, New Jersey. He has a granddaughter, Abigail. "I was stationed at Fort Campbell [Kentucky] when the USFL first started," Leon says. "Me and a friend went in on the 'buddy system.' The two of us used to always brag about Sam. There was a guy there from Georgia, and he always used to talk about Herschel Walker. Sam owned Herschel. *Owned* him. We used to have fun messing with the guy."

Caroline Bennett

Like her mother, Bennett was a private duty nurse, but eventually entered the ministry. For many years, she was the pastor of McLaughlin Pentecostal Faith Church in Long Branch. She was a community leader and served as president of the Urban Ministerium. Caroline was 17 years older than Sam, but had a big influence on his faith. She died in 2023.

LONG BRANCH HIGH SCHOOL (1973–77)

Frank Glazier

Glazier stayed at Long Branch High School just three years. He left in August 1978 to become the head coach at William Paterson College. He was there for four years (1978–81) and had a 17–22–1 record. He left coaching after that, moved to Florida, and devoted most of his time to Glazier Coaching Clinics, which he started in 1976 when he was still at Long Branch. Glazier died in January 1993 at the age of 59, but the Glazier Clinics are still going strong.

Ed Balina

Ed was a four-year starter for Frank Glazier at William Paterson College. He retired from the US Postal Service in 2025 after a long career there. He and his wife Susan have three grown children. They still live in Long Branch. He still remembers his last conversation with Sam shortly before his death. "He told me that one of his biggest regrets was that he wasn't going to be able to walk his daughter Sierra down the aisle when she got married," he says.

Bob Biasi

Bob was one of the most respected defensive coaches in New Jersey. He was Long Branch's head coach from 1991 to '94 and led the Green Wave to a 10–1 record in '93. He also served as an assistant at Long Branch, Ocean Township, and Shore Regional high schools. He was inducted into the Shore Conference Hall of Fame in 2025. "Even after Sam made it big in the NFL, he would still come back to Long Branch and visit," says Biasi. "I remember him coming to one of our awards banquets once and handing out trophies to the kids. He sat down and ate with us. He was great with the kids. The whole town loved Sam. He was such a good guy. Kindhearted and humble. But when he got out on that field, he was vicious."

Jim Simonelli

Simonelli, who taught Sam Mills "the triangle," was a longtime high school coach and administrator. At Long Branch, he served as the vice principal, principal, athletic director, and head football coach over the course of his career. He was also an adjunct professor at Monmouth University. He was involved in lifeguarding most of his adult life. Jim died in August 2025 at the age of 78. "You go to Long Branch and mention Sam, and it's a sense of pride for the whole community," Simonelli said. "You walk into the gym and his two jerseys are right there on the wall. His Carolina jersey and his Long Branch jersey."

Bill Hill

Hill and Mills became close friends in high school when Sam was playing for Long Branch and Bill was a star running back at Howell High School. Hill, who also played baseball, was drafted by the New York Mets and spent a year in their minor league system before walking on as a cornerback at Rutgers. He later played for the New Jersey Generals and the Dallas Cowboys. Since 2021, he's been the head coach at his alma mater, Howell. Bill made the 10-hour drive to Charlotte to see Sam just before he died. "When he was playing for the Saints, I got pretty sick," says Hill. "My oxygen level was real low. I'm lying in bed one day, and my wife comes in and says you've got a visitor. It was Sam. That's the kind of guy he was."

Ken Mandeville

Matawan High was the No. 1-ranked team in the state of New Jersey, and Mandeville was their star quarterback in '76 when Mills and Long Branch ended their 24-game win streak. Mandeville went to Syracuse, where he was switched to fullback. He had 1,000-plus career rushing yards and 13 TDs for the Orangemen.

Tim Fedroff

Sam Mills called the Carteret High quarterback the toughest player he ever had to tackle. That included all of the NFL players he faced over his 12-year career. Fedroff received a scholarship to the University of Maine, but his football career was cut short by an injury.

Craig Blackman

Blackman, the Sparta High School wrestler who beat Mills in the New Jersey state finals in 1977, attended Franklin & Marshall College, where he was an EIWA champ and finished fifth in the NCAA tournament in 1980. He was also a member of the US Junior Freestyle team. Blackman has been a social studies teacher at Indian River High School in Chesapeake, Virginia, and he was the wrestling coach there for several years. He followed Sam's football career closely. "What a story of resilience and determination," he says. "It's inspiring just thinking about what he had to go through. But he wouldn't quit."

Frank Maloney

Maloney, one of the many coaches who mistakenly thought Sam was too small to play for a major college program, had a 32–46 record and made just one bowl appearance in seven seasons at Syracuse. After getting fired in 1980, he left coaching and joined the Chicago Cubs organization, where he spent 29 years in their ticket office, 27 of them as the team's ticket director. He retired in 2010. He died of brain cancer in 2020 at the age of 80.

MONTCLAIR STATE (1977–81)

Fred Hill

Hill spent seven years as Montclair's head football coach (1976–82), including four seasons coaching Mills. He also coached Montclair's baseball team from 1977 through 1983. In '84, he was hired as the head baseball coach at Rutgers University, where he coached for nearly 30 years. He sent 72 players to pro ball. His 1,089 wins at Montclair and Rutgers are the 11th most in college baseball history. Hill died in 2019 at the age of 85.

Rick Giancola

After serving as an assistant on Fred Hill's staff (1976–1982), Giancola replaced Hill as Montclair's head coach in '83. He held that role for 40 years before retiring in 2022. He had a 260–143–2 career record. Montclair won 12 NJAC titles and went to the NCAA Division III playoffs nine times under Giancola. Rick says Mills was always grateful for the opportunity Montclair gave him. "We were playing a road game once in Delaware against Wesley," he says. "It was a nice day and we were doing our taping outside the locker room. Out of the corner of my eye, I see a guy by the fence. It was Sam. I can't remember who he was playing for at the time, but he had a game close by in Philly or Baltimore or Washington and stopped by to say hello. That's how he was. Another time, our intramural flag football team won the regional championship and was playing in New Orleans at the Superdome. Who do you think shows up? Sam. He says to them, 'Hi, guys. My name is Sam Mills. I was a Montclair graduate.' Everybody's jaw fell down."

Terrence Porter

Porter was an all-conference wide receiver for Montclair who caught 62 passes as a senior. He is in the school's Sports Hall of Fame along with Sam. Porter played in the CFL with the Montreal Alouettes (1982), had a training camp cup of coffee with the Chicago Bears, and played in the USFL with the New Jersey Generals (1983). He served as an assistant coach at Montclair in the mid-'90s, then enrolled in New Brunswick Theological Seminary. He's been the pastor at Pilgrim

Baptist Church in Red Bank, New Jersey, since 2003. He was the officiant at Sam's 2005 funeral service. "When I was in camp with the Bears, I got to know Mike Singletary," he says. "It was amazing the similarities between Singletary and Sammy. That quality of person. The humbleness. Mike was more vocal than Sam. Sam could swear and spit. But he would never raise his voice if you messed up. He always would try to encourage you."

Vinny DeMarinis

After playing alongside each other at Montclair for four years, Vinnie and Sam were reunited in the USFL with the Stars, where they played together for three years. "In 2003, Sam was coaching for the Panthers and they were in the Super Bowl," he remembers. "My son Vinny was 12 at the time. He calls Sam the day before the game and leaves him a message. He says, 'Hi, Sam. This is little Vinny. I just wanted to wish you luck. And tell [Jake] Delhomme not to panic. Everything is going to be okay.' The next day, three hours before the game, the phone rings. It's Sam. He said, 'Where's your son? He left me a message. I want to talk to him.' My son gets on the phone and talks to him for a good 15 minutes. *Fifteen minutes!* Right before the Super Bowl. That's the kind of guy Sam was."

McKinley Boston

Boston, who was Montclair's linebackers coach when Sam played there, later received a doctorate in education from NYU and was a visiting scholar at Harvard. He was the athletic director at several colleges, including his alma mater Minnesota, New Mexico State, Rhode Island, and Kean College. "The thing that jumped out at you more than anything with Sam was his leverage," he says. "He had great control of his lower body. I noticed right away that he had the ability, despite his size, to just get under players and keep his body under control. He could stop a 300-pound lineman in his tracks because he just had that natural ability in his lower body."

BROWNS TRAINING CAMP (1981)

Jim Garrett

After spending the first part of his career in coaching, Garrett switched to scouting in the mid-'80s. He worked for the Cowboys for 16 years before retiring in 2003 at the age of 73. He passed away in 2018. Garrett was big on fitness. Back before most hotels had gyms, Garrett would take weights with him on scouting trips. He would run a couple of miles around the hotel parking lot, then pull the weights out of his trunk and use them.

Jason Garrett

Jason played eight years in the NFL, seven of them with the Dallas Cowboys as Troy Aikman's backup, winning two Super Bowl rings. He later was the Cowboys' head coach for nine years (2011–19). Since 2022, he has worked as an analyst for NBC, primarily on their *Football Night in America* studio show. The Whale House in Monmouth Beach, where Sam worked out for Jason's father, remains in the Garrett family. One of Jason's sisters owns it.

Bill Cowher

After missing the 1981 season, Cowher came back and played in nine games for the Browns in '82, then was traded to Philadelphia, where he played two more seasons. He joined Marty Schottenheimer's coaching staff in Cleveland in '85. In '92, he was hired by the Pittsburgh Steelers as their head coach. The Steelers made the playoffs 10 times in 15 years under Cowher (1992–2006) and won the Super Bowl in 2005. His 149 wins are the 25th most in NFL history. He joined *The NFL*

Today on CBS as a studio analyst in 2007, and he has been with them for nearly two decades. He was inducted into the Pro Football Hall of Fame in 2020. "One of the reasons I respected Sam so much was because he was like me," says Cowher. "He knew the idiosyncrasies of every offense. You have to have athletic ability to make it in the NFL. But he was also smart. He had a great feel for the game, a great passion for the game, a great understanding for the game. He studied the game. He would eliminate plays when they lined up because he already knew what to anticipate."

Dick Ambrose

Ambrose, who was nicknamed "Bam-Bam," played nine years for the Browns at inside/middle linebacker. He started 103 games. He attended Cleveland State University College of Law while still playing, and became a lawyer after he finished playing. He practiced law for 17 years, then spent another 17 as a Common Pleas court judge in Cleveland. He retired in 2021.

Sam Rutigliano

Rutligiano, who recommended Mills to Philadelphia Stars GM Carl Peterson and told him not to cut him until he saw him hit people, spent seven seasons as the Browns' head coach (1978–84). He had three winning seasons. After he was fired, he became an analyst for NBC Sports and ESPN for three years, then was hired by Jerry Falwell to be the head coach at Liberty University (1989–99). He left Liberty with the intention to retire from coaching, but then spent seven years as an assistant in NFL Europe.

Marty Schottenheimer

Schottenheimer, who was the Browns' defensive coordinator in 1981, cast the deciding vote to cut Mills that summer. He replaced Rutigliano as Cleveland's head coach in '84. In '89, he was hired as the

Kansas City Chiefs' head coach by Carl Peterson. Schottenheimer spent 10 years with the Chiefs and took a lot of good-natured grief from Peterson for cutting Mills. Schottenheimer was also the head coach in Washington (2001) and San Diego (2002–06). His 200 career wins are the eighth most in NFL history.

TORONTO ARGONAUTS TRAINING CAMP (1982)

Dale Lindsey

Like Mills, Lindsey ended up in the USFL. He was the Boston Breakers' linebackers coach in 1983, then spent two seasons as the defensive coordinator for the New Jersey Generals. Both teams were in the same division as Mills' Philadelphia Stars. "I had the misfortune of seeing him every year, twice a year when I was in the [USFL]," Lindsey said. "I was thinking, *What a dumbass I am. The guy is running around making plays on us and you didn't keep him [in Toronto].*" Lindsey would serve as an assistant with seven different NFL teams over the course of his career. In 2013, he was named the head coach at the University of San Diego, where he had an impressive 80–30 record over 10 years.

PHILADELPHIA STARS (1983–85)

Jim Mora

After leaving the Saints in 1996, Mora was hired to coach the Indianapolis Colts in 1998. The Colts drafted Peyton Manning with the first pick in the draft that year. Mora coached them for four seasons, winning 13 games in his second season and making the playoffs twice. He was fired after the 2001 season by Colts GM Bill Polian when he refused to fire his defensive coordinator, Vic Fangio. Jim lives with his wife, Connie, in Palm Springs, California. Now in his 90s, he still golfs multiple times a week. His 125 career NFL wins are the 32nd most in league history. His iconic 2001 "Playoffs? Playoffs?" rant made a comeback in 2025 in a popular DraftKings commercial.

Carl Peterson

Peterson, the architect of the Stars' two USFL championship teams, was the general manager/chief executive officer of the Kansas City Chiefs (1989–2008). The Chiefs made six straight playoff appearances from 1990 to '95. He was an adviser to Stephen Ross when he bought the Miami Dolphins in 2009 and also served as chairman of USA Football until 2017. "Sam was dwarfed size-wise, but he always knew and saw and anticipated," says Peterson. "I never saw anyone with his ability to read the play almost at the snap. He was like a quarterback who knows immediately where to go with the football. He knew where to go as soon as the ball was snapped."

Bill Kuharich

Kuharich joined Mora in New Orleans after the USFL folded in 1986 as the team's personnel director. He was named the Saints' president and general manager in 1997 and stayed with the organization through 1999. He worked in scouting with the Kansas City Chiefs (2000–2008). He later worked in the Cleveland Browns' front office (2014–15). "Sam was one of the first guys who stayed in shape year-round," Kuharich says. "There were no mandatory offseason workouts back then. No OTAs. But Sam would be there every day working out. He'd say, 'I have to work every day, and I have to work hard every day, so that when I get to training camp, it's easy. And when I get to the games, it's real easy.'"

Terry Bradway

Bradway joined the New York Giants scouting staff after the USFL folded. He was with the Giants for five years and earned two Super

Bowl rings. He spent a decade as a scout and personnel executive with the Kansas City Chiefs. In 2001, he was named the general manager of the New York Jets. The Jets made the playoffs in three of the five years he served as their GM. Bradway has worked for five different NFL franchises over the last 40 years, including the Carolina Panthers, where he has been a part-time scouting consultant since 2022. "Being in Carolina now, that *Keep Pounding* thing that Sam inspired is real," says Bradway. "Twenty years after his death, it's still real. To have a legacy and a spirit like that when you've been gone as long as he's been gone, it's really something."

Bob Moore

Moore joined the Kansas City Chiefs as their public relations director in 1989. He held that role for more than two decades. In 2010, he became just the second team historian in NFL history (there are now 20) with the Chiefs. He helped design the team's Hall of Honor. He is still the Chiefs' historian emeritus and assists with special projects. Bob lives in Monmouth Beach, New Jersey.

Vince Tobin

Tobin spent seven seasons as the Chicago Bears' defensive coordinator (1986–92). The Bears led the league in points allowed in two of Tobin's first three seasons there. He was later the head coach of the Arizona Cardinals for five years (1996–2000). He had just one winning season and finished with a 28–43 record with the Cardinals. Vince was on dialysis for kidney disease and was unable to attend Sam's Hall of Fame induction ceremony in 2022. He died a year later. "Sam never had a bad practice," Tobin said. "He kept proving himself every day."

Vic Fangio

The Dunmore, Pennsylvania, native, who spent his first season with the Stars sleeping in the basement of Veterans Stadium, is considered one of the NFL's top defensive minds. He was the Denver Broncos' head coach for three years (2019–21), and he has served as a defensive coordinator with seven different NFL teams, including the Philadelphia Eagles, where his defense finished first in yards allowed and second in points allowed and helped the Eagles win the Super Bowl in 2024.

Joe Pendry

Pendry, who was the Stars' first offensive coordinator and ran the tryout camp that Mills attended, spent more than two decades as an NFL assistant. He was the Carolina Panthers' offensive coordinator when Mills signed with them in '95. He finished his career as Nick Saban's offensive line coach at Alabama before retiring in 2010.

Glenn Howard

Howard signed with the New York Jets after the USFL folded. But they found bone chips in his knee and he flunked the team physical. He spent a year as a volunteer assistant at his alma mater, Paulsboro (New Jersey) High School, then became the head coach there a year later. Howard went on to become one of the winningest football coaches in New Jersey high school history. He had a 316–70 record in 35 years at Paulsboro. His teams won 14 South Jersey Group I titles and had a 63-game win streak from 1992 to 1998. Glenn retired from coaching in 2021. On Sam's one-bad-practice-from-getting-cut approach, he says: "It was the inner force that drove him and made him supercompetitive. He never took anything for granted."

David "Duck" Riley

Riley had an opportunity to be a replacement player during the NFL strike in '87, but he turned it down. He became a successful coach and administrator in South Jersey after the USFL folded. He coached at Rancocas Valley and Cinnaminson, and he later spent 16 years as the athletic director at Willingboro High. In 2014, Riley was inducted into the South Jersey Sports Hall of Fame. He said playing on the Stars with Sam was an incredible experience. "In all of my years in sports, I never experienced anything like that," he says. "Being around a unique group of guys where nobody was hating on each other, where everybody was enjoying each other, I never experienced that before or since."

Joe Conwell

The Philadelphia native started 21 games for the Eagles in 1986–87 after the USFL folded. He is currently a senior vice president for a commercial real estate company in the Philadelphia area. He calls Mills the best teammate he ever had. "There was a reverence for Sam amongst the team," he says. "He just had a quiet stature within the team. But the thing about him was, he had a way of connecting with people. He had a natural way of making everybody, including myself, feel like you were an important part of the team and that he was interested in you as a person."

George Cooper

Cooper played 10 games for the San Francisco 49ers in 1987. He later served as a chaplain at his alma mater, Michigan State, and worked at the Ford Motor Credit Company for nearly four decades before retiring in 2023. George is Marcus Mills' godfather. Sam was the best man at his wedding. "We ran down [to city hall] on Tuesday, our off day, to get the [wedding] license," Cooper remembers.

George Jamison

Jamison spent 12 years in the NFL after the USFL folded, including nine with the Detroit Lions. He made 177 career starts for the Lions and the Kansas City Chiefs. He and George Cooper drove from Michigan to attend Sam's 2005 funeral. "There was no variance with Sam,"

Jamison says. "He was consistent, he was constant. With him being a family man, everything we saw in Sam inspired us and influenced who we became as men."

Mike Johnson

Johnson spent 10 seasons in the NFL, eight with the Cleveland Browns and two with the Lions. He made 125 starts and earned two Pro Bowl invitations. "I played next to Sam for two years," Johnson says. "It was to my benefit, for sure. Everybody talked about his height. But it didn't mean anything. He just happened to be 5'9". He played with power. A lot of power. I had to learn how to do that."

John Bunting

Bunting played for the Stars for two seasons (1983–84), then retired and coached their linebackers, including Mills, in 1985 when they won their second straight USFL title. He was the head coach at Rowan University from 1988 to '92. The '92 team finished 12–1 and made it to the NCAA Division III semifinals. He spent eight years as an NFL assistant and was the St. Louis Rams' co-defensive coordinator in 1999 when they won the Super Bowl. In 2001, Bunting was hired as the head coach at his alma mater, the University of North Carolina (2001–06). Bunting said Mills was the only guy he ever played with who beat him to the film room.

Antonio Gibson

Gibson and Mills played together for eight years, three with the Stars and five more with the Saints. He is now a retired performance training consultant who enjoys mentoring and training his young granddaughters, who play volleyball, basketball, and soccer. Antonio lives in College Station, Texas. "I played with three or four Hall of Famers in New Orleans," he says. "Without question, Sam was the best player I've ever played with in my career. Also, outside of my family, he might've been the best person I've ever met. I say that with no hesitation. Me and so many other people were just so fortunate that Sam crossed our paths."

Bart Oates

Oates went on to play 11 seasons in the NFL, including nine with the Giants. He won two Super Bowls with the Giants. He was a five-time Pro Bowler. He earned his law degree from Seton Hall University Law School in 1990 while still playing for the Giants, and he spent 20 years after his playing career practicing law. In 2017, he was named the president of the NFL Alumni Association.

Chuck Fusina

Fusina played in seven games for the Green Bay Packers in 1986. After football, he partnered with a company that manufactures and distributes baseball and softball equipment.

Kelvin Bryant

Bryant signed with the Washington Redskins after the USFL folded. He spent five seasons there (1986–1990) and won a Super Bowl, but he never became the dominant player he was with the Stars. They already had George Rogers when they signed Bryant and used Kelvin mostly as a pass-catching third-down back. He had 40-plus catches in each of his first three seasons. He returned to his hometown of Tarboro, North Carolina, after leaving football and still lives there. Bryant was always a man of few words who didn't care for the limelight. His wife, Teresa, nicknamed him "The Reluctant Superstar."

Herschel Walker

Walker and Mills faced each other 17 times over the course of their USFL and NFL careers. They both spent the same 12 years in the NFL (1986–97). Walker played for four teams and finished with 13,084 yards from scrimmage and 82 touchdowns during his NFL career. He ran for the US Senate in Georgia in 2022 and lost in a runoff election to Democrat Raphael Warnock. Since 2025, he's been the US ambassador to the Bahamas, appointed to the position by his former USFL boss, Donald Trump.

Grasella Oliphant

Oliphant was Mills' first agent. He was an accomplished jazz drummer who played with Sarah Vaughan and other jazz luminaries in the '50s and '60s and released two albums of his own on Atlantic Records in the '60s. He gave up drumming in the '70s to focus on his family. He worked as a concert promoter and golf course manager and represented small-college athletes from the New York metropolitan area, including Mills and his former Montclair teammate Terrence Porter. He negotiated Mills' first contract with the Saints. He resumed his music career in the early 2000s, mostly in north Jersey jazz clubs. He died in 2019.

NEW ORLEANS SAINTS (1986–94)

Rickey Jackson

After spending 13 seasons in New Orleans, including eight with Mills, Jackson signed with the San Francisco 49ers after the 1993 season and won his first Super Bowl that same year. He played one more season after that, recording 9 ½ sacks in 1995 at the age of 36. His 136 career sacks are the 17th most in league history. Jackson was inducted into the Pro Football Hall of Fame in 2010. In 2023, he got his bachelor's degree in social sciences from the University of Pittsburgh at the age of 65.

Pat Swilling

Swilling is 35th in the NFL in career sacks with 107 ½. He played five more seasons after getting traded by the Saints, but had just one more double-digit sack season—13 with the Oakland Raiders in 1995. He got involved in real estate after retiring from the NFL.

Vaughan Johnson

Johnson left the Saints a year before Mills did, signing with the Philadelphia Eagles, but his body was shot. He played in just four games with the Eagles in '94 and retired at the end of that season. Johnson, like the other three Dome Patrolers, is in the Saints Hall of Fame, inducted in 2000. He was just 57 when he died in 2019 of kidney disease. Johnson was posthumously diagnosed with CTE.

Bobby Hebert

Hebert signed with the Atlanta Falcons after the '92 season. He spent four seasons in Atlanta, two of them as backup quarterback to Jeff George. He had a 7–18 record as a starter with the Falcons. After retiring, Hebert returned to New Orleans and became a successful broadcaster. He still hosts a popular afternoon talk show on WWL radio.

Brett Maxie

After retiring as a player following the 1997 season, Maxie got into coaching. He has been an assistant with seven NFL teams (Carolina, San Francisco, Atlanta, Miami, Dallas, Tennessee, Tampa Bay) and two college programs (Vanderbilt, Colorado). In December 2025, he joined Mills in the New Orleans Saints' Hall of Fame. "Our second year in Carolina when we went to the NFC Championship Game, we had Lamar Lathon and Kevin Greene, and I think they combined for something like 30 sacks," he says. "But Sam was the glue. He made it easy for them. All they had to do was rush the passer. That's all they had to do. Sam was going to handle the rest. He knew the defense inside and out."

Jack Del Rio

Del Rio had a successful playing career after the Saints traded him. He started 118 games for three teams, although the most memorable moment of his playing career might've been during the '87 strike when he showed up at Arrowhead Stadium in Kansas City standing in the bed of a pickup truck holding a rifle. He later got into coaching and was the head coach in Jacksonville (2003–11) and Oakland (2015–17). He had a 93–94 career record, and his teams made the playoffs three times in 12 years.

Tom Benson

After Jim Finks' death, Benson's Saints fell into a state of disrepair. From 1993 through 2008, they made the playoffs just twice in 16 seasons. Benson's popularity in New Orleans hit rock bottom in 2005 when he considered permanently moving the team to San Antonio after Hurricane Katrina had ravaged New Orleans and the Superdome. All was forgiven in '09 when the Saints won their first Super Bowl. Benson died in 2018 at the age of 90. His third wife, Gayle, whom he married in 2004, is the Saints' current owner. The team her husband bought for $70 million in 1985 is now worth an estimated $5.7 billion.

Brett Senior

Senior is a managing partner of Tier 1 Sports Management. He has represented over 700 professional athletes and coaches over the last 50 years, including Sam Mills. Senior is a graduate of Franklin & Marshall, where he was the captain of the wrestling team. "When we did Sam's last contract with Carolina, I think it put him at the top of the league's inside linebackers for compensation," Senior says. "Bill Polian was the Panthers' GM and Sam thanked him profusely. He said, 'I have to tell you, my first year with the Stars, I made $18,500.' Then he said, 'I love this game so much, I probably would've played next season for you if you had offered me that much.' Bill looked at me and joked, 'Geez, I wish he would've told me that 15 minutes ago. I could've saved a lot of money.'"

Steve Sidwell

After leaving the Saints, Sidwell was the defensive coordinator for the Houston Oilers (1995–96), New England Patriots (1997–99), and Seattle Seahawks (2000–02). He died in 2023. He was 78.

CAROLINA PANTHERS (1995–2004)

Jerry Richardson

Richardson owned the Panthers from their inception until May 2018, when he sold the team to David Tepper. The sale came five months after *Sports Illustrated* reported that at least four former female Panthers employees had received monetary settlements because of inappropriate workplace comments and conduct by Richardson, including sexually suggestive language and behavior. A statue of Richardson that had been put up in front of the stadium in 2016 was removed in 2020. Richardson died in March 2023. He was 86.

Bill Polian

Polian left the Carolina Panthers after the '97 season to become the president and general manager of the Indianapolis Colts. He was with the Colts for 14 years. During that time, they made 11 playoff appearances, had 11 double-digit win seasons, won eight division titles, and went to two Super Bowls, winning one. Polian was selected to the Hall of Fame in 2015. "Sam's career was pretty amazing," he says. "It's in many ways a Horatio Alger story. And a great story of someone who wouldn't take no for an answer."

Dom Capers

After getting fired by the Panthers in '98, Capers spent two years as the defensive coordinator in Jacksonville, then was hired as the head coach of yet another expansion team, the Houston Texans, in 2002. He spent four years with the Texans. He later was the defensive coordinator in Miami (2006–07) and Green Bay (2009–17). Since 2019, he has worked as a senior defensive assistant with five different NFL teams.

Jackie Miles

Miles, who first met Mills when they were both with the Philadelphia Stars, was the Carolina Panthers' equipment manager from their inception in 1995 through 2018. He then spent six years as the New York Giants' equipment manager before retiring in 2024. He lives in Wilmington, North Carolina. He found out that Sam had died from Pat Yasinkas, who covered the Panthers for the *Charlotte Observer* back then. "Pat asked me for a comment on Sam because he knew we were close," Miles says. "I just lost it. He's writing down my quotes and I was crying my eyes out. I really loved that guy."

Dan Morgan

Morgan's playing career was cut short by injuries and multiple concussions. He retired in 2007 after just seven seasons at the age of 29. Unlike his bowling buddy Mills, Morgan opted for scouting over coaching after his playing career. "You're either attracted to the front-office lifestyle or you're attracted to the coaching lifestyle," he said. "Sam wanted to be out on the field influencing players there. I took the other route." Morgan worked in scouting for the Seattle Seahawks and Buffalo Bills before rejoining the Panthers in 2021 as their assistant general manager. Since 2024, he's been the team's general manager and president of football operations. Carolina made the playoffs in 2025 for the first time in eight years.

Steve Smith

Smith played in the NFL for 16 years. He made five Pro Bowls and was a four-time All-Pro selection. He is eighth in career receiving yards (14,731) and 12th in receptions (1,031). He is one of just four players who have led the NFL in receptions, receiving yards, and receiving touchdowns in the same season (2005). His wife, Angie, gave birth to their son Boston one hour before Sam died. "As he was coming into this world, a great man was leaving it," Smith said. "I'm reminded every April 18 that I have a young boy that hopefully can impact another Steve Smith when he grows up the way Sam impacted me."

Kevin Greene

After spending the '97 season with the 49ers, Greene re-signed with Carolina in '98 and played his final two NFL seasons with the Panthers. He had 27 sacks in those two years, and he finished his career with 160 sacks, the third most in NFL history, behind only Bruce Smith (200) and Reggie White (198). Like Mills, he got into coaching after retiring as a player and won a Super Bowl in 2010 with the Packers. In 2016, he was inducted into the Pro Football Hall of Fame. Four years later, on December 21, 2020, Greene died of a heart attack at the age of 58.

Jim Skipper

Skipper spent 37 years as an NFL assistant, all of them coaching running backs. He met Sam Mills when both were with the Philadelphia Stars. They became close friends. After Sam retired as a player, they coached together for three years in Carolina on John Fox's staff. The last round of golf Sam played was with Skipper. On his close relationship with Mills: "It was unspoken. If you didn't know, you didn't know. We didn't really want people to know that we were that close. Because it's unusual for a player and a coach to have that kind of relationship. But I wasn't his position coach, and we had kids that were the same age. So, it was just a natural thing."

Kerry Collins

After getting released by Carolina during the 1998 season, Collins dealt with his alcoholism and had a long career. He spent 17 years in the NFL. He made 190 career starts with six different teams. He had a 12–4 record as a starter in 2000 with the Giants when they made it to the Super Bowl. In 2008, he was 12–3 with the Tennessee Titans. In 2024, he was named the offensive coordinator/quarterbacks coach at Spring Hill High School near Nashville. He is eternally grateful to Mills for trying to help him. "There wasn't a finer human being that I came across during my career," Collins says. "They just didn't come any better. From a character standpoint. From a moral standpoint. All those things."

Kevin Steele

Steele's four years with the Panthers was his only NFL job. He spent the other 39 years of his coaching career at the college level, including three different stints with Nick Saban at Alabama. He retired from coaching after serving as Saban's defensive coordinator in 2023. The three years he spent coaching Mills were one of the highlights of his career. "It just doesn't seem like he's gone," Steele said. "He was larger than life. I mean, he may have been only 5'9", but he played like a giant and lived like a giant."

Billy Davis

Davis has been an NFL assistant for more than 30 years, including his four-year stint on Dom Capers' staff in Carolina (1995–98) when Sam played there. He has been a defensive coordinator with three NFL teams—San Francisco, Arizona, and Philadelphia. Since 2024, he has been the Houston Texans' linebackers coach. "By the time Sam got to Carolina, he was like a father figure to some of those young guys," Davis says. "He was a listener. If Sam ever called somebody out, you could hear a pin drop. If he had something to say, it came from his soul, and it meant something. He would do that very rarely.

Only when it really, really mattered. The rest of the time, he just let his actions do his talking."

Charlie Dayton

Dayton, who was the Carolina Panthers' director of communications for more than two decades (1994–2015), was one of the NFL's best PR people. A half-dozen current league communications directors got their start working for Charlie. He was with the Panthers for the entirety of Mills' career, which was why it was appropriate that the Pro Football Hall of Fame honored him with one of its first Award of Excellence awards the same week in 2022 that Sam was inducted into Canton. Charlie has been happily retired since 2017 and living in Hilton Head, South Carolina, where he can usually be found on the tennis court.

Bruce Speight

Speight became good friends with Sam when he was a young assistant on Dayton's staff. In 2007, Speight was named the New York Jets' vice president of media relations. He spent 11 years with the Jets before returning to Carolina in 2018 to run the Panthers' communications department. He still treasures the time he spent with Sam. "I remember a scripture verse he had at his memorial service," says Speight. "He had picked it out. Philippians 4:6. 'Be anxious about nothing, but in everything through prayer and supplication with Thanksgiving, let your requests be known to God.' As I read it, it was one of the few times my wife ever has seen me cry."

John Fox

Fox coached the Carolina Panthers for nine years, from 2002 to 2010. He was also a head coach with the Denver Broncos (2011–14) and Chicago Bears (2015–17). He had a 133–123 career record. His teams made seven postseason appearances in 16 years. "One of the last things

Sam said to me was make sure you take care of my son [Sam III]," says Fox. "He was with me the whole time I was with the Panthers, and Ron Rivera, who replaced me, carried that on after I left."

Ken Flajole

Flajole spent six seasons on John Fox's staff in Carolina, leaving in '08 to become the St. Louis Rams' defensive coordinator. Flajole has coached for eight different NFL teams, and he owns two Super Bowl rings. At 71, he's still coaching. Since 2025, he has been a senior defensive analyst at Stanford. Flajole says he's never seen anything have the impact that Mills' courageous cancer battle and his inspirational *Keep Pounding* speech had on the Panthers and their fans. "After that day, in that organization, in that city, that mantra kind of took on a life of its own," he says.

George Seifert

Seifert never coached again after the Panthers fired him in 2001 on the heels of a 1–15 season. He settled into a quiet, private life in California after that. Even with that 1–15 season, Seifert finished with a 114–62–0 career record. His .648 winning percentage is the sixth best in NFL history among coaches who coached 150 or more games, behind only George Allen (.712), George Halas (.682), Don Shula (.677), Paul Brown (.672), and Tony Dungy (.668). All five are in the Hall of Fame.

Todd Andrews

Andrews, who created the statue of Sam Mills that stands outside Bank of America Stadium, is an internationally renowned sculptor based in Grass Valley, California. Besides the Mills statue, he also made six Panthers that sit outside the stadium. His work is displayed in public and private collections throughout the world.

AUTHOR'S NOTE

WHY SAM MILLS?

During the nearly three years I spent researching and writing this book, that was probably the question I was most frequently asked.

If you weren't familiar with his backstory, I can see why you might wonder why a writer from Philadelphia chose a linebacker who died 20 years ago and spent his NFL career in New Orleans and Charlotte as a subject for a biography.

If you *were* familiar with his story, a better question would be: Why the hell did I wait so long to write it?

The truth is, I've wanted to write a book about Sam for a very long time. I felt his story was that compelling, that inspiring, and given his death at 45, that tragic. Unfortunately, I've never been a great multitasker. I've always envied other journalists who could spend 50–60 hours a week covering a beat and somehow still find the time, energy, and discipline to write a book in their spare time.

In 2010, a good friend of mine, Leo Carlin, who spent more than a half-century as a front-office executive with the Philadelphia Eagles, asked me if I would help him write his memoirs. I told him I'd be honored.

We got started shortly after that and worked on it between seasons and playoff games and Super Bowls and scouting combines and drafts and minicamps and weddings and graduations and baptisms and confirmations and funerals.

What I thought would be a one-year project took more than 10 to finally finish. Then, in one of the worst pieces of timing in publishing history, *A Bird's-Eye View: My Mostly Wonderful, Always Unforgettable Half-Century with the Philadelphia Eagles* was released in 2020, smack-dab in the middle of the COVID pandemic. I'm just thankful I was able to get it done for Leo before he lost his valiant battle to Parkinson's in January 2024. Leo knew Sam very well. I hope they have a bookstore in heaven where both of them can enjoy *Just Give Me a Chance to Fail.*

I met Sam Mills in February 1983 when he was trying to win a roster spot with the Philadelphia Stars. I covered the Stars for the *Philadelphia Daily News.*

When it was announced that Philly would have one of the 12 teams in a new spring football league, my boss, Mike Rathet, assigned me to the new team. I would cover pro football for nearly 40 years for the *Daily News* and *Inquirer*. That included more than 30 Super Bowls. Covering Mills and the Stars was, without a doubt, the most enjoyable experience of my career.

After getting cut by the Cleveland Browns and the Toronto Argonauts, the Stars were essentially Mills' last shot. If they had cut him, he would've gone back home to Long Branch, New Jersey, and become a teacher. Noble work, to be sure, but it was his dream to play professional football. The 5'9" linebacker just needed someone to give him a legitimate chance.

You cover professional football for as long as I did, you tend to get cynical. Quite frankly, there are a lot of assholes in the game, as there are in life. Sam wasn't one of them. He was loved and admired by everyone who ever knew him. He was one of the finest human beings I've had the pleasure of covering and getting to know during my career.

John Founds met Sam when he was playing for the Stars. John had started a program in the early '80s called *Life After Sports*, which helped professional athletes find offseason employment and prepare for life after their playing careers were over.

Founds had helped Sam find offseason work in the Philly area when he was playing for the Stars. He also helped him finish up his college coursework remotely so he could get his degree from Montclair State. It was the beginning of a long friendship.

Fast-forward 20 years to June 2003. John's wife, Diana, had been diagnosed with leukemia. Sam, who was an assistant coach with the Panthers at the time, was spending a few weeks before the start of training camp in New Jersey, where the Mills family had a home.

Diana was at the Hospital of the University of Pennsylvania in Philadelphia, which was about a 60-mile drive from where Sam was staying. But he would make the drive every week he was in Jersey and spend hours by Diana's bedside, sitting and talking with her.

"They would talk about diarrhea [caused by her chemo treatment]," Founds remembers with a laugh. "Here's a big NFL star and they would sit there and talk about diarrhea. But that was the kind of relationship that they had. She was able to share with him what she was going through."

Sam would eventually return to Charlotte for the start of training camp. A few weeks later, Founds got a shocking early-morning call.

It was Sam.

"John, I was just diagnosed with cancer and they've only given me a few months to live," he said.

Many of the players I covered on those Philadelphia Stars teams were guys like Sam, who had already been cut by one or more NFL teams and were desperately trying to keep their pro football dream alive. Guys like Glenn "Moe" Howard, George Cooper, and David "Duck" Riley. Rejection was the common thread that brought them together.

That Stars team bonded quickly, and with Sam as their leader, they became the class of the USFL. He was the glue that kept that team together and focused. It would be the same in New Orleans and Carolina.

After the USFL folded, I watched Sam make a seamless transition to the NFL and become one of the best linebackers in league history. I watched him transform a Saints team that had never had a winning season into an annual playoff contender. I watched him go to Carolina and carry a second-year expansion team on his back to the conference championship game. I watched him inspire the Panthers seven years later with his courageous cancer battle.

Fame never changed Sam Mills. He was the same humble person when I interviewed him in Charlotte seven months before his death as he was two decades earlier the first time I sat down with him at the Stars training camp.

When he was dying, he had every reason to feel sorry for himself and ask, *Why me, God? Why me?* Instead of wallowing in self-pity, though, he was philosophical.

"It certainly makes you appreciate life a lot more," he told me in October 2004. "I remember last year when we went out to Arizona for a game after I was diagnosed. You look around and you say, 'Wow, what a beautiful country.'

"You hear people talk about a movie coming out this winter or next spring, and you think, man, I might not even make it that far.

They talk about road projects and developments going up that should be done [the next year], and you say I might not even see that.

"But that's the way life is every day anyway. You don't know whether you're going to be around the next day. But something like this brings it to the forefront. I remember after I was diagnosed, thinking, *They're saying I might not even be around for my 45th birthday.* But thank God I am."

Why Sam Mills?

That's why.

ACKNOWLEDGMENTS

A BIOGRAPHY HAS ONE writer but numerous travel guides who escort him on the journey through the subject's life. And I had some excellent guides to help me tell the story of Sam Mills' inspiring but too-short life.

I want to especially thank the Mills family, particularly his widow, Melanie, his two sons, Sam III and Marcus, and his brother Leon for their help and cooperation with this project. It would have been impossible to tell Sam's story without them. Thank you for trusting me. I hope you're pleased with the result.

It was Leon who provided me with the idea for the title of the book when he told me how his brother, even before he was cut by the Cleveland Browns and Toronto Argonauts, would tell him almost every day, "Man, I wish they would just give me a chance to fail."

I interviewed more than 80 people from every period of Sam's life and career, including two—Vince Tobin and Jim Simonelli—who unfortunately passed away before the book was published. May they rest in peace. Were it not for Vince, who died of kidney disease in 2023 at the age of 79, Sam Mills' life story would've been about a terrific industrial arts teacher and high school football coach rather than a Hall of Fame linebacker.

Tobin, who was the Philadelphia Stars' defensive coordinator when Mills signed with them in 1983, was the one and only person willing to believe his eyes and ignore the fact that the guy who was knocking the shit out of people on the football field happened to be just 5'9".

Simonelli, who played for Sam's high school coach, Frank Glazier, in college and later was an assistant on his staff at Long Branch High School, was tasked by Glazier with the all-important job of teaching his star pupil how to read "the triangle"—the two offensive guards and the running back. After Sam learned the triangle, he became, in Simonelli's words, "a beast."

Simonelli was one of the many people who were very helpful to me in painting a picture of Sam's early years in Long Branch. Some others, besides his family, whose help was invaluable were Eddie Balina, Bill Hill, and Bob Biasi.

Balina, a lifelong friend of Sam's, was on the Green Wave football and wrestling teams with him. Hill was a star running back at a rival high school, Howell. Sam and Bill became good friends.

Biasi, like Simonelli, was a defensive assistant on Glazier's Long Branch staff. His amazing like-it-happened-yesterday recall of Sam's career at Long Branch, particularly the big games against Matawan and Carteret during his senior year, was invaluable.

I can't thank Philadelphia Eagles defensive coordinator Vic Fangio enough for agreeing to write the foreword for this book. Vic loved Sam. Despite his busy schedule, he was always quick to get back to me when I had questions. And I had many. I expected nothing less from a fellow northeastern PA guy.

Sam was a coach's dream. He was the proverbial coach on the field. He watched more film than Siskel and Ebert. He would have the week's defensive gameplan committed to memory before the rest of the team even had a chance to look at it.

I remember talking to Peyton Manning once after a Colts playoff win over Rex Ryan's New York Jets. He referenced something he had seen on film from *four years earlier* when Ryan was the defensive coordinator for the Baltimore Ravens that had tipped him off to something Ryan called in the playoff game. Sam Mills was the same way. He had an uncanny understanding of offensive tendencies and would relay the info to the rest of the defense before the snap.

Every coach I spoke with for this book gushed about Sam. Fangio has had a picture of Sam on the wall of his office at every place he's worked for the last 20 years. Jim Mora, Tobin, Dom Capers, John Fox, Kevin Steele, Billy Davis, Jim Skipper, Joe Marciano, Rick Giancola, McKinley Boston, Biasi, and Simonelli could've talked for hours about Sam. Their stories brought their experiences with him to life in the book.

I want to give a shout-out to some other former coaches who were of great help to me in writing this book. Jason Garrett, the former Dallas Cowboys head coach and current analyst on NBC's *Sunday Night Football* broadcast, took me inside his father Jim's important relationship with Sam. If not for Jim Garrett, Mills probably wouldn't even have signed with the Stars.

Hall of Fame coach Bill Cowher, who played for the Browns, was a big help in providing details of Sam's training camp experience with the Browns at Kent State in '81. So were two other former Browns players, Dick Ambrose and Doug Dieken.

Dale Lindsey was the Toronto Argonauts' defensive coordinator when they cut Mills. He recounted Sam's 1982 training camp experience with the Argonauts. Lindsey said Sam made coaches in two countries look bad. He was right.

Two other Hall of Fame coaches, Dick Vermeil and Bill Parcells, were invaluable in giving me their perspective on the evolution of the game and the transformation of the linebacker position in the '70s, '80s, and '90s.

Thanks also to Brett Senior, Sam's agent and dear friend, who gave me an invaluable glimpse into Sam's humanity.

I interviewed dozens of Sam's former teammates at Long Branch, and at Montclair, and with the Stars, Saints, and Panthers. Many thanks to all of them for their help and for sharing their memories of Sam. Topping that list are Antonio Gibson, who played with Sam in the USFL and then with the Saints and was one of his closest friends, and Reverend Terrence Porter and Vinny DeMarinis, who were Sam's teammates at Montclair, as well as former Panthers wide receiver Steve Smith.

Thanks to Craig Blackman for reliving his battle with Mills in the 1977 finals of the New Jersey state wrestling tournament. Thanks also to Todd Andrews, the California sculptor who created the statue of Sam that stands on the east side of Bank of America Stadium in Charlotte. Todd's telling of the story of Saints fans putting Mardi Gras beads on the statue after a Saints-Panthers game, and Panthers fans being ready to fight them because they thought they were trying to desecrate the statue rather than pay homage to Sam, was precious.

Thanks also to Jackie Miles, Carl Peterson, Bill Kuharich, Terry Bradway, Dan Morgan, Bill Polian, Joe Pendry, and John Founds for their valuable assistance with the book. Morgan, who is the Panthers' current general manager, was Sam's regular bowling partner and accompanied him to some of his chemo treatments.

Thanks also to the many communications people from the teams that Sam played on for their help and assistance. Many of them had personal, as well as professional, relationships with Sam. This includes Bob Moore and Mike Kaine from the Stars, Doug Miller and Justin Macione from the Saints, and Bruce Speight, Charlie Dayton, and David Monroe from the Panthers. Bob, Justin, and David provided several of the photos in the book, as did Ed Balina, Brett Senior, and the Mills family.

Thanks to my fellow Hall of Fame selectors Darin Gantt and Jeff Duncan for sharing their thoughts on Sam finally getting into Canton in 2022 in his 20th and final year as a modern-era candidate. Gantt and Duncan, who made the presentations on behalf of Mills at the meeting, were very persuasive. Job well done, guys.

Thanks to my editor/publisher, Brendan Cahill, for believing in this project and showing me why a book needs to be written much differently than a newspaper story. Thanks also to my friends and former *Philadelphia Daily News* colleagues Mark Kram and Mike Sokolove for their advice and brutal honesty on this project, especially early on. Kram and Sokolove are both critically acclaimed authors whose opinions I value. Thanks also to my agent, Bob Deforio.

Finally, this book doesn't get written without my wife, Shelley. As she was during my newspaper career, she was always there to provide encouragement and support when I was wondering whether I would ever finish this book or find someone to publish it.

Thank you so much. I love you.

Navigator Books Pledge of Quality

We hope you have enjoyed reading this book as much as we have enjoyed publishing it for you.

At Navigator Books we are dedicated to bringing the best books by the best authors to readers everywhere in the categories of History, Biography, Memoir, and Historical Fiction. We stand behind the quality of this book, and we guarantee your satisfaction.

If you are dissatisfied with this book for any reason, please notify us via email at inquires@navigatorbooks.com with a proof of purchase, and we will send you another of our titles of your choosing of equal or lesser price at no charge.

Sincerely,
The Team at Navigator Books

INDEX